THE SACRED AND

THE SECULAR UNIVERSITY

# THE SACRED AND
# THE SECULAR UNIVERSITY

*JON H. ROBERTS AND JAMES TURNER*

*With an introduction by John F. Wilson*

PRINCETON UNIVERSITY PRESS

PRINCETON, NEW JERSEY

# bof
5417

Copyright © 2000 by Princeton University Press
Published by Princeton University Press, 41 William Street,
Princeton, New Jersey 08540
In the United Kingdom: Princeton University Press,
Chichester, West Sussex

*Library of Congress Cataloging-in-Publication Data*
Roberts, Jon H.
   The sacred and the secular university / Jon H. Roberts and James Turner ; with an
introduction by John F. Wilson.
     p.  cm.
   Includes bibliographical references and index.
   ISBN 0-691-01556-2 (cl)
    1. Universities and colleges—United States—History—19th century.  2. Universities
and colleges—United States—History—20th century.  3. Secularism—United States—
History.  4. Humanities—Study and teaching (Higher)—United States.  5. Science—
Study and teaching (Higher)—United States.  I. Turner, James, 1946–  II. Title.

LA636.7.R62  2000
378.73′09′034—dc21                         99-055426 (alk. paper)

*March 21, 2000*

*To Anna Belle Roberts*
*and the*
*Memory of Robert E. Roberts*

*and to*
*Peter and Christopher Turner*

# CONTENTS

# FOREWORD

IN MARCH 1996, as part of Princeton's 250th Anniversary Celebration, Princeton University hosted a several-day conference on higher education in the United States. The conference focused on new works of scholarship and consisted of separate sessions that addressed widely varying subjects, ranging from assessment of the current status of the humanities to analysis of the financing of higher education, and from the challenge cultural diversity poses to contemporary colleges and universities to the impact of intercollegiate athletics on students. Among the sessions, one was dedicated to religion and higher education in American colleges and universities.

The session on religion addressed a historical topic rather than a transparently current issue, namely, the changing relationship of religion and American colleges and universities at their core—more specifically, knowledge was reorganized, roughly between the Civil War and World War I. This topic concerned the shape of academic endeavors that came to play such a large role in twentieth-century higher education. Changes in "higher education" in the course of that half century proved to be immensely important, indelibly transforming old institutions and fostering the growth of new ones. The Morrill Act (1862) stimulated the founding and development of America's great land-grant institutions, oriented toward greater access to higher education, professional training, and increasingly technical subjects. New concepts of the research university, appropriated from Germany, but with quite uniquely American characteristics, led to new-modeled institutions in both public and private higher education and caused or influenced the remodeling of existing ones (like the colonial colleges). Faculty members became increasingly specialized in their scholarship and oriented toward research over and beyond the teaching that had been their central activity. Disciplinary boundaries developed and were increasingly defined with reference to external professional societies. Faculty members' loyalties began their shift away from institutions and toward these disciplines, a transition that has accelerated through the twentieth century. So there is no sense in which colleges—let alone the increasing number of universities—"held constant" between the end of the Civil War and the outbreak of World War I. And there is no sense in which religious activities and interests within them were unaffected by these changes. But the chief direct effect upon religion was its changed relationship to the scholarly and teaching missions of college and university faculties.

The objective of the conference session was to focus on the salient adjustments at the core of the universities as they began to develop as central institutions in what we have come to term the knowledge industry. From colonial days onward, most colleges had been founded under the auspices of, or in association with, religious groups or movements even when their purposes were not explicitly linked to the training of clergy. While many of the newer universities in the nineteenth century were public and lacked such direct links, they, too, embodied assumptions about their missions, and the courses of study prescribed for students at least in a general way "privileged" broadly Christian assumptions if not a specific denomination or tradition. The means through which this occurred ran a wide gamut. Among them were stipulations concerning the number of trustees who should be clerics or lay folk representing particular religious bodies, support for extracurricular (and often student-run) activities, and the salient role of moral philosophy as the capstone of the curriculum in a course required of all seniors. The religious culture carried by these and other elements was so widely suffused, and deeply ingrained, that its status was "presuppositional" rather than explicit. But it was no less influential and important for this reason. Accordingly, the marked development of higher educational institutions after the Civil War directly challenged assumptions and practices through which religion was embedded in American higher education.

The program at the Princeton Conference focused on central elements in the arts and the sciences in this period of change, the half-century that transformed faculties, curriculums, and facilities. One essay explored the interaction between the claims of science and the role of religious presumptions and commitments—often focused in the same individuals. A parallel essay explored the emergence of the humanities as a construct that incorporated and transformed study of the various expressions of culture—languages and literatures, historical records and artifacts—that comprised the materials passed to and through Western learning, including the religious traditions. The conference also included a discussion of the changing role of the intellectual in this same period. In the lively discussion at the conference session, it was clear that if we claim that these changes were "secularizing," that is to use this term in a very technical fashion rather than in its more conventional sense, which implies a broad rejection of, or even hostility to, religion. More precisely, we should describe the process as one of differentiation.

Thus many of the scientists understood their work, and the reasons for their work, in implicitly if not explicitly religious (usually Christian) terms. Indeed, progress in science was often construed as disclosure of divinely authored works and frequently entailed a response that incorporated not a small degree of deference or even piety. Of course, the social sciences developed in part from the long-standing commitment to moral philosophy as prerequisite for liberally educated citizens as well as through commitment to social reform, so that (in origin at least) they embodied a component of political and social idealism. As for the humanities, they emerged almost as "religious" subjects, challenging students to appropriate truth for themselves in ways reminiscent of more conventional piety.

In these decades that led up to the end of the nineteenth century and initiated the twentieth, roughly from the Civil War to World War I, large-scale adjustments took place in the subjects studied and taught in American colleges—whether free-standing or university-based. Reconstellations of courses and curricula took place no less in the universities. Projecting from these changes, it is not surprising that formal study of religious subjects and interests would be largely (if not systematically) excluded from the pace-setting colleges in the period between World Wars I and II. But this outcome was not, by and large, the initial intention of those who presided over the development of colleges and universities in this critical era.

Jon Roberts and James Turner have reworked and expanded their contributions to the 1996 Princeton conference as the substance of this volume. Their thoroughly researched and carefully argued presentations invite readers to revisit stereotypical generalizations and to rethink the premises developed in the late nineteenth century that underlie the modern university. At the least, their arguments challenge crude versions of the secularization thesis as applied to higher education. They also have the potential to open new lines of inquiry along promising lines. The first set of chapters invites us to recognize the interplay between religion and science as it occurred in terms of assumptions, motivations, interpretations, and conclusions on the part of scientists—and religious folk, too. The strong thesis of Part II, about the humanities and their dependence on philology as paradigmatic for the study of cultural subject matters, challenges us to rethink the emergence of modern disciplines and their possible future. By presenting these contributions together, we hope that the lively discussion occasioned at the conference session will be replicated in additional thoughtful exchanges about how American universities enter the twenty-first century. For higher education now faces an era offering challenges that at least equal those that confronted many of the same institutions 150 years ago. And religion, having failed to dissolve or disappear, emerges as an even more complex subject meriting the respectful—if critical—scholarly attention of higher education.

We are grateful to our colleague John F. Wilson, Dean of the Graduate School at Princeton, and Agate Brown and George L. Collord Professor of Religion, for organizing the agenda of this segment of the conference and bringing this volume together.

William G. Bowen

Harold T. Shapiro

# ACKNOWLEDGMENTS

JON ROBERTS is principally responsible for Part I, on the sciences, James Turner for Part II, on the humanities. But having discussed each other's successive drafts over a period of years, we have reached agreement on all substantial issues and regard ourselves as collectively responsible for the book as a whole.

Both of us wish to acknowledge the generous support of the Mellon Foundation, which provided funds that made the research for and writing of this book possible, and the even more generous assistance of John F. Wilson, who has overseen this project since its origins, giving freely of his time and intelligence, despite the demands on his energy made by his position as dean of the graduate school at Princeton University. To that university and its president Harold Shapiro and to the Mellon Foundation's president William Bowen, we are grateful for the opportunity to present early versions of this work at the conference celebrating Princeton's 250th anniversary. The many archivists and librarians who cheerfully aided our research deserve more thanks than words can afford.

For helpful comments on earlier versions of the manuscript, we are both grateful to George Marsden and two anonymous readers for Princeton University Press. In addition, James Turner thanks Jean Heffer, François Weil, and Pap Ndiaye of the École des Hautes Études en Sciences Sociales and the members of the History Department Colloquium and of the Intellectual History Seminar of the University of Notre Dame for their kind criticism. He also appreciates the willingness of Professors Stephen Alter and Caroline Winterer to let him raid their well-stocked stores of ideas and information.

Jon Roberts thanks Christine Neidlein, Colleen Angel, and the other members of the staff at the University of Wisconsin–Stevens Point Interlibrary Loan Office for gracious, often heroic assistance. Members of the Department of History at the University of Wisconsin–Stevens Point gave him helpful feedback when he presented an abridged version of his contribution to this book at one of the Department's monthly brownbag lunch sessions. William B. Skelton provided a careful and intelligent reading of an earlier draft of this work. Ronald L. Numbers has read three versions and each time provided Roberts with his typically superb editorial and substantive advice. Daniel Thurs, a graduate student at the University of Wisconsin–Madison who is currently writing a dissertation on the history of the meaning of the term *scientific method* in the United States, graciously gave Roberts confidence that his own views on that subject were on target. His special appreciation, as always, to Sharon (ILYS) and Jeff. They continue to make it all worthwhile.

THE SACRED AND

THE SECULAR UNIVERSITY

# INTRODUCTION

## JOHN F. WILSON

T HIS VOLUME focuses on a particular period of American history, essentially the decades between the Civil War and World War I. And it concerns two broad subject areas central to the development of higher education in the course of these decades. The book starts from a simple observation that modern American universities began to take shape during this era, thus effectively differentiating from antebellum colleges (institutions from which a number actually descended). Several elements in this transition are well known and broadly acknowledged. The more important of them include (but are not limited to) (1) the founding and growth of additional public universities (land-grant institutions) especially by means of resources made available through the Morrill Act (1862), (2) the influence of European ideals of scholarly inquiry transmitted through increased numbers of American students who returned from courses of study in European institutions (primarily German), and (3) the refinement of scientific procedures as an increasingly powerful approach to knowledge, especially in its role as an engine for exploring the natural world (but not altogether excluding society as a subject). Of course, additional factors, some specific to higher education, some more generally present in the society, also affected this development of the modern American university. Among them we should especially note the expansion of technology and industry, the increasing utilization of state and eventually federal legal systems, and a growing perception of the need for effective government. All of these factors, along with others as well, played significant roles in remaking higher education during these decades.

While at the conclusion of the Civil War the nation's colleges largely continued along the lines of their prewar organization, by the end of the century the configuration of higher education had dramatically changed. A few universities were explicitly founded to embody the new style (the best example and limiting case being Johns Hopkins), while others, like Harvard, developed from earlier colleges. Additional public universities had begun to take shape, especially in the states more recently admitted to the union. Possibly most important, formal disciplines were consciously organized, an innovation that would produce the familiar departmental structure of faculties (like economics and history as well as literary studies). Although numerous reformers and/or visionaries played noteworthy roles in these years, these developments certainly took place without the benefit of any overall design or prescription of a system. Changes that summed to an emerging new era in American higher education occurred without clear central direction, as they did in other dimensions of post–Civil War America.

One of the broadly gauged and widely accepted generalizations about this era has been that, within the universities, religion was effectively displaced or marginalized. This especially seems to be the case when comparisons are drawn with the roles played by religious bodies and leaders in the earlier development of colleges or even in the continued founding of colleges and universities by religious groups in this and subsequent periods of American history. This point is sometimes rendered in a critical way as a proposition that this new kind of institution, the modern university, was essentially secular. This book undertakes to interpret more precisely the role played by religion in this decisive recasting of higher education in America.

The chapters that follow focus on one slice of this subject, namely, how religion was affected by the *intellectual development* of these universities at their core, whether as new or reconstituted institutions. It should be evident, of course, that religion was involved with these institutions in numerous additional ways as well, for example, through the presence of YMCA programs or ministries sponsored by denominations. As important as these activities may have been, and as strong as their parallels to contemporary extracurricular developments like the rise of Greek fraternities or the expansion of intercollegiate athletics, they do not concern us in the current study, which observes the strong restriction noted above.

Both of the topics defining this book are set in this period of thoroughgoing change in American higher education. Part I concerns the expanding domain of science, whether in the work of geologists or biologists, in the promising world of physics—natural philosophy being made experimental—or in the nascent social sciences. Part II concerns the humanities, for at least equivalent energy was dedicated to study of the human realm of cultural products—literature, language, archaeology, architecture, art, and so on—as the central intellectual endeavor that supplanted the moral philosophy that had served as the core of earlier collegiate curriculums. While the coverage of each topic is necessarily limited in focus, both were at the center of this "university movement" whether it occurred through the reconfiguration of older colleges or by means of founding institutions on the new model. Development of these institutions essentially comprised a new era in higher education. This observation is especially pertinent with respect to those universities that evolved in the late nineteenth century from points of origin that directly linked them to the earlier collegiate tradition.

## THE PUNCTUATED HISTORY OF HIGHER EDUCATION IN AMERICA

The universities developed during the decades after the Civil War represented the coming of a new and different era in American higher education. While many particular institutions bridged this divide, conveniently associated with (but not substantially linked to) the Civil War, the more basic point is that the playing field of higher education shifted. Indeed, continuing the image, the game changed, in objectives as well as in rules. To understand the significance of this period in higher education, we should recognize that a quantum jump occurred with respect to this sector of American society. Before the war, undergraduate colleges populated the landscape along with assorted training academies for such professional competencies as law and medicine that were commonly freestanding. In the post–Civil War era, the universities took shape as new kinds of institutions with different sources of support, different social functions, and different educational objectives. While familiar names (examples being Harvard or Columbia) remained attached to many of them, the actual institutions were dramatically recast shortly after if not during this period at least in terms of the assumptions on which they were based and that, in turn, defined them.

A contemporaneous change in the history of American corporations represents a useful reference point. Like colleges, corporations had been very much a part of the social landscape beginning in colonial times. Like universities, corporations became immensely consequential in the later decades of the nineteenth century, for they served as vehicles for the rapid industrial expansion and the marked economic transformation of the period. But there was a fundamental difference between the earlier and later forms of the corporation. In the earlier period, corporations were chartered individually by singular state legislative acts to serve some public purpose; in the years following the Civil War, a new pattern emerged; namely, general laws of incorporation were set out by the states that made the practice routine in the service of private goals. Yet the same name or designation—*corporation*—identified these significantly different entities. Similarly, while usage associates pre–Civil War colleges with post–Civil War universities, it is wrong to presume that the earlier college was simply a precursor to the latter university—or that the latter was only a projection of the former into a subsequent era.

Another close and possibly useful analogy to this shift from colleges to universities, which is associated with transition from pre– to post–Civil War periods (at least with respect to the landscape of higher education), is to be found much closer to our own time in the half century since World War II. Once again, new kinds of structures developed in higher education from existing institutions while remaining in continuity with them. In this recent era, what we know as research universities materialized very rapidly indeed, drawing on federal funds to sustain basic research. While government investment was primarily in those sciences and engineering fields relevant to the Cold War, it also carried over into support for work in related policy fields. Comparing higher education before World War II with its complexion at the end of the twentieth century highlights the dramatic reconfiguration that was wrought by this sustained government support for basic research. And even though the emphasis placed upon research and scholarship resulted largely from this government sponsorship, the ideal or model of research rapidly extended to affect the quadrants not necessarily benefiting directly from the federal funding—especially in the softer social sciences and the humanities. Thus, in the last half century of the twentieth century, a new kind of institution has developed, one without full precursors even though the familiar names and the similar degrees might suggest a high degree of continuity. The relatively sharp break that is implicit in the development of the research university from the earlier university is one helpful way to think about the relationship of the collegiate tradition of the antebellum years to the arts and sciences university of the following decades. In short, the map of American higher education was redrawn no less dramatically between 1870 and 1920 than it was subsequently reconfigured between 1945 and 1995. In both instances, radical change was embedded within superficial, or at least apparent, continuity.

## THE COMPOSITION OF THE NEW UNIVERSITIES

One distinctive feature in many late-nineteenth-century universities was their frequent association with existing professional schools, or their role in founding new ones, in fields such as law and medicine. The movement to standardize the training of professional workers rapidly gathered momentum toward the close of the nineteenth century, leading to the creation of academies directed toward training professionals to undertake particular activities (like social work, public health, or teaching) that often clustered around—and were often incorporated within—universities. However influential and important these initiatives were (and more attention will be given to them subsequently), there was an even more fundamental impulse at the core of the university movement after the Civil War. This was simply that the "arts and sciences" were conceived of as subjects of inquiry to be sustained through research and scholarship. Such a vision drew inspiration from the German university ideal of professorial research. Thus graduate study in arts and sciences disciplines, culminating in programs offering the Ph.D. degree, became the essential hallmark of the modern American university, perhaps even more than the array of professional schools gathered around it.

This basic development characterizing late-nineteenth-century universities entailed graduate activities and the degree programs accompanying them. It separated these institutions from the older colleges even though they might share comparable undergraduate curriculums and even though graduate students typically remained only a small fraction of the student body. For some of them, and Princeton is a salient example, there was great ambivalence about whether to take the plunge and enter the world of universities or to remain identified essentially as a college. For other existing institutions, there seems to have been little or no significant equivocation about this step. In still other cases, especially in the great developing universities of the land-grant tradition, an orientation toward practical research and the availability of its results in no way qualified their simultaneous commitment to the definition of disciplines in the arts and sciences framework. In any case, of course, the continuing links to the earlier collegiate tradition included competition with the colleges that remained undergraduate institutions. Another and increasingly important direct linkage was that graduate preparation and receipt of an advanced degree from a university eventually became prerequisite to faculty appointment at the colleges—as well as in the universities themselves.

## THE SEPARATION OF RELIGIOUS SEMINARIES AND THE SECULARITY OF UNIVERSITIES

At this point a further observation will help to situate this book. The simple comment is that, among the array of educational institutions populating the antebellum United States, many represented seminaries sponsored by religious bodies or movements. Their first order of business was to train professionals for service in the sponsoring religious communities. But they also became centers for the preservation and extension of religious knowledge—as well as its "application" in American society. In many respects these institutions—which were Catholic as well as Protestant, and eventually paralleled by counterparts representing traditions of the Jewish community—were similar to the schools of law, or of medicine, that were located throughout western lands as well as eastern regions. But in at least two perspectives there were significant differences.

One of the salient differences was that the federal system constituted a national framework of law. This in spite of the great number of state legal systems, which varied in minor ways only (except for that of Louisiana, which drew on the Napoleonic Code). There was no structural parallel among the religious communities. In law, appeals to the federal system were always a possibility; no such superior order or higher standard encompassed the increasing numbers of religious systems giving institutional expression to the denominational religious life of Americans. So centrifugal forces in the religious arena remained strongly in play and were not held in check or counterbalanced by institutions or activities parallel to the centripetal ones that marked the American legal system. Under these circumstances there were few if any incentives for religious seminaries to associate with each other, let alone for them to join universities; indeed, the incentives worked in the other direction. Religious communities derived benefits from acting independently, effectively sustaining through independent "denominations" the component elements that comprised the religious landscape of the relatively new nation.

These dynamics have remained in play throughout subsequent periods of American history even though numerous attempts have been made to develop ecumenical organizations, and significant energies have certainly been expended to launch transdenominational and interfaith movements. At its most basic level, there is no functional equivalent to federal law in the world of American religion. And in terms of an institutional counterpart there is no parallel to its hierarchical court structure that heads up in a "supreme court." Religion in American culture had been plural from colonial times. Nothing happened to challenge or moderate that reality in the decades from the Civil War to World War I. The degree of its pluralism also increased across that period, as it has since, fostering separation of professional training in religious circles from the development of universities (thus helping to marginalize fundamental scholarship in religious subjects internal to the different traditions).

A related observation about the special status of religion in American culture derives from citing the schools of law as a point of comparison. Many of the early ones were brought into relationship to the university centers that, especially after the Civil War, attracted them. Others that had an independent existence were displaced by law schools founded at or by the new universities. Certainly some regional or sectional law schools remained independent of, or unaffiliated with, universities throughout the twentieth century. But the broad pattern was to attract both the study of law and the function of preparing those who would practice it into the university orbit within higher education. In this respect seminaries and other institutions founded to provide religious training followed a markedly different trajectory. While a few divinity schools were attached to older colleges that elected to become universities (Harvard and Yale provide examples) no comparable development occurred among public universities. So the seminaries (where religious learning was preserved, adapted, and in turn transmitted) remained largely separated from the rapidly changing world of the developing universities.

Recall how universities attracted specialized schools offering a range of professional training in many other areas as well, such as medicine, education, business, public health, and nursing. Contrast with this their very different interaction with those serving religious traditions and communities. This marked disjunction signals the special place of religion in American culture and suggests the problems it has posed for the society. Not surprisingly, these features are very much reflected in the realm of higher education. In sum, the anomalous status of religion in the United States meant that this subject would be problematic within the world of higher education that came into being in the late nineteenth century.

The preceding paragraphs have simplified a highly complex background and, for the sake of intelligibility, reduced it to broad outline. They make it evident why a relatively straightforward thesis about the "secularization" of higher education in the United States is plausible. Indeed, it has been fashionable in some circles to argue the case that, whether by design or neglect, religion had been largely excluded from American universities so that by the end of the twentieth century higher education could be described as a "zone" relatively free of religion. Accordingly, on the threshold of the twenty-first century, there is a relatively widespread conviction that American higher education has proved to be thoroughly secularized, indeed, aggressively inhospitable to religion, and that this outcome had been prefigured in the design and development of American universities beginning circa 1870.

## The Intellectual Agenda of the Modern University

The purpose of the present book is certainly not to challenge the perception that higher education is very largely independent of the control that some members of religious communities believe they at one time exercised over it—and/or now wish that they could exercise over unruly institutions. Nor is it to contest the observation that, generally, higher educational institutions keep their distance, intellectually speaking, from religious beliefs and religious truths. Its purpose, rather, is to frame an alternate understanding of how and why religion's relationship to higher education changed as the modern university took shape. On the one hand, we have already explored the separation of universities from the prior collegiate tradition; on the other, we have also noted their independence from institutions providing professional religious training. Both are at best secondary factors, external to the question at hand, however, while a third factor is more central. This factor concerns the particular way in which the "arts and sciences" disciplines developed as the core of the modern university. Comprehending this factor requires more attention to the complex changes taking place in higher education and throughout the society. It also requires an informed view of the very special place of religion in our culture and its relationship to the institutions that are its carriers. The present book does not attempt to achieve this through constructing a sustained history of higher education in America, nor by chronicling the stages that led to professionalized leadership of these institutions. Rather, it suggests this conclusion by focusing more narrowly on several subjects that have been identified already. One of its perspectives is to direct attention to the critical period of the late nineteenth century, in which the "arts and sciences" emerged as the central and regulating core of the university, which was, simply, a new kind of institution. The other point of view is to highlight basic changes in the approach to knowledge under the arts and sciences, first, in the steady growth of scientific fields and, second, in the synthesis of the humanities that would define the cultural subject matter.

Accordingly, this book challenges the presumption that, because colleges founded early in American history largely depended on sponsorship by religious communities, they (and their successors) lost a particularly essential part of their identity when—and most certainly if—they developed independently of those beginnings. Such is presupposed by those who advance a "hard thesis" alleging the secularization of higher education in America, effectively arguing that a birthright has been stolen.

## SPECIALIZATION AND RELIGIOUS DIFFERENTIATION

The current chapters propose that a positive impulse, *specialization,* was a hallmark of the intellectual development that was at the core of higher education in the critical period between the Civil War and World War I. Since at least the middle of the nineteenth century, the impulse to specialize or differentiate functions has characterized virtually all modern social institutions as they have developed, including religious institutions as well as educational institutions at all levels, certainly including those of "higher education." So it should occasion no surprise that with respect to both the world of science and that of the humanities, specialization emerged as a primary driver of change. This thesis is developed in the pages that follow in different but complementary ways as befits the differences between sciences and humanities.

Part I, concerned with "The Sciences," takes as its point of departure the essential synergy between science and religion that had characterized the preceding era. The interpenetration of Protestant theology and natural science thoroughly characterized antebellum colleges. In effect this relationship sustained a program of apologetics. A fundamental impulse underlying these earlier scientific studies was finding in the world of nature evidence for the workings of divine order if not a divine mind. And the moral philosophy that served as the capstone of collegiate study was based on this evidence, namely, confidence that divine intention formed the framework of human endeavor. On the philosophical side, this rested on their confidence in the Scottish Common Sense approach to knowledge; on the ethical side, the program rationalized and endorsed Christian belief and behavior in a nineteenth-century Protestant version.

In the sciences, the critical departure from this hegemonic construct took place in the 1870s. The central step was the impulse to endorse a more specialized pursuit of science. Progress in this endeavor was tightly linked to a reduced range of its operation. In this adoption of "methodological naturalism" a more specialized understanding of science directly undercut its usefulness to apologetics. Explanation required a more rigorously controlled linkage between effects and their putative causes. Thus practitioners of science sought isolable problems that could yield answers in place of large-scale and conjectural explanations. This reduction in scope was linked to skepticism as an operative principle, and once embraced, it dramatically limited the opportunity for religious truths to be "grounded" in scientific claims. "Methodological naturalism" was the critical innovation.

The development sketched above holds no surprises for readers at the end of the twentieth century. What may occasion surprise, however, is the insistence that the individual scientists pursuing their more focused objectives did not understand their own motives to be antireligious or opposed to a broader grounding of religious claims. On the contrary, many of the more prominent scientists of the day portrayed their own work as furthering the objective of establishing religious truth. Some nonbelief operated, but scarcely the antithetical attitudes posited in more conventional understandings of this epoch as driven by secularization.

Even the purported "warfare" alleged to exist between science and theology, and forming the title for a well-known book, does not in fact support this kind of hypothesis. As interesting, support for science was often grounded in expectation of practical payoffs from its progress. The fine distinctions that we routinely make between engineering and science were not so self-evident as these activities developed a century ago.

Part I builds another related and important story on this recast understanding of the relationship between natural science and religion in the decades following the Civil War. This is an account of how the social sciences also developed in these same decades as the attempt to transfer or apply such scientific procedures and goals to the study of society. Sociology, psychology, economics, certainly political economy, and ideally history cast themselves in this camp. An older perspective on these endeavors emphasized that these disciplines derived from the moral philosophizing of the earlier antebellum era. And in the sense that subject matters remained relatively comparable, as well as in the sense that ethical concerns may have been shared across that divide, it is important to acknowledge that linkage. But in the authors' view, the self-conscious commitment to scientific procedures is much more telling. And chief among these was the same impulse to specialize in the sense of limiting inquiry to well-defined data, carefully collected and fully presented. In sum, a critical outcome of this inquiry is the conclusion that a strong methodological commitment to scientific procedure, on the model of the way the natural world was being studied in the new university setting, applied as well to study of society. In the branch of scientific endeavor relating to society, there was just as little residual linkage to the old apologetic world of natural theology as there was among those interested in nature. In this sense there was as great a potential for a secular worldview to seem to inhere in the social as in the natural sciences.

Part II concerns the invention of the humanities, a complementary intellectual endeavor. These chapters explore how the humanities emerged as a central project at the heart of the modern American university in the course of its late-nineteenth-century development. Drawing from the ancient interest in classical languages and civilizations, it emerged as a construct from the philological orientation of the German university. That languages and literatures were context-dependent, and that understanding the reciprocal relationship between context and content was essential to establishing historical interpretation, became the compelling framework within which human artifacts must be studied. This ideal informed the emerging interest in art and architecture that together presented, along with literary records, the available materials through which to recover the human past. So "philological historicism"

became the paradigm for pursuit of knowledge, or the controlling epistemological framework, in arts and sciences studies of the human world.

Philological historicism turned out to have universal implications as a
method, applicable to understanding the entire range of human endeavor, including the endeavors associated with science. It was compatible with specialized disciplinary studies that had an independent and
different taproot in the scientific realm. This orientation legitimated a
range of activities. The paradigm included the assumption that the study
of languages, literatures, artistic creations, and archaeological remains—
indeed, much of the array of disciplines of the *arts and sciences university* as we know it—was prerequisite to any substantial knowledge. Such
a program was not so much antireligious as it was a substitute for the
earlier formulations (based on Scottish Common Sense philosophy) that
had been presupposed by the Protestant religious communities throughout the nineteenth century. This relationship explains the basic compatibility between such a program and the religious thought of Protestant
liberalism in America, as well as its essential challenge to more traditional and conservative religious formulations. The displaced Protestant
approach to the scriptural record—as well as to nature—had little credibility, however, in light of the new paradigm through which warranted
knowledge was construed by philological historicism.

In this view, the emergence of scholarly interest in the Scriptures of
the ancient religious traditions—represented in the development of
courses in the Bible in the decades of our studies—simply confirms how
older presumptions about the status of theologically warranted truth
had been revised. Joined to the cognate approach through archaeology,
the ancient traditions of revelation (available to be confirmed through
explorations in Palestine) became a cultural subject for study rather than
a deposit of revelation. In this sense, the humanities—understood as
subject matter as well as approach—came to substitute for the older
claims that knowledge was unified because it rested on Christian claims
to universal truth. And within the new model of university learning and
the derived curriculum, the humanities displaced—indeed, replaced—
the moral philosophical center of collegiate studies in the earlier era.

If one asks about the new location of religious truth so available to
be studied and finally claimed, it was in the inner life of human consciousness and sensibility. Here was the true centering subject for the
liberal arts now modeled from arts and sciences university materials
rather than from earlier collegiate traditions. And humanities studies
so understood were entirely compatible with—indeed, complementary
to—specialized scientific endeavors. So the *arts and sciences university*
could be an integral construct, having wholly replaced the religious and

theological commitments of an earlier period with specialized pursuit of knowledge and the promise of a progressively unfolding new era. As different as the humanities were, they melded with, and reinforced, the new world of the sciences.

## SOME CONSEQUENCES OF A DIFFERENT PERSPECTIVE

Our primary objective in exploring the intellectual driving forces of modern American universities in this perspective is to secure a truer and more effective understanding of the relationship of religion to that emerging university. The essential argument is that specialization by disciplines in the pursuit and evaluation of knowledge and an emphasis on ongoing inquiry replaced the religious and theological presuppositions that gave coherence to the earlier collegiate tradition. This thrust, rather than a conscious—or even self-conscious—drive for secularization of the academy, stands behind the new arts and sciences university that took the place of the older collegiate institutions. And this new "center" was not explicitly antireligious, although it directly challenged particular theological formulations rooted in the ubiquitous Scottish Common Sense school of philosophy that had been uncontested in the antebellum colleges. In fact, it supported religious sensibility in a Romantic mode, for it was based upon new paradigms for truth that discredited the older ones dominated by particular Protestant versions of natural theology and moral philosophy.

Several significant implications follow from such a viewpoint. For one, it permits the conclusion that, if ecclesiastical control over higher education has indeed dramatically declined, there may have been some positive outcomes with respect to openness toward religion. One such outcome is that, as modern institutions, arts and sciences universities are certainly freer to attend to the manifold religions of our society, and of the world at large, acknowledging their variety and responding to their vitality. Another positive development has been the challenge such a perspective offers to recognize the power that religions exercise in modern societies, power to organize and sustain evil causes as well as good ones, indeed power that derives from the interpenetrating of economic, political, social, psychological, and cultural factors with religious ones. Such honest, critical, and discriminating views of this subject were (and necessarily are) hidden wherever *particular* communities or traditions were (or are) accorded privileged status within, or effective control over, the faculty appointments and curriculums of colleges and universities. Of course, in many instances the roles played by these communities or traditions, in earlier eras as well as our own, reflected (and do reflect) undoubted altruism and generosity, as well as dedication to the education of ongoing generations. But the intention to do good has never alone sufficed to ensure such an outcome, nor that whatever the outcome may be, it is done well!

In many respects, educational institutions (ranging from preschool nurseries to advanced-studies institutes) have flourished in the last half century. And increasingly we recognize that, like (or perhaps even more than) most sectors of modern American society, education is not homogeneous or even necessarily coherent. It harbors divergent—even diametrically opposed—impulses and is not encumbered by any necessity to reconcile or even correlate them. At the secondary level, partisans of school choice do daily battle with defenders of public schools, and those advocating religiously motivated home schooling vie with corporate efforts to apply the vaunted efficiencies of American business practices to local school systems. At the college level, the diversity is staggering, ranging as it does from colleges committed to particular religious traditions, denominations, or even singular charismatic figures to for-profit technical academies.

That education is not a coherent realm, religiously speaking, is self-evident. And for sensitive folk that may indeed be grounds for disenchantment, disappointment that its effect may be to raise questions more than to provide answers, or to challenge individuals to make moral determinations on their own rather than as a consequence of obedience to authority or deference to precedent. But whatever else is the case, the incoherence of education is not evidence for its being antireligious unless there is an unexpressed premise that acknowledging a particular kind of hierarchical order must be a condition for authentic loyalty to and respect for religion. It is not inappropriate or necessarily wrong for individuals and/or groups to lament this state of affairs, indeed, to argue vociferously against it. But such a point of view has the status of an opinion, and for it to be warranted as a critical judgment, it must be fully explicated in terms of the assumptions that are made and the values that are implicit. And at the least, if such claims are advanced as historical interpretations, the grounds for them ought to be fully and critically supported.

The following chapters by Jon Roberts and James Turner ought to challenge unreflective assertions that modern universities are necessarily secular in the sense of displaying hostility toward religion. (That individual professors have at times expressed overt or covert hostility to religion is another matter.) Instead, they ought to encourage readers to recognize that these are very special and precious kinds of institutions. In their modern instantiation they are independent of religious controls—institutional or ideological—but capable of openness toward religiously inclined folk and intellectual interest in the kinds of knowledge claims such persons might make. But the framework for incorporating interest in religion entails ground rules that have been exceptionally significant in shaping the modern world. Both scientific inquiry and humanistic scholarship as practiced in the contemporary university developed out of very special relationships with religious traditions. For some, that may appear to have entailed abandonment and divorce. From another perspective, however, it appears less a divorce than a reengagement at a new and more profound level.

It is axiomatic that the clock cannot be turned back or that we cannot go home again either in literal or metaphorical ways. But as the twenty-first century opens we can revisit the past and possibly discover different truths than had been found there and distilled by earlier generations. In the particular case of these materials, our authors suggest that, as the modern college and university curriculum took shape, there was less overt hostility to religion, or rebellion against its authority, than we often suppose. Indeed, the development of disciplines and their associated professional guilds did not comprise an exclusive realm of secular knowledge. Rather these bold ventures at once acknowledged the forces shaping the modern world and sought to adapt the older tradition of collegiate scholarship and teaching to a necessarily new era. As we contend with yet another period of rapid change in contemporary universities, we might take confidence from their achievement as well as undertake to learn from their mistakes.

*PART ONE*

THE SCIENCES

# Chapter One

## RELIGION, SCIENCE, AND HIGHER EDUCATION

ISTORIANS HAVE LONG maintained that a "revolution" occurred within American higher education during the late nineteenth century and that one of the major sources of the revolutionary impulse was science. In the name of reform, colleges and universities became more secular. The Christian faith lost its central place within higher education, and evangelical Protestants were displaced from their role as the major intellectual arbiters of American culture.[1]

This scenario contains a good deal of truth. Higher education did become more secular in the late nineteenth century, partly because of a gradual disjunction of scientific loyalties from theological concerns and partly because of a growing tendency to make the ethos of science the foundation of higher education. The mechanics of the process of secularization, however, were considerably more complex than historians have thus far suggested. The conventional account tacitly assumes that science was an independent variable and religion a dependent one. For much of the nineteenth century, however, the status and prestige of science depended to a great extent on its close association with Christian theology. The tendency of scientists to detach themselves publicly, if not always privately, from this association and their ability to create an even more central role for themselves within higher education should not be regarded as givens. Only if we contextualize those processes can we hope to answer a question posed by the historian George Marsden: "How was it that distinctively Christian teaching could be displaced so easily from the central and substantive role that it had held in American higher education for over two centuries and in the universities of Christendom for many centuries before that?"[2]

In order to understand how academic science established independence from religious concerns while increasing its status within higher education it is necessary to focus on ideas promoted by the professoriate. For too long the history of higher education has been written from the perspective of college presidents and trustees. This is not always inappropriate. The views of presidents and other officials often exerted enormous influence on the life of the institutions over which they presided. During the late nineteenth century, however, learning became more fragmented, and the task of running a college or university became more complicated. As disciplines and courses of study became increasingly specialized, and as presidents became increasingly oriented toward administration and town-gown diplomacy, they inevitably found their intellectual roles somewhat more attenuated. It became increasingly difficult for them to claim in any truly meaningful sense to represent the life of the mind in their institutions. To be sure, they continued to voice global concerns in the ceremonial speeches that remained essential to their vocations. Moreover, their support remained crucial for educational reform. Nevertheless, scholars seeking to ascertain the changing relationship between science and religion within higher education must go beyond the views of presidents to the foot soldiers in the academic trenches—the faculty.[3]

Prior to 1870, colleges typically functioned as the intellectual arm of American Protestantism. Indeed, the Protestant churches had given birth to higher education in North America and had nurtured it for much of its history. Even institutions of higher education created under the auspices of the states, though typically nonsectarian and willing to leave the finer points of theology to denominational seminaries, nevertheless remained, in the words of University of Michigan president Henry P. Tappan, "under the protecting and nurturing wings of Christianity." As late as 1868 Illinois Industrial University (later the University of Illinois) included in its official inaugural ceremonies hymns, scriptural passages, and prayers. Its first president, John Gregory, lost few opportunities to emphasize his university's Christian character.[4]

Although colleges were often founded to train ministers, few institutions of higher education limited their student body to ministerial candidates. The central vocation of colleges for most of the nineteenth century was promoting the development of Christian civilization through the education of learned "gentlemen." The close association between religion and higher education became most visible in the extracurricular aspects of student life—in the establishment of compulsory chapel and the promotion of periodic revivals of religion on campus. In the academic realm the role of religion was slightly refracted by the colleges' commitment to imbue students with what the widely circulated Yale Report of 1828 termed "the *discipline* . . . of the mind." This commitment reflected the reign of faculty psychology, which conceived of the mind as a set of powers, or "faculties," that could be trained and even strengthened with appropriate exercises. In practice, commitment to disciplining the mind meant that colleges generally devoted their first two years to mathematics and classics. Thereafter they focused more on providing students with "*furniture* of the mind" by offering them a more diverse curriculum predicated on the assumption that nature and society alike could best be understood through the prism of Christian theology.[5]

This assumption did not lead colleges to engage in formal theological training; that was characteristically left to the seminaries. Instead it was reflected in a variety of courses that sought to integrate knowledge on Christian foundations. The preeminent manifestation of such courses was moral philosophy, characteristically taught as a year-long course for seniors by the president of the college. In some respects a catchall, moral philosophy was rooted in the curriculum of medieval universities and was transplanted to American colleges from English and Scottish universities. It dealt with the motives, duties, and goals of human activity, as well as the social relations of human beings. In most American colleges, the content of moral philosophy courses was strongly tinctured by Scottish Common Sense realism, which emphasized the ability of the human mind to apprehend truth about both itself and the external world, and the course usually contained at least some discussion of epistemology. Educators regarded moral philosophy as independent of theology. In fact, because they emphasized the rational examination of data derived from human experience (including the intuitions embedded within consciousness), they commonly viewed their conclusions as scientific rather than speculative in nature. The intent of the course, however, was to demonstrate that the data with which they dealt became intelligible and ultimately meaningful only if they were set within the framework of the Christian worldview.[6]

The sciences also fostered a religious interpretation of reality. Although students in the colonial colleges received at least some science instruction, it was not until about 1830 that the sciences began to play a prominent role within virtually all institutions of higher education. By 1850 four of the nine faculty members at the typical college were teaching science and mathematics.[7]

The increasing importance of science within the curriculum was only partly due to college officials' belief that study of the natural world helped to train the mental powers of their students. Some natural scientists asserted that their disciplines also promised to improve the quality of peoples' material lives. In 1868, Frederick A. P. Barnard, who had become president of Columbia after a career that included professorships in natural philosophy, mathematics, and natural history, declared hyperbolically that "the applications of truths of science to the industrial arts are so numerous, that there is scarcely any article we handle in our daily life, which does not furnish an illustration."[8]

Still, while claims for the practical value of science were common, they were not paramount in the justifications that scientists presented for giving science a prominent role in the liberal arts curriculum of American colleges. This is hardly surprising; as even a cursory examination of scientific journals reveals, few academic scientists concerned themselves directly with practical affairs. For their part, many Americans outside the confines of the academy saw little connection between the material progress of the age and the orientation of many academic scientists. As one observer snidely put it, the American population "believeth indeed in railroads; it thinketh well of steam; and owneth that the art of bleaching by chlorine is a prodigious improvement;—but it laughs at the profound researches into the laws of nature out of which those very inventions grew." In fact, one of the complaints most widely voiced about higher education was that it was insufficiently attentive to practical concerns.[9]

For a long time, efforts to cash in on enthusiasm for science's technological and material potential centered on the development of separate institutions and degree programs dedicated primarily, though never exclusively, to applied science. There thus emerged both freestanding schools, such as the Rensselaer (later Polytechnic) Institute in Troy, New York, and the Massachusetts Institute of Technology and beginning in the 1850s, "schools" or "departments" at already-existing institutions that offered degree programs serving as alternatives to the bachelor of arts. Harvard's Lawrence Scientific School and Yale's Sheffield School were the most renowned of the latter, but by 1870 more than thirty other institutions of higher education had introduced variants of the scientific school. Although such schools helped lay the foundations of science education in the United States, at the time that they were founded and developed, the majority of academics regarded the students in those schools as inferior to those pursuing the B.A. Not only were the admission standards typically lower, but the course of study was most often a three- rather than a four-year program.[10]

Usefulness, however, could be construed in a variety of ways. The Harvard classicist Edward Everett spoke for most academics of his generation when he declared in 1856 that "the great object of all knowledge is to enlarge and purify the soul, to fill the mind with noble contemplations, to furnish a refined pleasure, and to lead our feeble reason from the works of nature up to its great Author and Sustainer." The natural historian Joseph LeConte denounced the idea that the principal goal of science was increasing humanity's "material comfort and happiness." In reality, he averred, "the highest end of science is not to lead us downward to art, but upward to the fountain of all wisdom." The first permanent astronomical observatory in the United States, constructed at Williams College, was created out of concern that an overweening attention to practical affairs had come to characterize American life. At the dedication of the observatory in 1838, the individual who had directed the project declared that his most fervent hope was that students, in pondering the heavens, would be encouraged to contemplate "that fathomless fountain and author of being, who has constituted matter and all its accidents as lively emblems of the immaterial kingdom."[11]

Such sentiments appealed especially to the clerics who typically presided over antebellum colleges and often served as faculty members and to the denominations that frequently gave them support. Recognition of this fact doubtless encouraged proponents of science to place great emphasis on the claim that a study of natural phenomena would be spiritually edifying: it would attest to the glory, wisdom, power, and goodness of the Creator. Indeed, Edward Hitchcock, a respected geologist and clergyman who became president of Amherst College, adopted the view of many partisans of scientific investigation within higher education when he asserted that "the religious applications of science are its most important use."[12]

Scientists and nonscientists alike assumed that God had created the human intellect with a capacity for discerning connections between the creation and its Creator. From this perspective, they concluded that study of natural philosophy and natural history would provide "statements, specifications, facts, details, that will illustrate the wonderful perfections of the infinite Creator." As early as 1788, the College of New Jersey (later Princeton) tutor Walter Minto declared that the study of natural philosophy, "by leading us in a satisfactory manner to the knowledge of one almighty all-wise and all-good Being, who created, preserves and governs the universe, is the very handmaid of religion. Indeed I consider a student of that branch of science as engaged in a continued act of devotion." More than a half century later the young Charles Eliot justified his decision to embark on a career in science by emphasizing that "the study of Science, rightly pursued, ennobles and purifies the mind. He who studies Nature, studies the thoughts and works of God. God is revealed in His works as well as in His word, and he who reverently contemplates the works, worships as truly as he who reads the word." Louis Agassiz, who became the most eminent natural historian in the United States after emigrating from Switzerland in 1846, regarded "the analysis of the thoughts of the Creator of the Universe, as manifested in the animal and vegetable kingdoms" as the ultimate goal of natural history.[13]

For much of the nineteenth century natural scientists working in institutions of higher education played a pivotal role, both in the classroom and in their publications, in developing what Theodore Dwight Bozeman has felicitously termed a "doxological" view of science, that is, the view that the investigation of nature constituted a means of praising God. Their appropriation of science for religious ends, however, went beyond doxology to argument. Professional scientists took the lead in expounding natural theology, which focused on the evidences for God's

existence and divine attributes as revealed in the natural world. Hitchcock, for example, recalled that his title of Professor of Chemistry and
Natural History did not precisely convey the "grand object" that he had
in view when teaching: "That object was the illustrating by the scientific
facts which I taught, the principles of natural theology."[14]

Providing raw materials for evoking piety and defending theism was
clearly professionally advantageous in a period when clergy played key
roles in collegiate structures of power. It will not do, however, to ascribe
the eagerness with which many scientists pursued those tasks entirely to
calculations of professional advantage. Most natural philosophers and
natural historians appear to have found the doxological and apologetic
aspects of their vocations both spiritually engaging and emotionally sat-
isfying. Some even came to believe that "the more fully the man of science puts himself into sympathy with . . . the Almighty . . . the more
likely is he to make advances in scientific attainment."[15]

The eagerness with which many scientists used science for religious
ends is consistent with what historians have been able to uncover about
their backgrounds. Prior to 1870 many practitioners of science in American colleges were also clergy or recipients of some clerical training. Even
those who took other career paths characteristically embraced Christianity. In fact, the scanty evidence that we have suggests that as of the
middle of the nineteenth century the percentage of scientists within college faculties who were church members was considerably higher than
that in the population as a whole.[16]

The cultural significance of scientists' use of nature to evoke consciousness of nature's God was profound. Natural theology served as
the very foundation of Christian apologetics in post-Enlightenment
America. Many exponents of natural theology were convinced that they
could demonstrate that divinity lay at the very core of reality. In 1858
Harvard's Asa Gray wrote in his botany textbook that "the idea of plan
and system in nature supposes a Planner, or a mind which has ordered
things so, with intelligence and purpose; and it is this plan, or its evidences and results, which the naturalist is endeavoring to investigate."
A colleague at Harvard, the chemist Josiah Parsons Cooke, maintained
that evidence yielded by the systematic investigation of nature demon-
strated that "the existence of an intelligent Author of nature, infinite in
wisdom and absolute in power, may be proved with as much certainty
as can be any theory of science." Cooke concluded that there was
"strong reason to believe, on scientific grounds alone, that the universe
is still sustained in all its parts by the same ominipotent and omniscient
Will which first called it into being."[17]

The doxological character of science and its intimate association with
defense of Christian theism not only infused knowledge of the natural

world with spiritual meaning but also increased enormously the prestige of the scientific enterprise. By mid century if not before, educated Americans had come to endorse the principle that on matters relating to nature, scientific interpretations were normative. That principle inevitably reinforced the disciplinary autonomy of science.[18]

The relationship between science and Christian theology was not always cordial. Occasionally, especially during the period prior to 1830, American religious thinkers expressed concern that science served as a distraction from biblical study. In 1808, for example, the Princeton Seminary theologian Archibald Alexander lamented that "the great extension of the physical sciences, and the taste and fashion of the age, have given such a shape and direction to the academical course that I confess it appears to me to be little adapted to introduce youth to the study of the Sacred Scriptures." Archibald's concern, however, did little to shape the curriculum or priorities of higher education.[19]

More problematic was the relationship between the conclusions of science and the testimony of the Scriptures. On more than one occasion scientists arrived at conclusions that seemed irreconcilable with the prevailing views of the Bible. The nebular hypothesis of the origin of the solar system, the antiquity of the earth and human beings, and the widespread rejection of the idea of a universal deluge are only a few of the most noteworthy instances of such conclusions. Occasionally college officials responded to such conclusions by castigating the sciences that promulgated them. The trustees of South Carolina College, for example, removed geology from the curriculum in 1835 on the grounds that the science was playing fast and loose with the time scale seemingly prescribed by Genesis. Such measures, however, were the exception rather than the rule—and not because scientists knuckled under. Rather, a modus vivendi emerged. Scientists typically joined the clergy in asserting that God had revealed himself in both nature and the Scriptures and that, when properly interpreted, those two sources of revelation would prove consistent. In order to establish that consistency, however, they found it necessary to concede that the Bible was not a science book; scriptural revelation provided human beings with the essential tenets of the scheme of redemption, not a detailed knowledge of natural history. From this perspective, would-be conciliators concluded that as long as the findings of science did not conflict with doctrines central to Christian faith and practice, they could be accepted—and biblical interpretations could be revised accordingly. They thus came to interpret Noah's flood as a local event of little or no geological importance. Many, too, interpreted the "days" of Genesis as indefinitely long periods of time.[20]

Such efforts to reconcile science and the Bible, never uncontested, left some crucial issues unresolved. Nevertheless, the idea that it was appropriate to alter interpretations of scriptural passages periodically to bring them into closer accord with the verdict of scientists concerning the history and operation of natural phenomena passed muster with most Christians who thought about such matters. Daniel Coit Gilman, the president of Johns Hopkins University, thus observed in 1876 that "hostility toward scientific pursuits or toward scientific instruction has never in this country been manifested to any noteworthy extent by the religious part of the community or by theological teachers. In discussions relating to the sphere of science and religion, the teachers of religion have almost always been earnest in their approval of scientific research."[21]

The claim that the Bible did not provide a scientific account of the natural world inevitably gave scientists a freer hand. In spite of this fact, some scientists continued to insist on the harmony of science and the Scriptures. At Wofford College in South Carolina, for example, Warren DuPre devoted his inaugural lecture on geology in 1856 to showing that geological truth was wholly consistent with the Bible. Other scientists, such as the Yale geologist James Dwight Dana, went even further, claiming that the results of scientific investigation could actually shed needed light on the meaning of difficult scriptural passages. Whatever their position on such issues, however, men of science, as the precursors of modern scientists were commonly called, increasingly pursued their investigations of nature undeterred by biblical constraints. As time went on, the focus of their attention increasingly centered on the results of careful investigation of the works rather than the Word of God.[22]

Especially in courses focusing on moral philosophy and natural theology, scientists expounded their careful investigation of phenomena in order to demonstrate that religious meaning and significance infused all of reality. Indeed, for much of the nineteenth century the natural and human sciences provided the most fertile data for grounding theological inferences in the entire college curriculum. Courses using those data shared a number of important characteristics. First, by showing that thorough, often minute, investigation of individual facts yielded evidence of the beneficent design of God, they put a significant premium on the value of knowledge. Reflecting American Christianity's commitment to the Enlightenment as mediated through Scottish Common Sense realism, courses in natural theology and moral philosophy displayed great hostility to "speculation"—the desiccated fruit of the "airy region of metaphysics." Those courses encouraged students to forsake speculation and conjecture and to make reasonable inferences based on facts. Second, although moral philosophers and natural theologians did not in principle deny the value of faith, they tended in practice to minimize its role and to glorify instead *proof* and *argument*.[23]

The belief that empirical knowledge supported theistic convictions was among the most salient factors in prompting colleges to emphasize the value of the acquisition and transmission of knowledge long before the alleged "revolution" in higher education of the late nineteenth century. To be sure, learning in antebellum colleges remained oriented around the goals of molding character and fostering appreciation of the nexus between the creation and the Creator rather than extending the boundaries of knowledge for its own sake. In addition, in most colleges, undergraduate teaching rather than research was paramount, in the sciences as elsewhere. Nevertheless, historians who have suggested that the "old-time college" lacked an "academic culture" have not sufficiently appreciated the respect for understanding and learning present in higher education prior to 1870. And in some curricular areas, most notably the sciences, that respect grew into concerted efforts to acquire new knowledge.[24]

During the first two-thirds of the nineteenth century, men of science in Europe and the United States—both within colleges and outside them—became increasingly proficient at gathering facts and arranging them into meaningful patterns. Their successes in this so-called Baconian endeavor issued in an explosion of often rather esoteric knowledge. This, coupled with new theories and improved instrumentation, led to growing specialization within the natural sciences. By 1870 natural philosophy had fragmented into several identifiable research communities of chemists, physicists, and astronomers, and natural history had become subdivided into several new disciplines, most prominently zoology, botany, and geology. This specialization, which became more pronounced over time, increased the premium on obtaining "expertise" and further accelerated the acquisition of new knowledge.[25]

As important as the growth of knowledge and disciplinary specialization were, however, the most significant development within the natural sciences during the middle of the nineteenth century was a profound change in the norms of scientific explanation and discourse. Between about 1830 and 1870 men of science increasingly limited the range of their discussions and explanations to natural phenomena. In taking this position, they effectively disjoined their vocation from natural theology and essentially completed the detachment of the scientific enterprise from theology that they had begun when they had severed their investigations from prevailing formulations of the Bible.

The effort of scientists to describe phenomena in terms of "secondary" causes and natural laws was not new. As early as the Middle Ages, some natural philosophers were already expressing a desire to sharply limit recourse to the supernatural, and efforts to substitute natural agencies and laws for supernatural fiat became increasingly widespread after the seventeenth century. Still, during the early decades of the nineteenth century, few scientists hesitated to invoke the supernatural when naturalistic explanations were not at hand. Nor did their hesitation to do so abruptly disappear; as late as 1859 Darwin could write of "laws impressed on matter by the Creator" without obliterating the canons of scientific discourse. Many of the scientists whose views Darwin was contesting had even fewer qualms about invoking God. Indeed, it was precisely the willingness of academic scientists to invoke the supernatural in explaining the structure and operation of natural phenomena that accounted for much of the power that natural theology possessed within the colleges and, more generally, within Anglo-American apologetics. After about 1830, however, the range of phenomena that scientists believed to be describable in terms of naturalistic agencies widened significantly. Perhaps even more important, scientists began making concerted efforts to establish the principle that, in the words of the Wesleyan natural historian William North Rice, "it is the aim of science to narrow the domain of the supernatural, by bringing all phenomena within the scope of natural laws and secondary causes." It required little more than a nudge—albeit a theologically crucial nudge—to move from that position to the notion that no other form of description or explanation rightly deserved the name of *science*.[26]

Charles Darwin provided the nudge. Although it now seems clear that his theory of organic evolution was simply one in a long line of theories that substituted natural for supernatural agency, it effectively cut the Gordian knot between science and supernaturalism and triggered the establishment of "methodological naturalism" as the norm of scientific discourse. Darwin himself, who increasingly used natural agencies to account for the origin of new species and insisted that any alternative procedure was ipso facto unscientific, served as a particularly eloquent spokesperson for the naturalistic norm. During the ensuing controversy over the transmutation hypothesis, scientists sometimes expressed their commitment to that norm and its emphasis on sensible experience by expressing impatience with the unwillingness of special creationists to specify how "special creation" had occurred. They also echoed Darwin's complaint that special creation explained nothing. In truth, this complaint was groundless; the act of an omnipotent God's act of creation can explain *anything*. What critics meant in advancing their complaint was that the idea of supernatural fiat was inconsistent with the explanatory criteria that scientists had come to accept—and expect. Although many scientists continued for some time to reject the transmutation hypothesis, by 1860 Agassiz was already complaining that many scientists had come to regard "the idea of creation, that is, a manifestation of intellectual power by material means, as a kind of bigotry."[27]

Long after it had become clear that the scientific community had returned a favorable verdict concerning the transmutation hypothesis, many phenomena remained inexplicable in terms of naturalistic principles. Nonetheless, the triumph of Darwinism proved decisive in convincing scientists that "all events or phenomena whatever are part of a natural order, and are subject to general and ascertainable rules of sequence."[28]

The triumph of methodological naturalism, with its attendant detachment of scientific discourse from religious affirmation, was neither sudden nor universal. Many scientists continued throughout the late nineteenth and early twentieth centuries to discuss the religious implications of science in works addressed to nonprofessional audiences. Few explicitly attacked natural theology, and a minority even continued to espouse it in some of their publications addressed primarily to nonscientists. In addition, practitioners of nascent scientific disciplines, such as psychology, sometimes attempted to bolster their status within higher education by emphasizing that their inquiries would foster grander conceptions of God. Be that as it may, naturalistic description, which had begun as one of the products of scientific analysis, became increasingly a postulate of such analysis. And inevitably, methodology edged into metaphysics. Scientists began to assume that supernatural fiat was simply "not the way in which Nature does business." Their refusal to ascribe natural phenomena to supernatural agency, though rarely explicitly formulated, was no less adamant and programmatic for that. In effect, the very idea of what counted as an "explanation" had changed. From the vantage point of those calling for a more rigorously naturalistic methodology, the affirmation of supernatural activity in the face of mystery seemed to short-circuit scientific inquiry and to exhibit an odious form of sloth, a sin especially repugnant to good Victorians. The appropriate response to the inability to account for natural phenomena naturalistically was to solicit further scientific inquiry, not posit the supernatural. Increasingly after 1870, scientists preferred confessions of ignorance to invocations of supernaturalism.[29]

Methodological naturalism required scientists to assume not only that natural events were invariably describable in terms of natural agencies but also that those events would be intelligible to and decipherable by human intellectual and sensory apparatus. In view of the fact that these assumptions seem just as arbitrary as those of natural theology, the question of scientists' motivation for altering their position inevitably arises. It is too simplistic to ascribe the limitation of their discourse to natural phenomena as devotion to positivism, at least narrowly conceived as discipleship to Auguste Comte. Few natural scientists in the United States explicitly embraced Comte's work or his "Religion of Humanity." More important, during the late nineteenth and early twentieth centuries many retained their religious faith and thus had little sympathy with positivism's overt hostility toward religion. They commonly insisted that their efforts to expand the scope of scientific explanation and their programmatic exclusion of the supernatural from such explanation involved a reassessment of the nature of divine activity rather than a denial of it. The ability of human beings to account for natural phenomena by means of intelligible natural agencies, they asserted, constituted the strongest possible affirmation of God's wisdom. From this perspective, they reasoned that their work ought actually to intensify humanity's awe and respect for the Creator.[30]

A number of American scientists rejected the notion that natural laws and "secondary causes" were autonomous agencies. Like Isaac Newton and numerous other earlier students of nature, these scientists concluded that in describing phenomena in accordance with the norms of scientific discourse, they were simply thinking God's thoughts after Him. They also maintained that the term *scientific explanation* was something of a misnomer; science did not provide an ultimate *explanation* of anything. Instead it simply described the ways in which a Deity immanent within His creation had chosen to act.[31]

A variety of other formulas affirming the complementary nature of science and religion also proved popular. Some scientists, for example, maintained that while the proper arena of scientific investigation was phenomena accessible to the senses, the appropriate focus of religion was values. Others suggested that whereas science addressed "how" questions, religion focused on more ultimate "why" problems. However they structured such formulas, scientists conferred on their disciplines the right to examine nature and society in an uninhibited manner while largely leaving things of the spirit to theologians and the clergy.[32]

Two considerations closely associated with the internal dynamics of science proved particularly decisive in leading scientists to prune the supernatural from their explanations and discourse. The first of these was the thrust of the history of science. That history seemed to show that in numerous realms of inquiry, phenomena once thought to be the result of supernatural fiat turned out to be describable in terms of intelligible natural processes. This gave credence to the assumption that in principle there were no limits to the scope of naturalistic description.[33]

Just as important, each expansion of the realm within which the operation of "secondary causes" could be employed served to extend the research agenda of natural science. For example, the theory of organic evolution, which described the history of life in terms of processes familiar to natural historians, opened up the relationships of organisms through time to investigation and thus dramatically expanded the range of scientific inquiry. Many scientists understandably found the notion that the scope of their inquiries was in principle limitless utterly irresistible. The psychologist G. Stanley Hall, for example, recalled that "to conceive the whole world, material and spiritual, as an organic unity, to eliminate all breaks and supernaturalism, . . . gave me a totally new aspect of life. . . . I was bat-eyed to difficulties and impatient at objections, and had a blind spot in my mind for every break in the developmental order and implicit faith that if there anywhere seemed to be gaps it was only because we lacked adequate knowledge."[34]

The effect of detaching scientific discussion from theological discourse was profound. By the last third of the nineteenth century most scientists, Christian and otherwise, no longer judged the effectiveness of their efforts by whether they enabled human beings to "satisfy the aspiration of Reason to understand the wisdom of the Creator in his work." In fact, religious concerns became essentially extrinsic to the culture of science. Nonbelief (though not unbelief) became science's reigning methodological principle. Even for the sizable number of scientists who retained their commitment to Christianity, recourse to the divine in discussing natural and social phenomena seemed supererogatory. Their work in the classroom and laboratory became theologically neutral—compatible with theism and atheism alike. Just as important, as Hall's comment in the preceding paragraph suggests, elimination of the supernatural as an acceptable explanation of the structure, behavior, and even existence of natural phenomena provided the scientific community with a strong incentive to engage in additional inquiry in order to forge additional links in their ever-expanding chains of natural causes and effects.[35]

The determination of scientists to bring phenomena within the purview of naturalistic description evoked a mixed response from Christians outside the scientific community. In fact, much of the tension between science and religion between 1830 and 1900 centered on the issue of what sources of knowledge and what methodological principles were most appropriate to bring to bear in dealing with natural and social phenomena. Adding confusion to the discussion was the fact that prior to 1870, theologians and clergy had commonly conceded the legitimacy of scientists' efforts to expand the realm of "intermediate agencies" and natural law. Still, the assumption that *all* phenomena were candidates for naturalistic description proved controversial. More than one Christian expressed concern that "principles of order," described naturalistically, would "lose their personal character, become a nature of things, and wholly separate the mind of man from God." Many clergymen and theologians—most commonly those who embraced a "liberal" approach to Christian thought—sought to avoid that outcome by joining scientists in embracing an immanentist conception of God's relationship to the world. These thinkers, persuaded that scientists were the most appropriate interpreters of the natural world, held that science and theology offered complementary but different perspectives concerning natural phenomena: science described them by means of a naturalistic vocabulary, and theology affirmed that the causal efficacy underlying such phenomena came from the divine "energy" of the Creator. Other nonscientists, however, believing that supernatural activity lay at the heart of Christianity, evaluated the theological tenor of science in accordance with the degree to which it promoted belief in supernaturalism. Those thinkers tended to see science's repudiation of supernatural fiat as a betrayal.[36]

American colleges and universities, as institutions charged with the responsibility of making sense of reality, were among the prominent sites in which discussion of changes in scientific norms and the theological implications of those changes took place. Some colleges and seminaries, such as Princeton, Bowdoin, Andover Theological Seminary, and Columbia Theological Seminary, established professorships explicitly designed to focus on questions concerning the relationship between science and religion. Other colleges designed courses to show that science and religion could be reconciled. Franklin and Marshall, for example, required seniors to take a course in the "connection between Natural Science and Revealed Religion."[37]

Scientists themselves sometimes participated in efforts to reconcile science and religion. As late as 1896, for example, the geologist William North Rice began teaching an elective course for upperclassmen on "Relations of Science and Religion" at the Methodists' Wesleyan University. For the most part, however, once academic scientists abandoned the practice of drawing inferences from nature to the supernatural, they ceased viewing the promotion of natural theology as part of their vocation. Even scientists who persisted in believing that the orderliness discerned by science was a product of divine design and affirmed an immanent divine presence in the universe no longer maintained that science found its chief end in providing raw data for the inferences of natural theology.[38]

The absence of strong support for natural theology from scientists helped seal its fate within colleges and universities. Although it remained prominent in works written by clergymen and theologians and directed at lay audiences, natural theology failed to retain a strong constituency within higher education. Philosophers, possibly wishing to express their allegiance to the efforts of scientists to limit their investigations to empirically based data, became increasingly hospitable to a neo-Kantianism that, in drawing sharp distinctions between knowable phenomena and unknowable noumena, became increasingly uncongenial to natural theology. By the last decade of the nineteenth century most colleges and universities had abandoned the practice of requiring students to take a course in natural theology, and a number of influential institutions of higher education did not offer a course in that subject at all. Significantly, the three most distinguished universities that opened their doors in the late nineteenth century—Johns Hopkins University, the University of Chicago, and Stanford University—did not offer courses on natural theology. Even where the subject persisted as a course within philosophy departments, the expansion of offerings and students' increasing ability to choose among those offerings meant that it was no longer taken by all students.[39]

The severing of the close alliance between science and religion and the consequent relegation of natural theology to a position of relative unimportance had important consequences not only for the history of Christian apologetics in the United States but also for the role of science within higher education. In choosing to detach their inquiries from theological reflection, scientists were in effect renouncing a collaboration that had long proved instrumental in giving them a prominent role within the colleges.

Students of the natural world would not have demanded autonomy if past successes had not given them an ebullient optimism about the future capacities of scientific investigation. This optimism served as the springboard for a revisioning of the scientific vocation and the function of science. Even prior successes, however, did not render the prominence of science within higher education inevitable or guaranteed. It was incumbent on promoters of the scientific enterprise to persuade both college officials and potential patrons of higher education that notwithstanding its detachment from theological affirmations, science was an eminently valuable academic enterprise. For crusaders who wanted to provide additional resources to scientific practitioners in the United States, the need to provide science with a firm base of institutional support seemed even more compelling.[40]

After 1870, an arbitary but reasonable and convenient chronological marker for an important transition, a number of American intellectuals enthusiastically and aggressively attempted to justify, even privilege, scientific inquiry. Many of those intellectuals were among the some 800 scientists who were employed in American colleges and universities as of 1870. Those scientists were motivated to commend the study of natural phenomena not only by instinctive loyalty to their disciplines but also by a desire to retain colleges and universities as fruitful sources of employment and a hope to secure from those institutions support for ever more sophisticated and expensive research programs. Other apologists for scientific investigation, such as Charles Sanders Peirce and Chauncey

Wright, had received training in science and remained committed to the scientific ethos. Still others were philosophers or members of other disciplines who regarded the triumphs that had thus far occurred in comprehending the cosmos justification for hitching their philosophical and emotional wagons to the scientific star.[41]

The success that this heterogeneous, dedicated, and outspoken group had in promoting a "culture of science" within American colleges and universities during the late nineteenth and early twentieth centuries was more decisively determined by published works intended for a nonscientific readership than by the actual activities of academic scientists in their laboratories and classrooms. This is not to say that those activities were unimportant. They did much to provide currency to the belief that scientific inquiry could yield a rich, heretofore largely untapped, vein of solid knowledge. Nevertheless, in developing a convincing argument for the central importance of scientific inquiry within the academic mission of higher education, rhetoric—or more bluntly, perhaps, pontification—counted for at least as much as practice.

\* \* \* \*

Agents for scientific culture employed a variety of tactics to advance their cause during the late nineteenth and early twentieth centuries. For some time scholars have called attention to the way in which agents for scientific culture appropriated the moralistic ethos of Christianity in an attempt "to vindicate scientific inquiry as a religious calling." This act of arrogation helped to secure for science a favorable hearing in late-nineteenth-century America. There were, however, other important elements of the scientific apologetic that have received considerably less attention: its emphasis on the substantive truths and theoretical insights yielded by scientific inquiry, and its promise that further inquiry would yield knowledge by turning to good effect the Victorian bugbears of doubt, ignorance, and uncertainty. Both the products and the ongoing nature of scientific inquiry proved fundamental in shaping the status, fortunes, and agenda of science within higher education. Whatever the importance of the methodology of science might be—and that issue deserves attention—college presidents and the public were primarily interested in results. And what better way to demonstrate the value of scientific inquiry than by focusing on its ability to contribute to humanity's stock of knowledge? At the hands of its apologists, natural science became the paradigmatic knowledge-producing enterprise.[42]

As was the case with their predecessors, academic scientists and their allies emphasized that their ultimate goal was the pursuit of truth. Few expressed the concern voiced by Charles Darwin and a number of philosophers that the evolution of the human mind from animal instincts makes truth a suspect—or at least a merely conventional—category. Rather, most scientists appear to have assumed the existence of truth, even Truth with a capital *T*. Most, too, expressed faith that those possessed by the kind of "fanaticism for veracity" inspired by science would be able to derive that Truth from human experience.[43]

For true believers in the special sanctity of science, the really salient issue was not the possibility of apprehending truth, but the superiority of "rigid solid knowledge" to speculation, faith, tradition, and authority. The valorization of knowledge, rooted deeply within the history of Western civilization, had long been characteristic of American academic circles. Hostility to speculation, which often manifested itself in denunciations of "metaphysics," had been a prominent aspect of American intellectual life throughout the nineteenth century. Celebrants of scientific culture within higher education, trading on that animus, expressed impatience with alternatives to knowledge.[44]

Implicit in the invidious distinction that they drew between knowledge and other approaches to experience was the notion that knowledge was acquired in a different manner from other sources of insight. The term that enthusiastic supporters of science commonly gave to the means of acquiring knowledge about the world was *scientific method*. When one examines scientists' discussions of scientific method in an effort to ascertain what they meant by this concept, however, the picture becomes frustratingly opaque. *Scientific method* appears to have functioned as a catchall term covering a multitude of widely disparate practices. Some scientists, emphasizing the importance of carefully observing and recording natural phenomena, implied that science was an essentially passive, contemplative endeavor requiring humility and modesty, even "meekness." Others, probably the majority, drew on the post-Darwinian view of intelligence as active and functional to emphasize the "aggressive, dynamic," and experimental aspects of scientific investigation. Still other scientists endorsed both approaches. Henry S. Pritchett, president of the Massachusetts Institute of Technology, asserted that "the scientific method of study is characterized rather by a distinctive attitude of mind toward truth than by any new machinery for collecting facts." Pritchett submitted that "the scientific method insists that the student approach a problem with open mind, that he accept the facts as they really exist, that he be satisfied with no half-way solution, and that, having found the truth, he follow it whithersoever it leads." Most scientists made little effort to define the term at all.[45]

The philosophers who enlisted in the campaign to establish a vigorous culture of science within higher education and, more broadly, within American society often found themselves in no closer accord concerning the meaning of scientific method than natural scientists. Nor were the philosophers always diligent about providing careful definition. In 1894 John Dewey, who spoke tirelessly of the need for civilization to cultivate "the scientific habit of mind," defined the "method of inquiry" employed by science as "an organized, comprehensive, progressive, self-verifying system of investigation." Charles Peirce, another cheerleader for science, was not much more precise in his description of scientific method: "by taking advantage of the laws of perception, we can ascertain by reasoning how things really are, and any man, if he have sufficient experience and reason enough about it, will be led to the one true conclusion." Few celebrants of the scientific method even appear to have been conscious that the methods employed by sciences that aspired to nomothetic generalization were necessarily different from those embraced by the so-called historical sciences.[46]

Notwithstanding ambiguities, differences in emphasis, and instances of sloppy analysis, partisans of scientific culture could agree that the key to doing science—to producing knowledge rather than speculation— was to *think small*: to ask questions for which there were determinate and publicly verifiable answers. The realm that they demarcated for such questions consisted of phenomena accessible to "objective" examination and verification. In practice, they emphasized the role of the senses, albeit carefully monitored for possible sources of bias or distortion. The University of Chicago geologist Thomas Chamberlin, for example, asserted that it was not only "the tenet of all scientists" but the view of "most intelligent people generally" that "we get our knowledge or at least that which is surest, through our senses."[47]

The idea that science was unable to address "ultimate" questions had deep roots in American collegiate soil. From the outset of the inclusion of science within the college curriculum, theologians, clergy, philosophers, and scientists alike had coupled their praise of the value of systematic study of the natural world for furnishing data valuable to Christian apologetics with denials that such study could yield knowledge or understanding of first principles. The task of making inferences from scientific data to more fundamental ontological foundations had been the province of natural theology rather than science proper. Nevertheless, prior to about 1870 academic scientists had often been the most ardent proponents of and spokespersons for natural theology. By contrast, during the late nineteenth century most scientists in American colleges and universities seemed content to limit the scope of their efforts to the disclosure of intelligible patterns in the behavior of natural phenomena. They regarded speculation about the ultimate origins of matter, life, and mind and other philosophico-theological questions as outside their professional mandate. Indeed, to hear apologists for scientific culture tell it, the exclusion of such questions from the purview of scientific investigation was less an avowal of the limitations of science than a key to its success in producing knowledge.[48]

The studied indifference of scientists to first principles, coupled with their increasing emphasis on specialization, implied that scientific knowledge now, more than ever, resided in the details. As a result, in spite of the fact that champions of science in the late nineteenth century often criticized Baconianism for its unremitting hostility to "hypothesis," they continued to view the fact gathering that was such an integral part of Baconianism as the surest guarantee of real knowledge. Hence, a continued emphasis on the acquisition of facts was one of the major characteristics of scientific investigation within American higher education during the late nineteenth and early twentieth centuries. The botanist John M. Coulter was characteristic of American academic scientists in asserting that "facts are like stepping-stones. So long as one can get a close series of them, he can make advance in a given direction; but when he steps beyond them he flounders." For Coulter and others, each factual increment, however small, expanded the boundaries of knowledge.[49]

By the late nineteenth century, however, most Americans who addressed issues relating to scientific methodology recognized that simple fact gathering alone could not sustain a fruitful scientific empiricism. The acquisition of knowledge also required conceptual devices expressing relationships among phenomena. Thinking small did not necessitate eschewing theoretical statements that were clearly within the purview of natural science. "Hypothesis," Asa Gray wrote in 1880, "is the essential precursor of every fruitful investigation in physical nature." Hypothetical constructs seemed all the more necessary in the wake of the excision of the supernatural from scientific discourse, for the only alternative to confessions of ignorance was the promulgation of hypotheses positing natural connections among phenomena. But hypotheses were not simply instruments of last resort. The successes that science had already enjoyed in disclosing intelligible connections among phenomena seemed to confirm the value of working hypotheses and theories. Theoretical constructs were frequently patterned after the sequences and relations of cause and effect familiar in physical science, but this was not always the case. In the biological and human sciences, scientific discourse was often dominated by a functionalist vocabulary.[50]

The purpose and perceived value of theoretical constructs as well as their structure varied according to discipline. The physical sciences characteristically employed theories to achieve the goal of predictability. In other sciences, most notably the so-called historical sciences, such as paleontology and physical anthropology, this was clearly not possible.

Yet, in those sciences, too, hypotheses guided research agendas. By encompassing large groups of facts within their purview, theoretical structures served to make the cosmos intelligible and orient human beings within a complicated social and natural world.[51]

For science to play such a role effectively, its apologists emphasized, scientists were sometimes forced to convey harsh truths. The Tennysonian vision of "nature red in tooth and claw" was an early expression of an increasingly widespread suspicion that reality might well prove to be less amenable to human sensibilities than most people hoped and nature's more sentimental defenders believed. Accordingly, the late nineteenth century witnessed the emergence of an ethic that emphasized the desirability of an unflinching examination of the data and an acceptance of truth, whatever it might be. Partisans of a strong role for science within higher education were among the architects of that ethic.[52]

The principled determination on the part of partisans of scientific knowledge to eschew grandiose metaphysical claims in favor of more modest and achievable problems was reflected in their acknowledgment that the conclusions of science at any given time were simply probable rather than certain. The scientific revolution initiated by Charles Darwin, as well as frequent other lessons from the history of science, had made advocates of scientific culture understandably reluctant to hitch their wagon to determinate theoretical stars and in effect forced them to concede that absolute certainty was a chimera. Hence, one of the defining characteristics of the culture of science after 1870 as articulated by its spokespersons was its willingness to abandon conventional wisdom in the face of more accurate theoretical interpretations or additional facts.[53]

One should not, however, exaggerate the modesty or diffidence of the votaries of science. Although they refused to guarantee either certainty or infallibility from scientific investigation, they emphasized that such investigation was more reliable than any other form of inquiry. Many also maintained that one of the great virtues of scientific inquiry was that it was self-correcting and cumulative. For proponents of that view, "working hypotheses" became not so much exact copies of reality as cognitive instruments—William James called them acts of faith—serving to direct further inquiry and, often, add to humanity's stock of knowledge. As scientists pursued their calling, adding new facts and refining their theoretical structures, "in the long run" they would attain knowledge and glean truth. Charles Peirce expressed this position metaphorically: "The idea of science is to pile the ground before the foot of the outworks of truth with the carcasses of this generation, and perhaps of others to come after it, until some future generation, by treading on them can storm the citadel." From this perspective, science involved both patience and diligence. The University of Pennsylvania paleontologist Edward Drinker Cope suggested that "science is glad if she can prove that the earth stands on an elephant, and gladder if she can demonstrate that the elephant stands on a turtle; but if she can not show the support of the turtle, she is not discouraged but labors patiently."[54]

This doctrine of the cumulative and self-correcting nature of science enabled partisans of scientific inquiry to turn a seemingly formidable weakness—science's liability to error—into a source of strength: its acknowledgment of how much more still needed to be learned. While praising scientists for having already embarked on a steady advance toward knowledge and truth, defenders of science could thus emphasize the unsounded depths of human ignorance that remained. This conceptual framework did much to ensure that during the late nineteenth and early twentieth centuries, architects of the apologia for science within higher education would work tirelessly to extol the principle of ongoing inquiry. Those individuals held that just as past successes in describing natural and social phenomena in terms of natural agencies had led to an expansion of knowledge and a growing apprehension of truth, so science would continue to render experience more comprehensible. Such expressions of confidence, coupled with an acknowledgment of present uncertainty and ignorance, became the basis of a compelling argument for the need for sustained inquiry.[55]

The growing emphasis on continuing investigation rather than a body of established truths served as a foundation for an important alteration in the way that many professors envisioned their vocation. Prior to about 1870 the commitment of colleges to learning had manifested itself primarily in an emphasis on knowledge transmission. During the late nineteenth century an ever-increasing number of academics added knowledge production to their view of the appropriate mission of higher education. Scientists and their publicists were at the forefront of that enterprise. R. H. Chittenden, the head of Yale's Sheffield Scientific School, suggested that "the true teacher of science" needed also to be a student, "ever on the alert to interpret such signs as nature may make, quick to seize the opportunity to add to man's knowledge, to broaden and extend the limits of his chosen science, to keep in touch with the advances of the present and to harmonize these advances with the knowledge of the past, bearing clearly in mind that whatever is gained by scientific inquiry or research is never lost." G. Stanley Hall, reflecting on his early years as an experimental psychologist at Johns Hopkins University, nicely conveyed the ethos of the scientist as research scholar:

> We felt that we belonged to the larger university not made by hands, eternal in the world of science and learning; that we were not so much an institution

as a state of mind and that wherever and to what extent the ideals that inspired us reigned we were at home; that research is nothing less than a religion; that every advance in knowledge to-day may set free energies that benefit the whole race to-morrow. We believed that there was no joy in the world like the eureka joy of discovery in the heart of an investigator who has wrung a new secret from nature and advanced ever so little the gospel of truth, whether to confirm faith, prevent illness, deepen self-knowledge and that of society, or give man mastery over the physical, chemical, biological, social, and psychic energies that control the world to-day and will do so more to-morrow.[56]

Hall's sense of participation in a larger endeavor, which can be viewed as a new variant of an older "republic of letters" ideal, moved him to an enthusiasm that was widely shared. The desire of many young people to acquire knowledge rather than more material rewards in a society that seemed to some uncomfortably avaricious and vulgar was one of the considerations that led both to a huge migration of American students to German universities and a boom in graduate education in the United States. In contrast to proponents of the German university ideal, who believed that research should be limited to those who had a special genius for it, scientists who embraced the research ideal within American colleges and universities maintained that even individuals of mediocre ability and intellect could make genuine contributions to the store of scientific knowledge. And while scientists in universities with graduate programs undoubtedly received the most powerful inducements to produce as well as to transmit knowledge, even academics within smaller institutions frequently embraced and promoted the research ideal as a means of bolstering their careers and improving their teaching. At Denison College in Ohio, for example, Clarence Luther Herrick not only encouraged his students to engage in extensive microscopic and geological research but also founded a journal of science as a means of promoting research. Similarly, even at institutions such as Illinois College, the University of North Dakota, and Wooster College, where there was rarely as much financial support as a full realization of the research ideal required, scientists gave systematic inquiry an enthusiastic trumpeting.[57]

Scientists were certainly not the only people who experienced the thrill of discovery or who argued, as did the Johns Hopkins University physicist Henry Rowland in 1883, that "the true pursuit of mankind is intellectual." Nevertheless, natural scientists and their allies deserve primary credit for the increasing respect that the discipline-based research ideal commanded within institutions of higher education. The accomplishments of science, as well as the link that the apologists for scientific culture had constructed between knowledge and ongoing inquiry, constituted a particularly cogent case for making research within specialized disciplines a fundamental component of higher education. Recognizing this, William T. Sedgwick of the Massachusetts Institute of Technology declared that "one of the greatest services that science has ever done is to discover and popularize the model method of research which all branches of learning have hastened to adopt, and whose adoption has brought about the scientific spirit of this age."[58]

As Sedgwick recognized, the ethos of science exercised a much more pervasive influence within higher education during the late nineteenth and early twentieth centuries than it had earlier. The primary reason for this is that scientists and their allies succeeded in constructing a compelling argument that scientific knowledge and ongoing rational inquiry were the most reliable modes of acquiring truth. Their success cannot be accurately measured in the actual amount of natural science that students took as part of their curricular requirements. During the late nineteenth and early twentieth centuries burgeoning college enrollments and growing specialization led to a significant increase in the number of natural scientists within the faculties of colleges and universities. By 1910 the number of academic scientists in the United States had increased by more than a hundredfold since 1820. Yet, largely as a result of the elective system, most college students devoted less of their time to studying natural science after 1870 than they had before. A much clearer indication of the increasing influence of science within higher education was the expansion of the methods and approaches employed by natural scientists into new areas of inquiry. Precisely because the term *scientific method* remained so vague, professors in numerous areas of inquiry found it possible to invoke that phrase as a talisman in justifying the legitimacy of their efforts.[59]

## Chapter Two

## THE EMERGENCE OF THE HUMAN SCIENCES

DURING THE LATE NINETEENTH and early twentieth centuries spokespersons for areas of inquiry that dealt with the activities of human beings made concerted efforts to participate in the community of discourse established by natural scientists and their apologists by drawing on the techniques, methods, and theory-driven agendas associated with natural science. Indeed, one scholar has suggested that "one could write the history of much of social science during the past hundred years in terms of declarations that it has just become, or is just about to become, a genuine scientific enterprise."[1]

Unlike the natural sciences, which had long occupied an important place in the college curriculum, the areas of inquiry embodied in the human, or social, sciences had characteristically been woven into courses in moral philosophy. Proponents of autonomous human science disciplines—most notably history, psychology, political science, economics, sociology, and anthropology—therefore found themselves needing to provide a compelling justification for them. This was one of the reasons why social scientists allied themselves with natural science. They hoped that this tactic would give their disciplines the intellectual authority needed to ensure them an important role within institutions of higher education. In turn, such a role would increase employment opportunities as well as the credibility and power of the human sciences within American culture. These professional considerations, however, do not entirely account for the eagerness with which partisans of the human sciences sought to identify their efforts with the natural sciences. Many were also convinced that the work of physical scientists and natural historians provided essential guidance in attaining truth.[2]

Although separate courses in history and political economy could be found within some antebellum colleges, study of what later became the human sciences remained within the curriculum of moral philosophy at most colleges until after the Civil War. Harvard, for example, did not create a department of political economy separate from philosophy until 1879. Moreover, the separate courses that were established prior to the late nineteenth century bore little relation to the human sciences that emerged in that period. Courses in political economy taught in antebellum colleges, for example, characteristically remained linked conceptually to the humanistic and theological concerns of moral philosophy.

History, discussed in more detail in Part II of this book, was often taught as belles lettres in antebellum colleges.[3]

After the Civil War the growing specialization within the natural sciences undoubtedly contributed to the credibility of the claim that the creation of a series of independent disciplines dealing with human beings would be "in the interest of scientific progress." The ideals of ongoing inquiry and the production of knowledge celebrated by natural scientists and their allies may well have helped to sell the idea of carving up the territory relating to human nature, society, and culture into more manageable chunks than the kind of integrated—but often superficial—learning found in courses on moral philosophy. However, in contrast to the natural sciences, which became autonomous disciplines largely as a result of burgeoning knowledge and growing specialization, the emergence of the social sciences from moral philosophy was more a cause than an effect of the development of specialized bodies of knowledge concerning the nature of human beings and the dynamics of their cultures and societies. The primary engine driving the detachment of the human sciences from moral philosophy was the success of a growing number of thinkers in convincing college officials and literate Americans alike that it was appropriate to treat human affairs as objects of scientific analysis rather than philosophical speculation. E. L. Youmans, a prominent apologist for natural science, gave voice to that conviction when he observed in 1874 that "social science is but a branch of general science, having similar objects, and to be pursued by the same methods, as the other sciences."[4]

For intellectuals who shared Youmans's view, the separation of the human sciences from the more humanistically oriented moral philosophy courses in which they had been embedded for most of the nineteenth century seemed imperative. Indeed, these intellectuals found the underlying philosophical assumptions, the animating purposes, and the characteristic patterns of discourse of moral philosophy unacceptable. A different approach was needed, they believed, an approach sufficiently rigorous and empirical to capture the complexity of psychical, social, and cultural reality in a period of complex and tumultuous change.[5]

The direction that the human sciences took within American higher education during the late nineteenth and early twentieth centuries can be traced to several different sources. German scholarship, which many social scientists experienced firsthand between 1870 and 1914, affirmed the value of eschewing metaphysical speculation about ultimate causes and entities in favor of concentrating on empirical analysis and inductive generalization. The University of Wisconsin economist Richard T. Ely was only one of a number of American social scientists whose study at German universities proved to be the occasion for abandoning the search for "absolute truth" in favor of analyzing more mundane social realities. A German influence can also be discerned in the way in which practitioners within each of the social science disciplines during the late nineteenth century emphasized the importance of arriving at generalizations through the careful examination of the data of history and contemporary society. Finally, German universities reinforced the value of research as an ideal in American higher education.[6]

Most social scientists were more intent on associating their fields with the spirit and procedures of the natural sciences than on appealing to the traditions of German scholarship. In some fields, most notably history, practitioners tended to equate the *Wissenschaft* they had encountered in Germany with the systematic and empirical approach associated with the natural sciences. Peter Novick has suggested that "no group was more prone to scientific imagery, and the assumption of the mantle of science, than the historians." The determined attempt of historians in the late nineteenth century to ally themselves with the natural sciences could be seen at every turn. It was pervasive in the work of Henry and Charles Francis Adams, who viewed Darwin's work as the primary impetus for "a science of history." It manifested itself in the work of Frederick Jackson Turner, with his use of such biological terminology as "vital forces" and "organs." It also shaped the thinking of James Ford Rhodes and Herbert Baxter Adams, who compared historical methodology with the laboratories of natural scientists.[7]

Economists also allied themselves with the natural sciences. The Harvard political economist Charles F. Dunbar, for example, asserted in 1886 that "the economic law, the deduction of pure science, is simply the statement of a causal relation, usually between a small number of forces and their joint effect, possibly between a single force and its effect." The relation of any economic fact "to its cause and its consequences," he submitted, "is as certainly a question to be settled by appropriate scientific methods, as the perturbation of a satellite or a reaction observed by a chemist." Although Dunbar's commitment to a classical vision of economics found little favor with partisans of the "historical" school of economics who came to prominence in the United States during the 1880s, those economists, many of whom had been trained in German universities, were similarly committed to associating themselves with the ethos of the natural sciences. Ely, for example, termed the approach that he favored in treating economic behavior the "experimental" method, pointedly emphasizing that "it is in many respects the same which has borne such excellent fruit in physical science." Ely acknowledged that experiments in economics were not entirely the same as experiments in the natural sciences, but he held that "the whole life of the world" had been "a series of grand economic experiments," and he urged that by carefully examining the data of history and contemporary society it would be possible to ascertain the truth about the changing nature of human economic behavior.[8]

During the late nineteenth century, political scientists drew as much on traditions of German scholarship as on natural science, but in practice the former were eclipsed by efforts to apply to political phenomena the principles and research methods most closely associated with the natural sciences. This perspective prompted John W. Burgess, a political scientist instrumental in launching a school in that subject at Columbia University in 1880, to maintain that the task of the political scientist was to arrange "the facts of history in the forms and conclusions of science." Even after the "historical-comparative method" gave way in the beginning of the twentieth century to greater interest in contemporary political life, efforts to associate political science with natural science persisted. For example, Henry Jones Ford, a professor at Princeton, likened the study of political science to the study of evolutionary biology and suggested that the State be viewed as an organism. Other political scientists ignored such metaphors but continued to express preferences for inductive methodology, the role of comparative analysis, the use of experimentation, and the search for "laws" of political behavior.[9]

Among sociologists there was widespread consensus that natural science constituted both a source of cherished principles and a model of rigor to be emulated in obtaining real knowledge. Ulysses G. Weatherly, a sociologist at Indiana University, noted that Lester F. Ward's command of natural science was "always the envy of his fellow-sociologists." William Graham Sumner ascribed much of the "thirst for reality" in human affairs manifested in the growth of his discipline to "the modern study of nature." Sumner viewed sociology and biology as "cognate" sciences in that they simply dealt with a different "range of phenomena produced by the struggle for existence." Franklin H. Giddings, an eminent professor of sociology at Columbia University, suggested that "sociology is planted squarely on those new conceptions of nature—natural causation and natural law—that have grown up in scientific minds in connection with doctrines of evolution and the conservation of energy."[10]

The field of psychology was at least as conspicuous in appealing to natural science as those human sciences that focused on society and culture. During the late nineteenth century a growing number of "new psychologists" in the nation's burgeoning colleges and universities sought to detach themselves from speculative philosophy by emphasizing the importance of using methods associated with the natural sciences to study the human psyche. One source of inspiration for this declaration of independence was the theory of organic evolution, which implied that human beings were not unlike other animals and that the human mind, like the human body, was a product of transmutation. Another was the work of European physiologists and psychologists, which suggested the interdependence of mental and neurophysiological processes and provided American psychologists with some of the experimental techniques that they employed in subjecting consciousness to scientific examination and measurement. Perhaps the most important reason for the appeal of a natural scientific approach to psychology, however, was expressed by William James in 1876: "Physical science is becoming so speculative and audacious in its constructions, and at the same time so authoritative, that all doctrines find themselves, willy-nilly, compelled to settle their accounts and make new treaties with it." This perspective convinced many psychologists that aligning their work with science was the approach most likely to secure the support of university administrators and the respect of the public. It even led some psychologists, including bedfellows as unlikely as the eclectic William James and the doctrinaire behaviorist John B. Watson, to place psychology within the orbit of the natural sciences.[11]

As disciplines that self-consciously sought to ally themselves with the natural sciences, the human sciences were in a very real sense born with a commitment to methodological naturalism. Although historians have sometimes acknowledged that the efforts of social scientists to detach themselves from moral philosophy included a campaign to secure "complete independence from theological restrictions," they have devoted far less attention to the fact that this campaign involved determined efforts to limit the focus of the human sciences to the realm of phenomena susceptible to disciplined, characteristically empirical, inquiry. In making those efforts, proponents of the human sciences regarded the natural sciences as a worthy model to emulate.[12]

In contrast to moral philosophy, with its providential framework and its congeniality to the idea of divine supernatural fiat, the human sciences employed rhetoric, methodology, and explanatory formulas that were resolutely naturalistic. Indeed, the absence of God-talk was such a pronounced characteristic of the human sciences in the late nineteenth and early twentieth centuries that it is easy simply to overlook it or, alternatively, to take it for granted. Historians have tended to make far more of the religious backgrounds of American social scientists and whatever vestigial religious and moral elements remained within the human sciences than they have of the devotion to a different, more naturalistic focus of inquiry in the disciplines that emerged from moral philosophy.[13]

The differences between the human sciences and moral philosophy in this regard should not, however, be exaggerated. The moral philosophers, many of whom likened the moral universe to the Newtonian cosmos, actually began the process of detaching discourse about the social order from discussions of divine activity when they described the "laws" that God had embedded within the fabric of society and in the hearts of the human beings who composed it in terms of natural mechanisms such as self-interest, competition, sociability, and the calculus of pleasure and pain. In addition, the conviction that God had laid down laws of social and cultural interaction had led moral philosophers to enjoin their students to examine human phenomena carefully and to draw inferences about the nature of moral law from the actual fortunes of men and women. On the other side of the coin, even in the late nineteenth century, not all social scientists were scrupulous in avoiding allusions to the divine. The University of Michigan historian Andrew C. McLaughlin, for example, coupled his claim that the laws underlying the "hurly-burly of succeeding events in history" constituted a "natural process" with an insistence that "the impulses of God" underlay the process.[14]

Despite certain continuities, the emergence and development of the human sciences marked an important transition from its predecessor. A providentialist ethos pervaded moral philosophy. Moral philosophers may not have been averse to invoking "secondary" agencies in describing God's general providence, but they characteristically pointed out that such agencies *did* represent divine activity. If they frequently described God's moral government in terms of a series of laws, they lost few opportunities to praise such laws as the "harmonies of Providence." Moreover, God's role in moral philosophy was not mere window dressing. Rather, the conviction that the mechanisms shaping human activity were grounded in the divine will served to ensure their essential goodness. No less important, because God's general providence could be altered through special divine interventions, providentialism provided an intellectually cogent explanation of those occasions when there appeared to be exceptions to the moral laws governing individuals and society.[15]

The ideas and rhetoric of the human sciences stood in sharp contrast to the conceptual universe of moral philosophy. The most obvious difference is that in the late nineteenth century, references to God as an agent within the social order were conspicuous by their absence. Like the natural scientists and their apologists, most spokespersons for the human sciences appear to have believed that scientific analysis required investigators to attend to phenomena without invoking the Deity as an explanatory hypothesis. Indeed, the prospect that God periodically intervened by means of supernatural divine fiat in the social and cultural arena would have jeopardized the effort to render psychical, cultural, and social phenomena scientifically intelligible.[16]

As important as the abandonment of God-talk by practitioners of the human sciences was on the rhetorical level, the inclination to ignore the role of providence in human affairs went well beyond rhetoric. By the late nineteenth century, social scientists, possibly inspired by the example of their counterparts in the natural sciences, had become convinced that attributing the phenomena they investigated to the will of God was too facile and insufficiently explanatory. They sought instead to render the facts of social life into descriptions, even explanations, that employed natural, verifiable processes and mechanisms. In taking on that task, they joined natural scientists in conceding that phenomena were complex, puzzling, often mysterious. By the late nineteenth century, however, they were unwilling to use supernatural currency in gaining a purchase on those phenomena. For social scientists, as for natural scientists, ignorance seemed more worthy of science than professions of faith.

Lester F. Ward presented one of the clearest articulations of social scientists' determination to detach discussion of society from supernaturalism. Ward, who spent much of his life specializing in paleobotany with the United States Geological Survey, did not obtain an academic position in sociology until late in his career. Nevertheless, his *Dynamic Sociology* (1883) profoundly influenced many academic social scientists and earned him the title of founding father of American sociology. Ward envisioned all phenomena "as the parts of one whole or unit, and bound together by an absolutely unbroken chain." He insisted that it was appropriate to dispense with all first and final causes and rely on "efficient causes only." From Ward's perspective, the only "proper objects of knowledge" were "tangible facts; material objects; truths, laws, and principles, demonstrable either directly by the senses or deducible from such as are demonstrable, in such a manner that their negation is absolutely excluded." Convinced that "the only important knowledge is science," he urged that social phenomena be treated in the same way that scientists treated natural phenomena: "as both effects and causes, as terms in an infinite series of causation, deriving their own character from the immediate antecedents out of which they are evolved, and impressing that character upon the immediate consequents upon which their activities are expended." In his *Pure Sociology,* published in 1903, Ward addressed the tendency of the "theologically inclined" to attribute human events to the guidance of God with some scorn. "Science," he declared, "deals with phenomena and can only deal with phenomena." Sociology would thus achieve scientific standing only insofar as it took the position that "human events are phenomena of the same general character as other natural phenomena, only more complex and difficult to study on account of the subtle psychic causes that so largely produce them."[17]

Other sociologists concurred with Ward on the necessity of liberating social inquiry from the categories of supernaturalism. Franklin H. Giddings reminded his readers in 1894 that "in the universe as known to science there are no independent, unrelated, uncaused causes." The sociologist, Giddings asserted, "finds nowhere a social force that has not been evolved in a physical-organic process, nor one that is not at every moment conditioned by physical facts." Albion W. Small, who accepted the first academic chair in sociology in the United States, at the University of Chicago, in order to establish the scientific credentials of that discipline, recalled that from an early stage in his career two recurrent thoughts dominated his thinking: "first, that there must be some sort of correlation between human occurrences, and second, that the clues to that correlation must be found by checking up cause and effect between human occurrences themselves, not in some a priori." Small maintained that working sociologists must locate "social causation within human beings, instead of outside, above, beneath, or beyond them." The "sociological movement" in the United States, he noted, was the product of a *"deliberate and avowed purpose to work for a scientific interpretation of cause and effect in human society at large."*[18]

Edward A. Ross, who after graduating from Johns Hopkins in economics in 1891 taught sociology at Stanford, Nebraska, and Wisconsin, recalled that even before graduating from college he had abandoned "all attempt to ascertain the cause or 'ground of being' of things." A diary entry written by Ross in 1889 while he was studying in Germany confirms his recollection: "The philosophy that sets as its task the determination of the regular time-and-space order of groups of similar phenomena is the only one that is not doomed to disappoint." Somewhat later in his career Ross, though critical of crude efforts to apply laws of natural science to social phenomena, emphasized that it was better to invoke analogies between natural phenomena and social phenomena than to interpret them "providentially." Committed as he was to both "the *continuity* of social change" and the idea of "*resident forces* as causing change," he assumed that it was axiomatic that "sociology does not venture beyond the causes and laws of the phenomena it considers."[19]

Historians joined sociologists in committing themselves to naturalistic discourse and patterns of description and explanation. Ephraim Emerton, Harvard's Winn Professor of Ecclesiastical History, denounced the practice of invoking supernatural powers to account for historical events as indicative of an "unhistorical attitude of mind." For Emerton and other historians, whether historical events were described in terms of individual choice, large social forces, or "laws" of development was less important than the need to confine the discussion to the natural plane of existence and avoid the temptation to resort to the transcendent. In 1902 the University of Pennsylvania professor Morris Jastrow, an eminent student of the history of religion, gave voice to the view that by then had become dominant among historians: "Unless human history is to be explained by a thorough study of causes and results, and by an exclusive regard to human conditions, no explanation in the real sense of the word is possible. To have recourse to supernaturalism is to confess our inability to solve the problem on which we are engaged."[20]

The other human sciences also shunned supernaturalism. In economics, for example, in 1865 Arthur Latham Perry, a professor of history and political economy at Williams College, described political economy as "an examination of the providential arrangements, physical and social, by which it appears that exchanges were designed by God for the welfare of man." From Perry's perspective, "if the footsteps of providential intelligence be found anywhere upon this earth, if proofs of God's goodness be anywhere discernible, they are discernible, and are found in the fundamental laws of society." Even as late as 1890 Perry continued to value economics as a forum for discussing "the divine Purpose." By the 1880s, however, there was a discernible drift away from God-talk among economists. Both partisans of classical economics and members of the insurgent "historical" school avoided describing economic behavior in terms of divine providence in favor of making generalizations in accordance with observed phenomena. The *locus classicus* for a naturalistic approach to economics was Thorstein Veblen's classic article, "Why Is Economics Not an Evolutionary Science?" Veblen maintained that the key to creating a truly "scientific" economics was an abandonment of teleological thinking and all efforts to get beyond "the colorless sequence of phenomena." "The guiding hand of a spiritual agency," he maintained, "becomes less readily traceable as men's knowledge of things grows ampler and more searching." For his part, he found the "long and devious course of disintegrating animism" in economics all to the good.[21]

In political science, John W. Burgess articulated the prevailing hostility to providentialism. Burgess informed his readers that while it was perfectly acceptable to believe that God had "implanted the substance of the state in the nature of man," it was unnecessary to assume that the "direct intervention" of the Deity was involved. Moreover, he averred, in describing the development of the State, political scientists should limit their focus to the activity of human beings within history.[22]

The efforts of psychologists to develop a more scientific approach to study of the human mind went beyond the creation of laboratories and the establishment of suitable research strategies. It also entailed pruning their discourse of references to God and other spiritual forces. That endeavor was initially complicated by the desire on the part of some of the "new" psychology's founding fathers to refute materialism. In the 1870s and 1880s this desire prompted them to describe psychology as "Christian to its root and centre." During the 1890s, however, an increasing number of academic psychologists began to insist that psychology would not be truly scientific until it freed the study of mind and behavior from any connection with theological categories. Those psychologists remained judiciously noncommittal as to issues such as the existence of the human soul and the relationship between consciousness and neurophysiological processes. Their intent was simply to eliminate spiritual agency from their descriptive and analytic arsenal by limiting their focus to natural entities and processes. This intent prompted James Mark Baldwin to enjoin psychologists to "reason from a basis of fact and by an inductive procedure" by separating the "deposit" of verifiable data relating to the mind from the "speculative solvent" in which it resided. William James, though generally congenial to the idea of the supernatural, nevertheless promised readers of *The Principles of Psychology* (1890) that his treatment would "remain positivistic and non-metaphysical." Although James did not always keep that promise, he made it clear that he associated the development of a scientific psychology with a "fair and square and explicit *abandonment* of such questions as that of the soul, the transcendental ego, the fusion of ideas or particles of mind stuff." Psychologists more indifferent than James to spiritual concerns and especially anxious to emulate the natural sciences went out of their way to insist, as the Bryn Mawr psychologist James Leuba put it, that "it is no business of theirs either to reject or to affirm the transcendental existence of God."[23]

Anthropology was less clearly established as a distinct field of social scientific inquiry within institutions of higher education in the late nineteenth century than other disciplines in the social sciences. Nevertheless, a good deal of inquiry about the origin, behavior, and cultural development of human beings had proceeded outside the confines of the colleges and universities. Reflecting on the results of this inquiry, the Yale social scientist William Graham Sumner concluded in 1881 that "anthropology is more likely to give laws to metaphysics than to accept laws from that authority." The unwillingness of anthropologists to construe their inquiries in any other than naturalistic terms is hardly surprising, for the underlying premise of anthropological research in the late nineteenth century was that "man must be placed wholly within the domain of nature."[24]

The number of explicit statements repudiating the use of supernatural agency in discussions of social science fails to provide an accurate measure of the decline of God-talk in that arena. Many social scientists who avoided allusions to divine activity did so without comment and perhaps even without full consciousness of the implications of their position.

Others assumed that efforts to detach the social sciences from theology were, as Sumner—hardly a pussycat in such matters—put it, "best carried forward indirectly." Timing does much to account for the relative paucity of discussion concerning the role of God in social phenomena. By the time the social sciences were establishing themselves as autonomous disciplines, the natural sciences had already rendered exclusion of the supernatural from discourse quite conventional. Indeed, the notion that it was essential to restrict discourse and patterns of explanation to natural agencies and events had become one of the reigning assumptions in conceptions of what it meant to do science. Disciplines with aspirations to anchor themselves within institutions dedicated to scientific inquiry and the production of knowledge could ill afford to incur the taint of "speculation" by incorporating God into their analysis.[25]

By the beginning of the twentieth century, anthropologists, sociologists, and psychologists were subjecting religion itself to scientific scrutiny. Practitioners of those disciplines, in accordance with the secular precepts of science, treated religion as a phenomenon that had arisen as a result of human needs and impulses—through "secondary causes"—rather than from the promptings of the divine.[26]

The refusal to invoke supernatural agency in accounting for the behavior of human beings was not, however, simply a tactic designed to ingratiate social scientists with natural scientists and college officials. Implicit in that refusal was a sincere conviction that the best way of making sense of social and cultural realities was through the use of theoretical concepts invoking intelligible, discernible, natural connections among phenomena. Accordingly, practitioners of the human sciences coupled their abandonment of the providential framework of moral philosophy with assiduous efforts to formulate such concepts. They arrived at several that proved valuable in organizing data, most notably social evolution, cultural organicism, and preeminently, as in the humanities, historicism. And, as in the case of the humanities, those concepts substituted relationships among human beings for the nexus between God and His fallen children.[27]

Like many of their counterparts in the natural sciences, many social scientists concentrated primarily on discovering causal relations. Edward A. Ross, for example, argued that "laws of causation" were "the peculiar treasure of a science." From this perspective, he concluded that the number of causal relations that were discovered "is a true measure of scientific advancement." During the late nineteenth and early twentieth centuries social scientists yielded a spate of potentially useful causal agents. A useful summary of these agents can be found in the work of Thomas L. Haskell, whose discussion is worth quoting at length:

Social scientists in the 1890's, and in the Progressive era located the effective causation of human affairs sometimes in heredity, sometimes in environment; sometimes in the play of economic interests, sometimes in particular historical conditions, such as the frontier experience; sometimes in stimulus-response associations, sometimes in instinct, sometimes in culture, sometime in that alien area within the person but remote from his conscious mind, the subconscious.[28]

Dorothy Ross has suggested that the growing popularity of the social sciences resulted at least partly from the ability of their practitioners to minister to the anxieties of people no longer confident of the reality of divine purpose. There is undoubtedly some truth to this view. But the human sciences should be viewed as agents of secularization and not simply results of the process. A willingness to abandon discourse about the relationship of God to the social order and ignore questions of divine purpose in thinking about social reality signifies a shift of focus to the secular arena. Clearly, some social scientists, such as Lester F. Ward and Edward A. Ross, had abandoned their faith prior to choosing their careers. Some also regarded their professional inquiries as an appropriate surrogate for more conventional expressions of religion. Still, not all social scientists who participated in the removal of references to the supernatural from the interpretation of social phenomena were ardent secularists. Many had pious backgrounds and retained a Christian perspective in their personal lives. These thinkers apparently regarded the naturalistic turn in the social sciences as a comment on the *mode* of divine activity rather than a denial of its existence.[29]

*   *   *   *

Social scientists not only paid homage to the natural sciences in substituting naturalistic causal structures for divine agency but also emulated the efforts of natural scientists to produce knowledge by combining empirical facts with verifiable theories. As a group they were no less ambiguous and unsystematic than natural scientists in discussing what it meant to study phenomena scientifically. In the end, like most practicing natural scientists, most practitioners of the human sciences proved less interested in proffering a systematic explication of philosophy of science than in producing knowledge.

The precise nature of the knowledge that the human sciences were to produce, however, did not always seem entirely clear. The late nineteenth and early twentieth centuries witnessed a series of sometimes heated discussions within many disciplines as to whether the vocation of social scientists consisted primarily of eliciting the particularity of data relating to social phenomena or whether it resided in efforts to discover general principles, or "laws," of social behavior. Historians and other practitioners of the human sciences ultimately divided over this issue.

Most historians embraced particularity. Although a few, such as Henry Adams, persisted in attempting to discern scientific laws of development, most professional historians were leery about such an endeavor. For them the challenge of doing "scientific" history lay not in discovering laws or testing models of human behavior but in using a rigorously empirical method of investigation and in attempting to discern the chains of cause and effect relevant in accounting for specific historical events.[30]

Practitioners in the other social sciences also acknowledged the importance of particular facts and events, but like the natural scientists whom they viewed as exemplary, most of them emphasized the value of interpreting data within the framework of broader theoretical models and principles. They were convinced that effective research—and the key to making the human sciences "science"—involved developing theoretical models that could be tested against carefully arranged facts. They thus saw no conflict between allegiance to theory and commitment to empirical evidence. As Ely put it, "We must observe in order to theorize, and theorize in order to observe." Edward A. Ross expressed a common view when he asserted that by "patiently comparing social facts among themselves," it would eventually be possible to disclose "regularities" that permitted "the formulation of laws."[31]

From the very outset of the emergence of the human sciences from moral philosophy, however, some spokespersons in each discipline criticized their colleagues for being too quick to posit laws and broad generalizations. Although most of them did not in principle oppose theory, their recognition that scholarship in the human sciences was at an early stage prompted them to emphasize that theorizing should proceed slowly and cautiously. While the necessity of scrapping the "old apparatus" of explanation seemed apparent, it was considerably less clear just what a more theoretically sound description of human nature, culture, and society would look like. This prompted many social scientists to suggest that the most pressing need of the day was the acquisition of empirical data. As Ely succinctly put it, "The first thing is to gather facts."[32]

Over time, this emphasis on fact gathering converged with a growing conviction that the only way that real knowledge could be produced in the social sciences was "to isolate a relatively controllable problem." This conviction manifested itself in an increasing tendency after about 1900 to abandon univeralistic, "cosmic" models of social behavior, such as social evolution, in favor of more restricted patterns of analysis. Like the natural scientists, social scientists increasingly embraced research programs that yielded questions for which there were (in principle, at least) verifiable answers and theoretical principles that could be tested by systematic examination of manageable segments of data. Albion W. Small characterized this tendency as "a scientific achievement." It represented a recognition that "intensive operations upon details of the structure and processes of reality" were more fruitful than assaults on the "citadel of all reality." Small held that "putting fragments of truth together will make the fragments more truthful and the whole more symmetrical."[33]

This vision of the human sciences, institutionalized in graduate seminars and reflected in college classrooms, encouraged practitioners in those disciplines to place the same emphasis as their counterparts in the natural sciences on ongoing inquiry and research. Convinced that the intellectual problems involved in analyzing human phenomena were "as far as we know without end," social scientists concluded that knowledge could be attained only by means of a continuous process of investigation, a dogged "pursuit of truth." That pursuit, William Graham Sumner wrote in 1905, "gives us life, and it is to that pursuit that our loyalty is due." Like defenders of natural science, Sumner acknowledged, even reveled in, the fallible but cumulative nature of scientific knowledge—this in contrast to religion, with its false promises of "complete and final answers to the problems of life."[34]

During the late nineteenth and early twentieth centuries a number of spokespersons for the human sciences supplemented their emphases on the need for ongoing inquiry with the claim that the knowledge yielded by their investigations could be used to promote human welfare. Convinced of a link between truth and morality, they argued that this knowledge could empower human beings to engage in social engineering. For example, John Dewey suggested that the social order "is based on law and order, on a system of existing stimuli and modes of reaction, through knowledge of which we can modify the practical outcome." Dewey, as well as a number of other advocates of social science, held that knowledge of social phenomena would ultimately enable human beings to achieve ethical progress comparable in significance to the technological progress they had achieved through greater knowledge of the natural world.[35]

The belief that knowledge provided by the social sciences could serve as a springboard for improving society, reminiscent of one of the major preoccupations of moral philosophy, was especially prominent within sociology and the "new political economy" associated with Richard T. Ely but could be found in all of the human sciences. It helped lead many intellectuals to opt for a career in the social sciences, and then, persuaded that serving humanity was an essentially religious vocation, a number of them joined the vanguard of the Christian social gospel movement. Indeed, during the late nineteenth and early twentieth centuries discussions of the relationship between knowledge and ethical responsibility served as an area in which religion continued to exert at least some influence within the social sciences.[36]

Those discussions, however, rarely included much consideration of theology; they centered instead on the nature and dynamics of the social order. The University of Michigan economist Henry Carter Adams was one of a number of social scientists who concluded that the ethically oriented analysis of society served as a more authentic expression of Christianity than theological reflection. Even most of the social scientists who remained committed to Christianity in their personal lives assigned distinctly different functions to religion than they did to their academic disciplines. Henry Carter Adams and Richard T. Ely, for example, suggested that whereas the teachings of Jesus provided the ideal of society toward which human beings should aspire, the scientific analysis of the social order provided the knowledge necessary for them to realize that ideal. This notion that ideals are extrascientific while knowledge is the product of science, which also obtained currency within the humanities during the late nineteenth century, enabled Ely to write Daniel Coit Gilman in 1885 extolling the idea of using Johns Hopkins as a vehicle for promoting the development of "a sound Christian political economy." Other social scientists, however, gave religion an even more limited role. By the second decade of the twentieth century the only division of labor that most social scientists outside seminaries and divinity schools were prepared to countenance was one in which religion provided inspiration and emotional fervor, while the social sciences provided knowledge and guidance as to the direction in which society should move.[37]

Albion W. Small, who probably devoted as much attention as anyone to the appropriate relationship between Christianity and the human sciences, exemplified social scientists' unwillingness to accord religion a significant cognitive role. In 1894 Small and George E. Vincent, coauthors of the popular textbook *A Scientific Study of Society*, warned that "piety without knowledge of facts would work disaster in politics and economics." The appropriate source of knowledge about society, they argued, was sociology rather than Christian theology. Two years later Small noted that sociological elements actually had played relatively little role in the teachings of Jesus. Even if one conceded that "the New Testament contains the nucleus of all that men need to know about the spirit of ideal human society," it provided no blueprint for reaching that ideal. Rather, the scientific approach of the sociologist alone taught "the laws of cause and effect, physical and psychical, to which social beings are subject." As of 1896 Small had no objection to use of the term *Christian sociology*. By 1924, however, he had sharpened the distinction between Christianity and sociology to the point where he could assert that it was "as muddled to talk about 'a Christian sociology' as 'a Christian chemistry' or 'a Christian mathematics.'" "A Christian attitude," Small wrote, "no more makes a social than an electrical engineer."[38]

The increasing tendency of Small and other social scientists to draw sharp distinctions between the role of their disciplines and that of Christianity proved to be only one aspect of a broader tendency to dissociate social science from ethical inquiry in the name of science. Although an outspokenly "objectivist" stance did not reach full intellectual expression until after World War I, its roots can be found earlier. Throughout the late nineteenth century, a number of social scientists emphasized that the dispassionate analysis of society required a scientific temperament alien to the vocation of reformer. Some of these social scientists, such as William Graham Sumner, took this position at least partly because they opposed efforts to engage in social engineering. Even supporters of reform, however, held that the primary task of social science was not to change society but to understand it. Indeed, to hear many social scientists tell it, the most compelling "social problem" facing Americans was an inadequate understanding of social processes.[39]

In disjoining social science from normative claims, academic social scientists did not assume that they were making a choice between acquiring knowledge and serving society. Rather, they were simply seeking to restrict more sharply the boundaries, while simultaneously seeking to plumb more completely the depths, of their realm of expertise. That effort was largely the result of increasing awareness of the parameters appropriate to a "scientific" analysis of society. Many social scientists ultimately concluded that however eloquent they might be in arguing that the reform of society required the guidance of scientific inquiry, science and reform were in fact different enterprises. That conclusion was probably reinforced by the sense that discussion of values had the effect of undermining their claims to scientific respectability. A Dartmouth sociologist thus complained that sociology would "command respect" only when it relied on "observed facts" rather than untestable claims. From this perspective, most proponents of the human sciences within American higher education increasingly gravitated toward the notion that a division of labor should exist in which institutions of higher education would serve primarily as centers of social inquiry, while other institutions would concentrate on social reform.[40]

The increasing determination among social scientists to limit their analysis to disinterested inquiry and the production of knowledge also reflected the growing status of those values within academic life. At the outset of the late-nineteenth-century reform movement in higher education, college officials had welcomed the idea that a scientific analysis of the social order would yield insights and data relevant in mediating the often fierce cultural and social conflicts within American society. The success that the advocates of the human sciences had in convincing officials who presided over colleges and universities of the usefulness of their disciplines helps account for the especially rapid growth of those sciences in the United States. By 1900, however, many college administrators and faculty members alike had come to envision the academic role of higher education primarily in terms of the promotion of inquiry. Increasingly the status of the social sciences depended less on their ability to mediate conflicts in the social arena or direct social change than on their ability to serve as centers of investigation and the production of knowledge. Recognizing this, many social scientists during the early twentieth century joined natural scientists in basing their claim for a prominent place within the curriculum of higher education on the need to conduct inquiry, their possession of a body of phenomena accessible to empirical investigation, and their skill in producing knowledge through the use of a recognizably scientific methodology. Small, for example, asserted that the ability of sociologists to "retain the academic recognition they have won will depend on whether they turn out to be at least as scientific as the most responsible of their colleagues." The experience of the social sciences in specific institutions confirmed Small's claim. At Harvard, for example, the failure of sociologists to demonstrate that their subject possessed either a coherent "body of knowledge" or a theoretical structure permitting meaningful predictions precluded them from establishing their field as a separate department until 1931.[41]

Social scientists proved quite successful in associating their disciplines with the methodology and goals of the natural sciences. As early as 1880, Daniel Coit Gilman proudly noted that "some of the ablest intellects in the world are now applying to the study of social phenomena, the same industry in collecting facts, the same patience in weighing them, the same methods of analysis and synthesis" that had paid dividends in the natural sciences. At Johns Hopkins and at most other institutions in the vanguard of collegiate and university reform, the human sciences prior to 1920 rarely attained the intellectual status of the natural sciences. Some historians have rightly observed that proponents of the human sciences frequently boasted of having developed sciences before they possessed either a "firm body of scientific knowledge" or "commonly agreed-upon theory." For their part, natural scientists would on occasion express skepticism about the legitimacy of social scientists' efforts to depict their disciplines as rigorously scientific. Nevertheless, beginning in the late 1860s and accelerating with the development of research-oriented institutions, the human sciences managed to attain an increasingly influential role in the curriculum of American colleges and universities. A large share of the credit for that lies in the success that social scientists and their allies had in identifying their disciplines with the knowledge and inquiry associated with science.[42]

The relationship between institutions of higher education and the human sciences was not, however, simply that of patron and client. Those sciences played a vital role in assisting the natural sciences construct a strong scientific culture within colleges and universities. As advocates of, as well as participants in, that culture, social scientists did much to reinforce the efforts that natural scientists were making to ensure that the academic mission of higher education focused strongly on ongoing inquiry and the production of knowledge.

The human sciences took the lead in imitating the natural sciences, but similar efforts occurred elsewhere. Even in such humanistic disciplines as philosophy, discussed at greater length in Part II, the siren call of science sometimes drowned out other voices. Colleges and universities also revamped the curriculum in other areas of academic life—schools of medicine, law, and even seminaries—in accordance with the precepts and practices of science. It is little wonder, therefore, that in 1893 David Starr Jordan, president of Stanford University, observed that "more and more each year the higher education of America is becoming steeped in science; and in the extension of human knowledge the American university now finds its excuse for being."[43]

# Chapter Three

## KNOWLEDGE AND INQUIRY IN THE ASCENDANT

I T MAY WELL BE, as one historian of science has suggested, that "modern academic science" began "at the moment investigators began to care more for the approval and esteem of their disciplinary colleagues than they did for the general standards of success in the society which surrounded them." Nevertheless, academic scientists and their allies recognized that they could ill afford to ignore the outside world altogether. Accordingly, they sought to convince college presidents, trustees, patrons, and the public that the "culture of science" was crucial to the academic mission of higher education.[1]

On balance, advocates of science proved remarkably successful in their proselytizing efforts. During the late nineteenth century, college and university presidents characteristically embraced the idea that their institutions should be pushing back the frontiers of ignorance, especially in the sciences. A number of these presidents, in cooperation with their faculties, adopted structures for hiring and promotion that rewarded research. Just as important, the public supported institutions explicitly committed to the discipline-based research ideal. Both the quantity and the quality of scientific research improved within higher education after 1870.[2]

Despite the growing commitment to the notion of ongoing inquiry, most colleges and universities devoted relatively few resources to research prior to the twentieth century. Not only officials in the liberal arts colleges but even the majority of the most dedicated reformers of higher education continued to embrace the notion that teaching undergraduate students by transmitting the methods and knowledge already at hand was of central importance. For their part, most defenders of science within academe could hardly fail to recognize that college teaching was the major occupation available to academically trained natural and social scientists. Nor could they be unaware of the fact that many of the individuals who presided over colleges and universities, as well as many professors, continued to emphasize the centrality of character development in the classroom. They were therefore impelled to address themselves to the issue of the value of teaching their disciplines to the achievement of a liberal education.[3]

Toward this end, they characteristically argued that careful scientific study of phenomena would promote intellectual development and mental discipline, long thought to be of central importance in higher education. The study of science, broadly construed, even fostered such character traits as independent thinking, open-mindedness, tolerance, the love of truth, and skepticism. Apologists for science maintained that these qualities, which they associated with the kind of ongoing inquiry that they were trying to promote, enabled individuals to live in accordance with the imperatives of modern life.[4]

During the late nineteenth century, proponents of scientific culture held that the surest method for inculcating in students the character traits associated with the study of science was to employ laboratory and, especially in the human sciences, seminar instruction. Such instruction, they argued, taught students how to use scientific methods to produce knowledge and think for themselves. In this spirit, the Oberlin historian Frank Hugh Foster, arguing for the value of the seminar, declared that "no man is truly a student of any branch until he is an original student. He is never fully interested in study till he begins to pursue it for himself by original methods. Hence it is the duty of all institutions which will fit their students for the highest intellectual service in the world, to train them in this method." These arguments proved enormously resonant among college officials. In 1899 James B. Angell, president of the University of Michigan, observed that "no more important step in education has been taken than in the universal introduction of the laboratory methods in the sciences." Seminars, too, increasingly became part of the education of advanced undergraduate and graduate students in American colleges and universities.[5]

By thus centering their justification for science within the liberal arts curriculum on the central importance of the "attitudes of mind" that ongoing study of phenomena promoted, apologists for scientific culture enabled academic scientists to teach highly specialized facts and theories and applaud ongoing efforts to extend the boundaries of knowledge while claiming to be imbuing students with habits of mind appropriate to liberally educated individuals. They thus justified an education in science for promoting norms and values that were good for *everyone*, not just specialists in their disciplines.[6]

Not surprisingly, in view of the nature of the justification that was given to the teaching of science in the classroom, the continued emphasis of colleges and universities on teaching in the late nineteenth and early twentieth centuries rarely acted, ideologically at least, to discourage research. The growing emphasis on laboratory and seminar instruction during the late nineteenth and early twentieth centuries helped to ensure that the teaching of the sciences in the classroom would point in essentially the same direction as scientific research: toward ongoing rational inquiry into questions that had determinate, verifiable answers. In the view of many partisans of science both the process and the outcome of that process—the resolution of doubt, the elimination of ignorance, the relief of uncertainty—promised to minister to some of the deepest needs of American culture.[7]

Many promoters of the culture of science coupled their homage to scientific inquiry with determined opposition to perspectives that challenged or actively rejected "the necessity of questioning all things and proving all things." It is in this context that reports of "warfare" between science and theology became especially relevant. This discussion entered the public forum in 1869 with a published account in the *New York Daily Tribune* of a lecture on that topic presented by the president of Cornell University, Andrew Dickson White. It accelerated with publication of John William Draper's *History of the Conflict between Religion and Science* (1874) and reached its defining expression, perhaps, in White's two-volume *A History of the Warfare of Science with Theology* (1896). These works, as well as many others that embraced their views, repudiated the notion that the "restraints of religion" were necessary for fruitful scientific investigation. In place of that notion, which prior to 1870 had been endorsed by a number of scientists and nonscientists alike, Draper, White, and their allies held that fearless investigation and a commitment to "truth for its own sake" were the marks of the scientific temperament and the conditions for maximum scientific progress. They blasted Christian theology for restricting untrammeled investigation and for promoting ungrounded and intractable dogmata, intolerance, and obscurantism. At the same time they praised the work of scientists for encouraging well-grounded conclusions and open-minded inquiry.[8]

In retrospect, the latitude that colleges and universities gave natural and social scientists to pursue their investigations seems far more pronounced than theological opposition to such efforts. Few institutions of higher education seriously challenged the academic freedom of scientists. Despite occasional conflicts between theologians and scientists, the picture of ongoing "warfare" drawn by White and others constitutes a caricature of the historical relationship between science and religion. Nevertheless, those who constructed that caricature achieved their main goal: they convinced educated Americans of the desirability of giving students of nature intellectual independence.[9]

Apologists for science within higher education did not simply equate the scientific method with inquiry and promise that such inquiry would yield knowledge. They were also intent on convincing college presidents and the growing public constituency for higher education that the ethos of science, with its emphasis on acquiring and transmitting publicly verifiable knowledge, provided essential guidance as to what the paramount *academic* missions of colleges and universities should be. They were strikingly successful in achieving that goal. As early as 1869 William Watts Folwell, president of the University of Minnesota, announced in his inaugural address that "we have discovered what is that informing spirit which is to give life to the limbs and elements of the University; which can fuse, cement, and compact them into a harmonious organization. It is Science." During the decades that followed, Folwell's position was frequently repeated. At least part of the success that science enjoyed within higher education can be attributed to the intellectual backgrounds of many of the college and university presidents during the late nineteenth and early twentieth centuries. Many of those individuals— Charles William Eliot, David Starr Jordan, Thomas Chamberlin, Ira Remsen, and others—had been trained as scientists. They embraced an expansive view of the scope of scientific investigation and optimism about the capacities of science to find intelligible connections among phenomena. They also appreciated the notion of "thinking small" that proponents of science had been advocating. Eliot aptly captured that notion:

> Natural science has engendered a peculiar kind of human mind—the searching, open, humble mind, which, knowing that it cannot attain unto all truth, or even to much new truth, is yet patiently and enthusiastically devoted to the pursuit of such little new truth as is within its grasp, having no other end than to learn, prizing above all things accuracy, thoroughness, and candor, in research, proud and happy not in its own single strength, but in the might of that host of students, whose past conquests make up the wondrous sum of present knowledge, whose sure future triumphs each humblest worker in imagination shares.[10]

Appreciation of the value of science among college officials was not, however, limited to erstwhile scientists. Other college presidents—Daniel Coit Gilman of Johns Hopkins University, Cornell's Andrew Dickson White, and other less well-known figures—also became dedicated converts to the notion that scientific knowledge was, as Gilman put it, "another name for truth." Hence, four of the six first full professors whom Gilman hired were natural scientists and mathematicians. And when he listed the major achievements of the human intellect in the half century prior to 1897, each lay in the realm of natural science. For his part, Andrew Dickson White promised not only to minister to students' burgeoning interest in natural science but to "endeavor to inculcate scientific methods for their own sake." Toward that end, White's Cornell faculty agreed to require students to take courses in natural science at the beginning rather than the end of their undergraduate years.[11]

The close association that partisans of the sciences had made between their disciplines and the acquisition of knowledge through the process of ongoing inquiry led college presidents who extolled science to maintain that the academic mission of higher education was inextricably bound up with the constant quest for new truth. Perhaps the bluntest affirmation of that mission was presented by Stanford's president and one of the most distinguished zoologists of his day, David Starr Jordan. Jordan asserted that "in proportion to the extent to which it widens the range of human knowledge and of human power, in that degree does an institution deserve the name of university. A man content with the truth that now is, and without ambition to venture into the unknown, is not the proper man to be a university professor." Jordan's view found expression in the public statements of other college and university presidents associated with the reform of higher education. Eliot maintained that "truth is the motto of the University, and truth-seeking one of its chief occupations." The secret to discovering more truth, he suggested, was to proceed "little by little, step by step," by means of empirical investigation. When Gilman suggested in 1886 that "among the brightest signs of a vigorous university is zeal for the advancement of learning," he placed as much emphasis on the term *advancement* as he did on the word *learning*. In 1905 Angell suggested that whereas students during his college days had been expected to embrace received wisdom, contemporary institutions of higher education urged students to cultivate "the power and the passion for discovering new truth." Such commitment to ongoing inquiry goes a long way toward explaining the structure and imperatives of the academic world in the late nineteenth and early twentieth centuries.[12]

Some college presidents disagreed that higher education should be so exclusively bound up with the acquisition of knowledge and the promotion of inquiry. Noah Porter, who served as Yale's president from 1871 to 1886, believed that higher education had developed an unhealthy obsession with intellectual development. Porter warned that "intellectual activities and achievements not infrequently exclude frequent and fervent thoughts of God and become unfriendly to an earnest and religious life. The work of the scholar takes a more exclusive possession of his inner life than the occupations of other men." Porter, neither an obscurantist nor an opponent of science, believed that apologists for scientific culture promoted a "coreless" education inconsistent with the development of well-rounded individuals. "The division of labor in modern science and research, tends to make the devotee of any single department, narrow and dogmatic in proportion to the completeness of his mastery over his chosen field," he argued. "A thinker who is limited to a single species of phenomena or a single class of relations, is likely to be inappreciative or incredulous with respect to any other."[13]

No issue among college and university leaders was more controversial during the late nineteenth and early twentieth centuries than the degree to which knowledge and inquiry should dominate higher education. Some humanists, as the discussion in Part II makes clear, especially resisted equating higher education with the acquisition of knowledge and ongoing inquiry. In some respects, however, the controversy, though occasionally full of sound and fury, signified little. Proponents of the idea that institutions of higher education should focus on such goals as service and liberal culture characteristically believed that accomplishment of those goals involved strong doses of both knowledge and investigation. Even those who voiced concern about overintellectualization and the dangers of disciplinary specialization rarely differed significantly from those who viewed knowledge and inquiry as paramount goals in the way they described the ideal content and structure of the curriculum. Porter, for example, urged that colleges and universities committed to the Christian faith ensure through their hiring practices that their scholars professed Christianity, presumably because he assumed that this would affect the content of their scholarship and teaching. Porter refrained, however, from specifying just how that content would differ from what non-Christians taught. Princeton's James McCosh expressed concern about students attending colleges that stimulated the intellectual faculties without encouraging true religion, but the changes in the curriculum that he embraced had the intent and the effect of making it more rather than less intellectually challenging. McCosh concentrated his efforts to foster religion in the extracurricular arena.[14]

College officials who emphasized the preeminent importance of knowledge and ongoing inquiry in the academic mission of higher education were aware that these values had drawn the fire of some who were committed to the idea that institutions should place equal emphasis on spiritual edification. The outrage that surfaced in some Christian circles in response to the decision of Johns Hopkins University to allow Thomas Huxley to present a scientific lecture at its opening ceremonies without preceding that event with prayer indicated the concern that could arise about the irreligious tendencies of scientific culture. To counter such concern, many college officials emphasized the compatibility of zeal for knowledge and piety.[15]

Some went even further in attempting to defuse potential religiously inspired opposition to the intellectual tenor of academic life. In 1885 Gilman, having been embarrassed by the Huxley incident, advised his fellow university president James Burrill Angell of the University of Michigan to resist the temptation to hire faculty members whose Christian credentials were suspect, whatever their scholarly credentials might be. Gilman doubtless assumed that institutions of higher education could find plenty of individuals who endorsed both Christianity and scientific culture. More disingenuously, Gilman enjoined at least some of the members of his faculty to attend churches in Baltimore for the sake of appearances. When Charles Eliot Norton was asked to give the Percy Turnbull Lectures in Humanities at Hopkins during the early 1890s, he declined on the ground that as an agnostic, he could not make the affirmation of Christian faith that the founder of the lecture series required. Gilman responded that he would not allow such restrictions to constrain a lectureship at his university—but was careful to clear Norton's appointment with the lectureship's founder.[16]

There were, however, limits to the concessions that administrators were willing to make. A number of college officials, though aware that Christianity included affirmations based on revelation, faith, and the acknowledgment of spiritual forces not necessarily discoverable by scientific inquiry, refused to allow those elements to impinge in any concrete way on what they saw as the primary mission of the university, the promulgation of knowledge and inquiry. Some embraced the view most commonly associated with Andrew Dickson White that theologians had frequently made efforts to erect roadblocks to the open-minded pursuit of scientific investigation. Others, while admonishing institutions of higher education to be "fearless" and "determined" in their investigation of nature, commended the idea of leaving the activity of God, in Gilman's words, "unobtrusive." While those officials insisted that extension of knowledge left faith intact, they acknowledged that it also left it "restricted."[17]

Many of the most well-known college presidents and faculty members during the late nineteenth and early twentieth centuries were liberal Protestants, who were especially concerned with reconciling Christianity with the most up-to-date results of modern scholarship. Those liberals, together with others who maintained distinguished positions within the larger culture, played pivotal roles in securing for the "culture of science" a central place within American colleges and universities. Thanks to the work of George Marsden and others, we now know considerably more than we once did about the role that liberal Protestant opinion leaders played in altering the "soul" of the modern university. Nevertheless, we cannot fully understand what enabled liberal Protestants to embrace an ethos emphasizing knowledge and inquiry essentially detached from religious conviction without further analysis of the liberal worldview.

Such analysis would involve moving rather far afield from higher education and can only be briefly outlined here. It seems clear that at least three characteristics of liberal Protestantism allowed its adherents to countenance, even encourage, greater emphasis on disinterested scientific inquiry. First, during the late nineteenth and early twentieth centuries, liberal Protestants—and especially those influenced by the German theologian Albrecht Ritschl—tended to draw sharp distinctions between the factually based truths obtainable through scientific inquiry and the more value-laden, Christocentric truths of the Christian message. This rendered science less threatening. Second, much of the interest of liberal Protestants during the late nineteenth and early twentieth centuries focused on moral and social questions. In addressing those questions, many liberals found "scientific" forms of social and cultural inquiry to be useful instruments of analysis. Third, by the end of the nineteenth century, many liberals were less interested in constructing formal arguments for God's existence and attributes than in simply positing an immanentist view of God's relationship to the world. Immanentism, with its robust view of the divine presence, interpreted natural laws and "secondary" agencies as modes of divine activity. Although an immanentist perspective emphasized the distinction between scientific description and theological explanation, it had no quarrel with scientists describing phenomena subject to empirical investigation in terms of a continuous chain of natural causes and effects. In having "discovered and set forth the magnificent idea of the continuity of creation," Harvard's president Eliot wrote, modern science had actually "exalted the idea of God—the greatest service which can be rendered to humanity."[18]

In emphasizing the compatibility of piety and learning, college officials were reinvoking a hoary bromide. To be sure, they were more explicit and vocal than their predecessors in identifying the academic mission of higher education with the custodianship and creation of knowledge and ongoing inquiry rather than faith and the Scriptures. Their position, however, represents a heightened emphasis on, rather than a dramatic departure from, previous views of that mission. Throughout the nineteenth century, notwithstanding rhetoric acknowledging the need to create well-rounded individuals, faith and scriptural authority played a distinctly secondary role within higher education; academic life had tended to focus almost entirely on the promotion of learning. In principle, at least, Protestants had long embraced the ideal of free and open inquiry. The proponents of natural theology who had sponsored science in the antebellum curriculum had emphasized the importance of science in apologetics precisely because they believed that it could provide publicly verifiable data capable of grounding theological inferences. Although many colleges undoubtedly placed greater emphasis on the importance of harmonizing science and revelation in the period prior to 1870, the thrust of most of those harmonizing efforts had been steadily moving in the direction of altering biblical interpretations to comport with the findings of science.[19]

The educational ideal promoted by defenders of science proved compelling not only to the "captains of erudition" who presided over American colleges and universities but also to the literate public who served as higher education's constituency. Many members of a society beset with the doubts and uncertainties attending profound social and cultural change found themselves responding favorably to a message proclaiming that doubt was properly an occasion for inquiry, ignorance an opportunity for investigation, and uncertainty a necessary step on the ongoing path toward truth. The vision that celebrants of the culture of science successfully projected was that perseverance, patience, and effort—all cardinal Victorian virtues—would yield knowledge and ultimately truth. In this vision, skepticism became a prelude to knowledge, not a threat to faith. Ignorance became a call to inquiry, not the basis of an appeal to faith or authority.[20]

The actual products of scientific inquiry seemed equally beguiling. At the same time that science was offering people the excitement of confronting "experience" head on, it held out the promise of discerning intelligible order in that experience. Science traded in the currency of hard facts and verifiable theories; it exuded impatience with speculation and ungrounded ideas. To Americans living in a society abuzz with numerous philosophies clamoring for people's allegiance, the decision of academics to attenuate their discourse, to limit it to discrete, "doable" problems, must have seemed salutary, the very soul of tough-minded common sense. At the same time, through the use of its theoretical structures, science extended the promise of yielding some of the same fruit as religion: it could demonstrate that beneath the seemingly chaotic world of experience lay a comprehensible set of processes.[21]

The educated public's endorsement of the vision promoted by apologists for science does not entirely account for why institutions of higher education became more "culturally strategic" in late-nineteenth-century America. The need for a means of credentialing workers in an increasingly technologically oriented society also played a role. Still, the celebrants of scientific culture were instrumental in helping to create a consensus concerning the value of verifiable knowledge about nature, human nature, society, and culture. Thorstein Veblen identified this consensus when he observed that "modern civilization is peculiarly matter of fact." The effect of that orientation was to reinforce the idea that the mission of institutions of higher education was the promotion of knowledge and inquiry.[22]

The interwining of this mission with the ongoing acquisition and transmission of facts and principles involving sensible, characteristically verifiable, phenomena inevitably affected the status of religion in general and Christianity in particular within higher education. Although most colleges and universities did not become more secular in the sense of being actively hostile to religious belief, they did become less concerned with the dictates of Christian theology and the imperatives of religious faith. As the discussion in Part II makes clear, the very nature of disciplinary research undermined the kind of unitary view of knowledge implied in the Judeo-Christian worldview. Insofar as colleges and universities found a substitute for the moral philosophy and natural theology courses that had integrated knowledge in the antebellum colleges, that substitute was the humanities—and a secularized version of humanities at that—rather than the natural or social sciences. Just as important, the act of discovering and analyzing the operation of "secondary" agencies took priority over expressions of delight, awe, and thanksgiving in response to the activity of God. The determined efforts of practitioners of the natural and human sciences to avoid invoking the Deity in their professional discourse narrowed the space in American culture within which God-talk seemed appropriate.[23]

As higher education increasingly became identified with expanding the boundaries of verifiable knowledge, such knowledge became valorized in classrooms, seminar rooms, laboratories, and academic discourse. Truth claims based on alternative epistemologies—tradition, divine inspiration, and subjective forms of religious experience—increasingly lost credibility within the academy. In addition, the recognition that knowledge itself was fallible and progressive cast doubt on the legitimacy of venerable doctrines. Claims that ongoing inquiry would eliminate error and establish truth fostered an iconoclasm toward orthodoxies. "Research," the political scientist John W. Burgess observed late in his career, "implied doubt. It implied that there was, at least, a great deal of truth still to be found, and it implied that the truth thought to have been already found was approximative and in continual need of revision and readjustment." It is therefore little wonder that Charles Eliot concluded that "the very word education is a standing protest against dogmatic teaching." The resolute hostility of scientific culture to "speculation" may well have discouraged the development of attitudes of mind propitious to new, creative ventures in philosophical theology. Nor were these consequences entirely unintended; apologists for science made it a vital part of their agenda to give scientific knowledge a privileged place in the academic mission of higher education.[24]

Even more damaging to the fortunes of religion within academic life was the spirit of inquiry itself, which by its very nature undermined the status of the kind of belief, trust, and commitment that lay at the heart of religious faith. Trust in the testimony of others has played a crucial role in the growth of scientific thought. During the late nineteenth and early twentieth centuries, however, this was typically ignored by apologists for the culture of science, whose rhetoric emphasized instead that dogged inquiry constituted the key to the production of knowledge. Thomas Chamberlin offered a representative view of such rhetoric in 1899, when he identified a determined unwillingness to make affirmations without sufficient evidence as one of the reigning "canon[s] of scientific study." For proponents of such thinking, "proof," not faith, should precede belief. Even if they did not exclude in principle the legitimacy of propositions based on faith, they made the imperative to find out for oneself—the kind of inquiry allegedly pursued by science—preeminent over the willingness to take other people's word for things on which faith hinged. Just as important, in lauding the kind of cool, clear-eyed detachment that science seemed to require, partisans of scientific culture may well have undermined belief in the value of the kind of impassioned commitment that was fundamental to religious faith.[25]

Insofar as there has been an institutional locus for the "religion of science" since 1870, that locus has been higher education. During the late nineteenth and early twentieth centuries, colleges and universities became identified as institutions imbued with the faith that the only knowledge really worth having is obtainable through rational, "scientific" inquiry. If this now seems obvious to us, it is a measure of how completely higher education and the culture to which it has ministered have been captivated by that faith.[26]

# PART TWO

## THE HUMANITIES

# Chapter Four

## THE TRIUMPH OF THE HUMANITIES

DEVELOPMENT MAY be forecast; revolution cannot. No one in 1850 could have predicted the shapes into which academic knowledge would shift by 1900. In probably the least likely turn, a congeries of studies almost unknown to earlier American colleges rapidly gained prominence in the liberal arts curriculum. These usurpers, dethroning the Greek and Latin regnant for centuries, were "the humanities." Even against the background of the flux that has always typified American higher education, this outcome was extraordinary.[1] In what we usually regard as an Age of Science, and despite the powerful influences delineated in the preceding pages, it was not the natural or social sciences that provided the great novelty of academe, but the new humanities.[2]

The word itself was anything but new. *Humanity* in its academic meaning appeared in English in the later fifteenth century, arriving via French and Italian from Latin *humanitas*. The neologism originally served to distinguish secular studies (principally of Greek and Latin texts: the *literae humaniores*) from theological ones, that is, *humanity* as opposed to *divinity*. By Bacon's time *humanity* had come to demarcate classical learning from both divinity on one side and natural philosophy (science) on the other.[3] The word in Bacon's sense was still current, though not frequently used, in American colleges during the early nineteenth century.

Both its frequency and what it referred to soon changed dramatically. In 1850 the term still denoted principally the study of Greek and Latin, carried on through close attention to grammar and calculated to impose "mental discipline" on the unformed boys who inhabited classical (or "grammar") schools and colleges.[4] But by 1870 the officers of even fairly traditional colleges could already distinguish in their educational goals between "literary culture" or "liberal culture" and classical study. *Humanity* in its plural form soon attached itself to this broadening "liberal culture."[5] By 1900 the "humanities" meant a wide range of "culture studies," most new to the curriculum: literature, philosophy, art history, often general history as well. The humanities still included Greek and Latin; but even these traditional studies had got a new label—"the classics"—and acquired a novel literary orientation and cultivating aim.[6]

These arrivistes did not wander onto the scene by chance. As classical college evolved into modern university, knowledge itself changed in nature, and its traditional relation to religion grew problematic. This secularization of higher education was a vast and amorphous development, which George Marsden has recently described in commanding sweep; and academic secularization was, in turn, only one facet of a much broader social and intellectual phenomenon.[7] The deep and varied causes and effects of secularization, academic or general, can hardly be explored here; and to do so is not the intention now.

Rather, the rise of the humanities was intimately linked to embarrassments consequent upon secularization, and so, to understand the genesis and character of these new studies, we need to investigate their relation to the changing role of religion in higher education. Doing so, moreover, may incidentally provide some insight into difficulties that the emergent American university faced when knowledge lost its religious presuppositions, perhaps even into some long-term outcomes of this epistemological revolution.[8] The modest hope, then, is to comprehend better the origins of the humanities themselves and possibly to open an inch or two wider our window onto the changing character of knowledge under the strain of secularization.

To pursue such deeper meanings we first need a road map of the surface, that is, a quick sketch of the layout of the new humanities.[9] Then we must look into how they stood in relation to the growing specialization of academic knowledge in the Age of the University. Only after this apparent detour, but in fact essential background, can we begin to understand how the humanities affected religion in the academy, and vice versa.

Two of the subjects that clustered together under the rubric of the humanities in the later nineteenth century were not in fact novel at all, though much altered in outlook. One was philosophy, taught in some form even in the earliest colonial colleges.[10] The form, however, transformed itself with the introduction of Scottish moral philosophy beginning in the late eighteenth century, then again even more dramatically when philosophy joined the humanities.[11] Both of these changes we shall need to consider presently. The other "traditional" subject was classics—traditional in the sense that Latin and Greek had long formed the core of college education. But the rebaptism of these languages as "the classics," beginning in mid century, signaled a pedagogical revolution. Where Greek and Latin had once been valued for the mental discipline students acquired in conjugating Attic verbs and parsing Ciceronian periods, the new classics stressed the "cultivating" influence of the plays of Sophocles and odes of Horace. The study of ancient languages became (or pretended to become) the study of literature.[12]

Literature indeed loomed at the center of the humanities, but dating its entrance into the curriculum is surprisingly difficult. One early landmark juts up clearly, only to mislead the explorer. Harvard exposed students to continental European literatures as early as the 1820s, when George Ticknor took up the new Smith Professorship of French and Spanish languages and belles lettres. Henry Wadsworth Longfellow, his successor, continued until 1854 to lecture in Ticknor's historical-critical mode, adding Germany and Italy to Spain and France.[13] However, this early dose of European literature was homeopathic even at Harvard and, more important, remained an isolated aberration for decades.[14] It was the study of English literature that first spread among colleges.

The teaching of Shakespeare and Wordsworth, however, developed within a much older standard course in rhetoric, and hence a college's catalogs rarely spell out when such works began to be studied qua literature.[15] Confusion about timing is compounded because some colleges before the Civil War called their rhetoric teacher the professor of "belles lettres," a category that then included what later generations called literature. The University of North Carolina, for instance, required "the study of Belles letters [sic]" from its founding in 1795, but closer inspection of early catalogs makes clear that this meant grammar, rhetoric, and elocution. Princeton in the 1830s likewise denominated (surer of its French) the Rev. James Alexander professor of "belles lettres," but the reverend gentleman almost certainly expounded the glories of Milton and Burke as exempla for student writing rather than as objects of veneration in their own right. For in teaching grammar and composition, instructors often assigned literary passages as models for student emulation.[16] One wonders how much Milton's prominence in literature classes after 1860 owes to his earlier ubiquity in rhetoric courses: if you could parse *Paradise Lost,* you could parse anything.

But when exactly did Satan's tirades become the focus of aesthetic admiration as well as grammatical bewilderment? False dawns abound, trumpeted by institutional historians. Matthew Boyd Hope, we learn, lectured on "English literature" at Princeton in 1846–1847; Trinity College (predecessor of Duke University) required "English literature" of sophomores in 1856. However, the lecture notes surviving from Hope's courses and the explanations in the Trinity catalog show that in these courses literature still subserved composition.[17] Perhaps the first person to teach English literature as a subject independent of rhetoric—and, in that case, second only to Harvard's Smith Professors to teach any literature as such—was Francis A. March of Lafayette College, who famously introduced such a course in 1857.[18]

He did not wait long for imitators. The next year Andrew Dickson White began to teach at Michigan "the History of English Literature" and "the Masterpieces of our Literature," while James Russell Lowell offered English literature as a senior elective at Harvard. Yale dipped a

timid toe in the new wave in 1870, though at first confining literature
to the modern-minded Sheffield Scientific School. Yale's wariness, however, looked downright moss-backed: by the 1870s even the Agricultural
College of Pennsylvania and struggling little Austin College in Texas
required all their students to study English literature. The Agricultural
College explained that its course stressed "the critical reading of our
best English writers, from Chaucer to Shakespeare," aiming to introduce
"the Literature itself" rather than only "its history."[19]

By the 1880s literature was everywhere. Any new institution—no
matter how remote, no matter how feeble—offered it instinctively. Even
at the Illinois Industrial University, where the lamp of liberal learning
flickered feebly indeed, grammar gave way to literature by the early
1880s. And by the start of the new century English literature had displaced Latin and Greek "as the backbone of the humanities" even at
Yale.[20]

By then the whole skeleton was fleshed out, and just as close to the
ideal heart of the new humanities as literature, though a rarer exuber-
ance, was the still newer field of art history. In 1874 Charles Eliot Norton began lecturing at Harvard on "the History of the Fine Arts as connected with Literature."[21] This was by no means the first time an
American university had approached the arts; Princeton, for instance,
offered extracurricular lectures on the history of architecture from the
1830s into the 1850s and briefly featured a "Lecturer on the Fine Arts"
in the later half of that decade.[22] But Norton was the first regular professor of art history in the United States and really established it as both a
college subject and an academic discipline. The idea quickly caught on.
Princeton in 1883 established a School of Art, which included three
courses in art history—a general survey, a course on ancient painting,
and one on Italian painting.[23]

Art history did not spread through colleges as rapidly as literature, in
part owing to a severe deficit of competent instructors and textbooks.[24]
At a small college the same person might well teach both subjects,
though probably pretty amateurishly, as was the case at little Carleton
College in faraway Minnesota. Still, by 1900 or 1910, though rarely a
required study, an appearance by art history in the curriculum was de
rigueur in schools with high pretensions to modernity and quality in liberal culture, especially women's colleges.[25] Art history had—like its
more nearly ubiquitous cousin, literature—come to be recognized as in-
carnating whatever "culture" and the "humanities" meant. Looking at
Raphael conveyed the same value as reading Dante.

The relation of general history to the humanities was more uncertain.
As a distinct study history was almost as fresh as literature. True, textbooks in Greek and Roman history had for some decades prior to 1850

aided instruction in classical languages.[26] But the first American to teach history as a separate course seems to have been Jared Sparks of Harvard, appointed to the new McLean Professorship of Ancient and Modern History in 1838 ("modern" history at this time meaning postclassical).[27] In any event by the 1850s history as a distinct study raised no eyebrows. The University of North Carolina, for instance—no curricular pioneer—then required of its juniors ancient and medieval history in the first semester, modern in the second. But apparently not until 1857 was any professor in the United States charged with modern history exclusively; this was Andrew Dickson White of the University of Michigan.[28]

After the Civil War—perhaps even partly because of it?—history infiltrated American higher education as quickly as literature. Princeton added modern history in its big curricular revision of 1869 and went so far as "American Civilization" in the following year. Not only the self-consciously advanced Johns Hopkins University felt that it needed to offer history when it opened in Baltimore in 1876; so, too, did the self-consciously traditional Carleton College when it opened six years earlier—even though lacking a professor to teach it.[29]

However, unlike their literary counterparts, teachers of history seem usually to have touted their subject for its "practical" worth to students about to become citizens. Certainly Andrew White thought it "applied to the immediate needs of our time." Thus history's popularity owed at least as much to the desire to reform colleges in a utilitarian direction as to the movement to reshape them on the model of "liberal culture."[30] Moreover, as noted in Part I, most of the academic avant-garde regarded history (comprising then primarily political and constitutional history) as a "social science," not a humanity.[31] Still, when in the 1880s and 1890s people began routinely to speak of "the humanities," some continued to link history with literature. Nor, at smaller institutions, was it odd for the same person to be charged with teaching both.[32]

History nearly rounded out the circle of the humanities at the end of the century. Foreign literatures, taught extensively at first-rank colleges by the 1890s, fitted neatly into the space opened by English and need no further discussion. Comparative literature put in a first tentative appearance in 1891, at Harvard, in the person of Professor Arthur Richmond Marsh, but its flowering came decades later.[33] Music—as a humanity: a matter for lecturers rather than for instructors in voice or piano—was also beginning to poke its nose under the tent, but its full entrance likewise awaited the twentieth century, when cheap, facile, and faithful technologies of sound reproduction became readily available. In sum, then, within the humanities Literature sat at the head of the table, with Art History benignly by its side, their infants Music and Comparative Literature gurgling quietly, great-uncle Classics smiling proudly, cousin History occasionally dropping in to visit—and Philosophy at the far end, remote in genealogy though somehow kindred in purpose.

Yet what was this purpose? Why did the humanities surge so suddenly into prominence, when their most characteristic subjects, literature and art history, had never before figured in university education at all?

The first piece of the answer is fairly obvious. The classical education heavy with Greek and Latin, its raison d'être grown feeble with advancing years, its aging body patched up in makeshift ways since the seventeenth century, at last fell apart like the deacon's one-hoss shay between about 1870 and 1910.[34] This left a huge void to fill. Colleges experimented with various successor curricula, and the ensuing picture was extremely confused.[35] Harvard's famous embrace of free election was not only controversial but unusual. By the first decade of the twentieth century, probably most schools had greatly deemphasized classical languages (especially Greek) and limped halfheartedly toward letting students elect their own studies. As a rule freshmen and sophomores seem still to have faced largely required courses. These included remnants of the old curricula (Latin, mathematics, "freshman comp"), but the new humanities (English literature, history) filled in the gaps. Juniors and seniors appear generally to have enjoyed, or puzzled over, a high degree of choice in principle (though in practice a lot to choose from only at universities). The upperclass menu typically contained a large selection of humanities. So one reason for the popularity of the humanities was simple and practical: they provided "modern" substitutes for old studies fallen into disfavor.

Yet this hardly begins to answer the question; for why should colleges have offered English and art rather than larger doses of economics and chemistry? The answer hinges on an ideological problem created by the retreat from the classical curriculum and the move toward electives. It is probably fair to say that universities welcomed the elective system far more enthusiastically than did liberal arts colleges, but almost everywhere electives advanced or requirements remained chiefly for lack of cogent alternatives. Pieces of the rationale for the old curriculum—notably the idea of "mental discipline," which, as Part I indicates, enjoyed a long afterlife—could be salvaged for new ones, but the looser new curricula no longer fitted neatly under old justifications. It was hard to argue that reading George Eliot provided the same discipline as decoding the *Aeneid* (though not impossible: the self-protecting ingenuity of professors is not to be underrated). Without classical languages at the core, what was the point? What did "liberal education" mean? In particular, the spread of electives demanded a new understanding of curricular coherence, not just a clinging to relics of old requirements: why *these* electives? and, given electives, what made education coherent? Even most liberal arts colleges confronted these questions for their juniors and seniors. The conundrum pressed hardest on the new universities, where electives most expanded.

The handful of places like Harvard where free election ruled faced the problem in its clearest state. Even a cheerleader for the elective system like President Charles W. Eliot felt that students needed *something* to glue the pieces together, to enlarge their perspective on their specialized studies, to situate knowledge within the business of living as a moral being. In short, young barbarians required civilizing, even at Harvard, perhaps especially at Harvard. Eliot's cousin Charles Eliot Norton, who would come to exert more influence than any other individual in forming the self-understanding of the humanities, put Eliot's concern more formally when explaining in 1874 why the new study of art history was needed:

> In a complete scheme of University studies the history of the Fine Arts in their relation to social progress, to general culture, and to literature should find a place, not only because architecture, sculpture and painting have been, next to literature, the most important modes of expression of the sentiments, beliefs and opinions of men, but also because they afford evidence, often in a more striking and direct manner than literature itself, of the moral temper and intellectual culture of the various races by whom they have been practised, and thus become the most effective aids to the proper understanding of history.[36]

Norton's rhetoric expressed tolerably well the outlook of all the new humanities—one might say, in more recent argot, "culture with an attitude." And that attitude begins to suggest why the humanities moved to the center of liberal education in the curricular crisis of the late nineteenth century. But the attitude requires scrutiny if one is to understand its force—and to grasp what the triumph of the humanities implied about academic knowledge as a whole. For the humanities prospered, not simply because they filled a curricular vacuum, but because they responded to a general crisis in the academy.

## Chapter Five

## THE BOON AND BANE OF SPECIALIZATION

T HE HOUSE OF LEARNING underwent more than minor redecoration in the United States during the latter half of the nineteenth century. And it will startle no one to hear that the radical rearrangement of knowledge involved increased emphasis on research, professionalization and specialization among the faculty, and the slow alienation of academic knowledge from its once sturdily Protestant view of the world, as already described in connection with the sciences. But the precise character of this revolution, and its link with the contemporaneous revolution of the humanities, needs specification.

This can begin by sweeping away the lingering dust of one hoary popular myth, continuing the housecleaning begun above in the discussion of the sciences. University reformers did not heroically discover in 1869 or 1876 that professors could do research. Granted, before 1850, erudition was possibly more at home outside than inside the academy, and few professors really qualified as learned. Granted, too, research became a much more widespread academic ideal in the second half of the century. But it is easy to overestimate research even in the best universities during the crucial decades of the late nineteenth century. In his inaugural address as president of Harvard in 1869, that great reformer Charles Eliot, while expecting "the strongest and most devoted professors" to "contribute something to the patrimony of knowledge," firmly insisted that "the prime business of American professors in this generation must be regular and assiduous class teaching." And it is equally easy to forget that research was far from discounted in the old, religiously oriented colleges. George Ticknor began his great history of Spanish literature while teaching at Harvard; Joseph Henry carried on his influential researches in electromagnetism while teaching at Princeton. Yale, stalwart of the classical curriculum, nurtured a whole school of Christian scholars: William Dwight Whitney, arguably the most eminent scholar produced by the United States in the nineteenth century, blossomed in it.[1]

No, the novelty was not research as such, but the beginnings of a certain kind of specialization in knowledge. (These distinctions matter, being often blurred in retrospect.) Specialization (beyond the obvious separation of, say, chemistry and Greek into different courses) would have seemed utterly out of place in college education before 1850, had anyone given it a thought. A minority of professors—probably a small one—did pursue research in special fields, as Ticknor did in Spanish literature and Henry in electromagnetism; but research did not imply academic specialization in the sense current after 1900. Only in the natural sciences had expertise even begun to regard itself as "specialized." Possibly Henry saw his experimental work as carried on within a specific "discipline," but Ticknor viewed himself as a man of letters, not a specialist in Spanish literature.[2]

And even for those professors who pursued research, their scholarship had only the thinnest connection with academic duties. Ticknor actually completed his history after resigning from Harvard, and even if one charitably assumes that students benefited from his erudition, the advantage was solely theirs: Ticknor's teaching was far too elementary to nourish his scholarship. Professors in his era did not teach specialized courses (what we would think of as "upper-level" courses), nor did students "major" in a "discipline." Either would have breached the conception of college work.

For the classical college did not wish to equip one student differently from another. Rather, it intended to discipline each student's mental faculties through the same general studies and to furnish every brain with the same broad smattering of information. College study thereby laid a basis for more advanced learning either in a professional course or through informal reading—though perhaps some superstructure actually rose on the foundation more often in the president's dreams than in the graduates' lives.[3] Putatively modern and "useful" courses of study did begin to proliferate from the 1820s, providing alternatives to the inherited curriculum centered on Greek and Latin. But they offered alternative forms of general education, a different track to a different degree, not a more specialized education.[4] Even when postgraduate study in the arts and sciences first glimmered—as feebly it did at Harvard in the 1830s and Michigan in the 1850s—it offered more extensive culture, not training for specialized research.[5] And the first college to experiment seriously with electives—Harvard in the 1840s—aimed to enliven general education, not to create a more specialized one.[6]

Harvard's intentions soon changed. Charles Eliot began his 1869 inaugural address by dismissing earlier American writings on higher education as having "no practical lesson for us to-day." He went on to speak of his hope of giving the "young men" who attended the College not only "an accurate general knowledge of all the main subjects of human interest," but also "a minute and thorough knowledge of the one subject which each may select as his principal occupation in life." Eliot even regarded the old-time college's "lack of faith" in "the value of a discipline concentrated upon a single object" as "a national danger." This insistence on applying to college education "the principle of division of labor" undergirded Eliot's campaign to expand drastically the elective system.[7]

Underneath this robust faith in the division of academic labor lay a new conception of knowledge. Knowledge seemed to Eliot necessarily subdivided into specialized domains. (Was it coincidence that he was a chemist?) This ideal of specialization went far beyond simple admiration of expertise—a disposition that has thrived as long as scholars have owned mirrors. For expertise as such implies nothing more than familiarity with many details of one or more sites on the map of knowledge. What was changing was whether a scholar could seriously aspire to roam from one site to another far away.

Previously, he could; for the map of knowledge was a seamless whole. This conviction of the unity of knowledge had framed learning at least since the seventeenth century.[8] In American colleges between the Revolution and the Civil War the belief expressed itself most explicitly in a course called "moral philosophy" or "moral science." Although briefly sketched in Part I, this study requires now fuller explication. Hatched in the Scottish Enlightenment and exported to Britain's North American colonies shortly before their fit of ingratitude in 1776, moral philosophy within a few decades established itself throughout the new United States as a kind of capstone course for college seniors, usually taught by the president. "Moral philosophy" embraced much more than the word *philosophy* now suggests: something like metaphysics plus natural theology plus ethically oriented human sciences.[9] Adam Smith's *Wealth of Nations* originated in the moral philosophy course he taught at Glasgow, a fact that gives some sense of the subject's range. In its American variant the course showed, in principle at least, how to relate varied bodies of knowledge to each other and to the larger whole. The distinguished psychologist and academic entrepreneur G. Stanley Hall never forgot Mark Hopkins's moral philosophy course at Williams College in the 1860s; young Stanley and his classmates "certainly felt at the close" that "we had had a bird's-eye view of human knowledge, effort, and affectivity."[10]

Scholars had similar license to soar. In the Anglophone world as late as the 1870s and 1880s researchers in most areas of knowledge could employ whatever methods, pursue investigations across whatever fields, they thought fit. Charles Eliot Norton in the 1880s was an internationally recognized academic authority on medieval church architecture, Italian painting prior to 1600, ancient Greek archaeology, and Dante; in 1896 he published a seminal essay on Donne. He also worked competently, if more derivatively, on William Blake, J.M.W. Turner, and the seventeenth-century American poet Anne Bradstreet, inter alios. True, in practice, expertise in natural history offered scant help to a student of government. But both parakeets and politicians comprised parts of a single universe of knowledge, undivided by any epistemological principle. Norton's friend Charles Darwin, no intellectual slouch, roamed from zoology and botany (where he was expert) into philology (where he was an amateur) without perceiving any methodological barricade.[11]

A younger generation of academic specialists did start to throw up such barriers in the later nineteenth century. And it signifies that they were *academic* experts, for they nurtured their new conception of knowledge within universities rather than importing it from without. Their implicit ideal, or at least operative principle, was not simply specialization—the need for which scholars had long appreciated—but *disciplinary specialization* more precisely.

For brevity, *specialization* hereafter will signify "disciplinary specialization," but it is important to understand the difference. Mere specialization had earlier implied only mastery of a particular subject. It neither limited authority over that subject to a distinctive cadre of methodologically acculturated experts nor restricted a scholar from pursuing very different subjects. Charles Norton had indisputable claim to specialized expertise in several fields—but in no "discipline." The novelty of disciplinary specialization is obscured by the fact that *discipline,* like *humanity,* is an old academic term that acquired a new meaning after 1850.[12] But novel it was.

The decisive distinction of the new specialization, separating it from older forms of specialization, was not narrowness of range but acknowledgment of disciplinary isolation. Norton's longtime friend and Harvard colleague Francis Child earned a Ph.D. from Göttingen and thereafter limited his research to early English literature. He made an enduring reputation as renovator of Chaucer studies and editor of the prodigious *English and Scottish Popular Ballads.* But no more than Norton did he perceive barriers of disciplinary method or approach dividing his scholarship in English from his friend's in art and archaeology. To be sure, archaeologist and philologist needed special technical skills, but still they labored at different sites on the same spectrum of knowledge. Disciplinary specialists eventually would claim Child as one of their own by concentrating on his single-minded work and ignoring his own view of its relation to the larger world of scholarship, but disciplinarity had no room at all for a methodological freebooter like Norton—whose formal education had ended at eighteen with a bachelor's degree. It declared that, in principle, scholarly competence required restricting oneself to one's "discipline."[13]

Disciplinary specialists thus began to snip apart the previously undivided map of knowledge into separate territories. Between these "disciplines" they started to erect methodological fences hard for nonspecialists to scale. They declared, though still uncertainly and confusedly, two revolutionary dogmata: that knowledge does *not* form a whole but, on the contrary, properly divides itself into distinct compartments, and that unique methodological principles and scholarly traditions govern life within each of these boxes. The implication, seen only dimly by many academics even in the early decades of the twentieth century, was that a specialist in any one discipline could work satisfactorily in another only by a strenuous feat of reacculturation. This emerging urge to repudiate the unity of knowledge both prefigured the more radical antifoundationalism of the next fin de siècle and mirrored the nineteenth century's larger flight from universalism, seen in such movements as racism and nationalism; what connections subsist among these phenomena, if any, merits reflection.[14]

Yet it would be utterly wrong to claim disciplinary specialization as epistemologically dominant in the late nineteenth century: on the contrary, it was no more than a babbling infant. Rarely did a professor openly avow that the apparent "unity [of the world] does not come from investigation" but is merely "something we have read into" reality. Far more commonly academics still believed, at least implicitly, in the extrahuman and objective unity of knowledge, grounding their conviction, if not in the old Scottish Common Sense realism, then often in a vague idealism, occasionally in a more rigorous neo-Hegelianism or neo-Kantianism imported from Germany.[15]

If disciplinary specialization was hardly thundering across the academic prairies in 1890, why mention it? The reason is the *developing* shape of academic knowledge and the concerns expressed about it. This new specialization, differing from older expertise in the degree to which it fragmented knowledge into disconnected portions, *did* come to dominate academic knowledge in the United States during the twentieth century.[16] And although far from triumphant during the later nineteenth century, indeed often still inarticulate, the tendencies which solidified into disciplinary specialization in the twentieth century were already present then. Contemporaries did commonly recognize them, though differing widely in assessing their direction and power. The term *disciplinary specialization,* then, serves here as a kind of ideal type: a convenient shorthand to label these tendencies toward fragmented, disciplinary knowledge—inclinations often alluded to in the 1880s and 1890s.

For the drift toward disciplinary organization of knowledge was just beginning to accrue cogency—from small adaptations in academic practices, minor adjustments in attitude, gradual replacement of old professors by younger ones with tighter focus and stronger sense of the distinctiveness of their particular study. The hotbed of specialization after 1870 was the handful of research-oriented universities; smaller colleges usually had little inclination for it and less space. And even many practicing specialists remained convinced in theory of the ultimate unity of knowledge, however poorly their faith comported with the realities of their research. So any notion that this new ideal developed with consistency in the decades after 1850 is absurd. That it impinged much on the consciousness of the average professor is unlikely.

That it nonetheless did pervasively if erratically affect attitudes is patent. Daniel Coit Gilman, founding president of the new Johns Hopkins University, made specialization the first requisite for a professor. "The day has gone by," he declared in 1875, "for *a* professor of science or *a* professor of languages or *a* professor of history." Not quite: in the same year, Harvard hired Norton. But henceforth the omnivorous scholar who ranged across different fields of knowledge did get a cooler and cooler reception, especially in universities, and not just in the natural and social sciences. A professor of Greek at North Carolina warned a university committee in 1913 that classical art and archaeology "are now taking a high stand in all the larger Universities" and, "to be properly pursued, must be in the hands of a specialist." A University of Michigan professor explained in 1892 that a graduate student aiming at an academic career should strive for "an independent scholarly grasp" of one or two delimited topics; imparting a "general education" was "not the proper function of a university professor."[17]

One sees the bite of the new specialization not just in such rhetoric, but also in the growing tendency of university professors who believed in God, as most did, to keep their religious beliefs in one box and their academic ones in another, a novel phenomenon already noted among the scientists discussed earlier. This segregation was no accident: knowledge in a proper discipline was, after all, self-contained. Hence the new specialization worked, along with other forces, to exclude religious belief as an *intellectual* tool within the university. Especially in the hothouse atmosphere of self-consciously advanced research universities, religion tended to retreat to ceremonial occasions and the extracurriculum, though impudently flourishing there.

The less "progressive" universities, along with most liberal-arts colleges, sustained Christianity unselfconsciously in the classroom, but the rhetoric of specialization nonetheless penetrated even the remotest outposts of higher learning in the United States. In the medium-sized town of Sherman, Texas, not far south of the Red River, a tiny "female college and conservatory" touted its advantage in having "a specialist in each department." A hundred miles down the road, on the outskirts of Fort Worth, the new Polytechnic College of the Methodist Episcopal Church, South, proudly announced, "Every teacher here is a specialist in his or her department. This fact tells, without comment, that the instruction here imparted is equal to that afforded anywhere in the South." By the 1890s the advantages of specialization were often assumed "without comment."[18]

Not, however, without unease. The difficulty was felt perhaps especially intensely among those charged with teaching the rising generation. For, if imported from laboratory into lecture hall, specialization could prove toxic to a coherent education. If one field of knowledge had no essential connection with another, how could the curriculum hold together? How could students gain a comprehensive view of the world into which they were about to launch themselves? As late as 1898 the United States commissioner of education (and Hegelian philosopher) William Torrey Harris insisted, "Higher education seeks as its first goal the unity of human learning"; only afterward might students properly specialize.[19] A little of this and a little of that did not add up to a general education when this and that had nothing to do with each other or with anything else. In short, the elective system was the logical outcome of specialization.

In just such terms, boiled in invective rare among university administrators, Princeton's James McCosh let fly at his brother president Charles Eliot in 1885: "I hold that in a college with the variety there should be unity. The circle of the sciences should have a wide circumference but also a fixed centre." "In a college there may be, there should be, specialists," McCosh granted, "but not mere specialists, who are sure to be narrow, partial, malformed, one-sided and are apt to be conceited, prejudiced and intolerant."[20] McCosh's awkward distinction between "specialists" and "mere specialists" suggests a groping to distinguish traditional experts from embryonic disciplinary specialists. In his view the latter made coherent education impossible.

His opinions prevailed far more widely than Eliot's, especially in liberal arts colleges, bound as they were to local communities rather than to national or international scholarly affiliations. Disciplinary specialization and free election were yet ominous thunderclouds rather than a storm sweeping higher education. They hovered mainly over one or two older universities like Harvard, a few brash new foundations like Johns Hopkins. "There are few observers of American life," reported Bliss Perry as late as 1904, "who believe that specialization has as yet been carried too far"; still, he insisted, it needed "examination and correction in the interests of true human progress."[21]

Certainly, for an orthodox Presbyterian like McCosh, who presided over a college-becoming-university still explicitly Christian in character, specialization posed a sufficiently distinct threat to rail against. The particular form of curricular coherence under attack at Princeton and elsewhere, after all, was inspired by Scottish moral philosophy—as no one appreciated better than McCosh, who was by birth a Scot, by vocation a philosopher, and by fate the last great defender of Scottish philosophy as its American hegemony crumbled.[22] And the unity of knowledge insisted upon by these Scots and their New World disciples was inseparable from their Reformed Protestant beliefs. Disciplinary specialization could not only shatter the coherence of education but, if taken as governing axiom, sever the historic connection between academic knowledge and Christian beliefs.

For Christianity posited a single reality, with some kind of rational coherence integrating it. This assumption flowed from elemental Christian beliefs: a single omnipotent and all-wise God had created the universe, including human beings, who shared to some extent in the rationality behind creation. Given this creation story, it followed that knowledge, too, comprised a single whole, even if finite and fallible human beings could not perceive the connections clearly or immediately. And Christianity generated an intellectual aspiration, even imposed a duty, to grasp the connections, to understand how the parts of creation fitted together and related to divine intention.

To see the consequences of these convictions, consider the extraordinary range of influence of another Scot, Adam Smith, as a founder of the social sciences. Smith produced distinct systems of ethics, law, and most famously political economy, "each conform[ing] to the requirements of the Newtonian method in the broad sense of that term." But these *different* systems also cohered *as a whole,* not simply because Smith was by temperament a system builder—though he was—but because all assumed unselfconsciously a single divine plan. Such an axiom was nearly universal in Smith's day and remained similarly unquestioned among American academics until the 1860s; that Smith personally had a very distant relationship to Christianity only testifies to this assumption's enduring force. Nor did one have to dote on the Scots to believe it. Henry P. Tappan, the University of Michigan's prodigiously influential first president, owed more to French and German thinking about universities, but he assumed just as readily as McCosh that all knowledge necessarily cohered.[23]

This presupposition in no way inhibited the growth of *specialized expertise*—witness Smith and McCosh themselves—but it did put a brake on *disciplinary specialization.* So long as academic axioms remained Christian, specialization could not develop as epistemological principle but only as untheorized practice, as it did in the mathematized areas of natural science long before the late nineteenth century. And even this limited sort of specialization evolved under the reins of a strongly felt need to embed science in larger systems of natural theology.

Put differently, specialization might make *practical* sense for a physicist like Joseph Henry or a botanist like his younger contemporary, Harvard's great Asa Gray, but specialized knowledge made *intellectual* sense only if connected (at least in theory) with other areas of knowledge as a part of an overall divine system. As Henry believed, "The tendency of science is to higher and higher, or rather I should say wider and wider, generalizations, and could we be possessed of sufficient intelligence we would probably see all the phenomena of the external universe, and perhaps all those of the spiritual, reduced to the operation of a single and simple law of the *Divine* will. I cannot think that any fact relative to mind or matter is isolated."[24]

This assumption began to weaken in the later nineteenth century, despite support from the Protestant convictions still pervasive in American higher education. It weakened in part because of the passing away of the moral philosophy course that had used to explain and certify the unity of knowledge.[25] It weakened in part because of the daily practices of researchers (such as the scientists discussed in the first part of this book), more and more focused on minute studies apparently unconnected to questions outside "the field," less and less likely to invoke the Creator or any larger matrix of knowledge—whatever their own beliefs in such matters. It weakened in part because growing numbers of American scholars, leaders of the American university revolution, got postgraduate training in German universities, where links between Christianity and academic knowledge had frayed if not snapped. It weakened in part because a small but influential cadre of actual agnostics sprinkled the faculties of American universities after 1870, to whose presence scholarly discourse had to accommodate itself. And it weakened in part because of the methodological consequences of the Darwinian revolution and the wider shaking of epistemological certainty that Darwin represented, not just within the sciences.[26]

Weakening did not necessarily spell demise—indeed, probably most college presidents in 1900 would have echoed Joseph Henry—but it did call for bracing of the dikes. Fortification was needed in two respects, in theory mutually supportive: reinforcement of the links binding knowledge into a single whole and shoring up of Christianity within the curriculum. For the erosive effects of disciplinary knowledge threatened Protestant university leaders like McCosh with two related disasters: the sapping of coherence from academic knowledge and the stripping away of its connections with the divine. Nor was the threat simply to effective teaching, though the elective system did become the great bogey; the character of knowledge itself was at stake. As Henry Tappan declared in 1858, "All branches of learning are cognate, and require for their successful prosecution, cordial cooperation and mutual support. Nay, they are logically interdependent, so that to separate them would be to render their development impossible." Tappan's axiom still held sway in American academe into the twentieth century, but no longer unquestioned sway. Both the unity of knowledge and its transcendent meaning needed defense.[27]

Only at a few places like Hopkins and Harvard, where secularization had gone unusually far, did danger appear to press immediately. But the decline of moral philosophy within colleges everywhere, and the rise of a more obviously secular culture outside, created concern about the future as the nineteenth century wound down. There were many sources of secularization in higher education, and disciplinary specialization was only one. But together with the spread of naturalism, it was the main methodological or epistemological manifestation of secularization and, therefore, a focus of concern. Nonetheless, the tone of educational leaders rarely suggested the wolf at the door: more often buoyant zeal to bring Christian learning up to date.

It was generally in this spirit that academics—and not only Protestants—evolved a variety of strategies for subduing the threat of disciplinary specialization and of intellectual secularization more broadly. Protestants, often evangelicals, did still hold the reins in the great majority of universities and colleges, private and public.[28] So one natural arrangement was to introduce distinct courses on the Bible; these began to appear after the middle of the century and proliferated near its end.[29] However potent in inculcating a generic Protestantism, Bible requirements in effect conceded that Christianity needed to be taught in discrete new courses precisely because it no longer ruled all learning in moral philosophy. Moreover, catechizing students did nothing to resolve the looming epistemological crisis. With the fading of Scottish philosophy and the stirrings of the new specialization, a framework broader than the old Protestant one but still compatible with Christianity was needed to reinforce the unity of knowledge.

In this context the rise of the humanities makes fuller sense. For the new humanities—though scarcely the only solutions advanced—did address precisely these problems. This was far from their sole appeal. Compared to the old classical curriculum, subjects like English and history sported a tough-minded air of practicality, however odd this later sounded; and, conversely, rubbing up against Shakespeare and Michelangelo gave young people a cultural sheen alluring to the post–Civil War haute bourgeoisie and the aspiring petite.

Yet, for their teachers, the humanities' highest merit seemed to lie in their capacity to restore coherence to knowledge and to sustain its religious character. This is not to say that all teachers of the humanities despised specialization. Many, maybe most, valued "graduate specialization" and approved "technical courses" at that level, and as scholars of

Greek temple architecture or Provençal philology they increasingly pursued their own research along disciplinary lines. The hobgoblin of consistency haunts professors no more than other mortals. The "ideal of undergraduate instruction" among humanities instructors, however, was anything but "specialistic." It was rather (as a Latin professor in Texas imagined) that of "an intimate spiritual exchange between pupil and teacher."[30]

That literature and art possess peerless power to ward off specialization and promote "spiritual exchange" is not intuitively obvious. Indeed, teachers of the humanities had no arcane wisdom; they drew upon notions widespread both within the academy and without. But they deployed these commonplaces with greater éclat and effect than colleagues in geology or sociology. To see why, we must first distinguish the threat of an incoherent knowledge from that of a knowledge severed from religion. Then, in exploring responses to the first, we must set philosophy temporarily aside from its literary and historical kindred among the humanities; for it was these latter, the core subjects of "liberal culture," which pioneered a new way of making knowledge cohere. They owed their success in no small part to the fact that the remotest origins of these humanities threw them athwart the new tendencies to disciplinary specialization.

# Chapter Six

## TWO IDEALS OF KNOWLEDGE

D ISCIPLINARY specialization and most of the humanities actually derived from two different approaches to knowledge. European education had since antiquity encompassed two more or less distinct wings: rhetoric (roughly, the art of persuasion) and philosophy (roughly, the science of demonstration). This division in turn reflected a more basic divide between what we would call two modes of knowledge.[1]

We would say two modes of knowledge: *they* did not, for one of these types of "knowledge" counted in the Middle Ages and Renaissance only as "opinion." *Opinion* then meant something close to what *probabilistic knowledge* does now, that is, knowledge of facts, which might attain a very high degree of probability ("moral certainty") but could never reach absolute certainty. "Opinion" or probabilistic knowledge formed the educational realm of *rhetoric;* for, where proof was strictly impossible, one perforce resorted to persuasion. The other type of knowledge ("truth"; "science") we would subdivide into perhaps three areas: immediate intuition (such as that $2 + 2 = 4$); divine revelation; and logical demonstration from the unquestionable axioms provided by intuition and revelation. This sort of "science" was the educational domain of *philosophy,* which dealt with true knowledge. In philosophy complete certainty was possible, though at the price of a certain abstraction from mundane reality.[2] Philosophy had lorded it over knowledge in the Middle Ages and continued to dominate university education through the seventeenth century.

Yet, outside the universities, Renaissance humanism rehabilitated the prestige of rhetoric—and its kindred study, philology. *Philology* is a term that in the nineteenth century grew remarkably flexible in the studies it covered. But in earlier times it was understood as the branch of scholarship devoted to reconstructing, analyzing, and interpreting ancient texts. Philology was already sophisticated in the ancient world, but when the western Roman Empire fell upon hard times, so did it.[3] Its resuscitation in the Renaissance goes far to explain why there was a Renaissance, for philology enabled the recovery of the heritage of classical antiquity. Later, northern humanists like Erasmus turned their attention increasingly to a different sort of ancient text, the Scriptures, and in doing so founded modern textual criticism of the Bible. For all its varied achievements, though, humanist philology did nothing to bridge the ancient gap dividing rhetoric from philosophy, probable opinion from demonstrative certainty, language from science. "All knowledge," Erasmus averred, "falls into one of two divisions: the knowledge of 'truths' and the knowledge of 'words.'"[4]

Yet a kind of epistemological revolution did occur in the seventeenth century: in history, in law, in theology, in the understanding of probability, and most notably in natural science.[5] Put succinctly, factual data graduated from mere "opinion" to "knowledge." The heightened respectability of empiricism was less a matter of redefining concepts than of redistributing prestige. Demonstrative knowledge alone still claimed absolute certainty, but it often now appeared abstract, arid, irrelevant. Empirical knowledge still aspired only to moral certainty at best; but it gave human beings the kind of information they needed to regulate their lives, govern their states, manage their countinghouses, and control nature—a type of knowledge that came to seem far weightier to John Locke and many others than mere philosophical propositions. This revolution elevated probabilistic experimental knowledge into true science, thus helping to define modern science. Even Newton's putatively demonstrable laws required probabilistic knowledge for their discovery.

Yet, as the boundary between "science" and "experience" became permeable, that between philosophy and rhetoric continued to resist penetration. Probabilistic knowledge had become true science, and thus the experimental sciences, at least when aiming to discover general laws, proudly donned the ancient mantle of philosophy ("natural philosophy"). But although science now had a probabilistic component, the division between true science and the studies centered on language remained.

By 1800 these traditional two sides of learning had crystallized into two great models of knowledge. One was nomothetic (that is, law-seeking) natural science. It was embodied most fully in Newton's mathematical laws of motion but also was busily transforming the study of electricity and extending its reach to chemistry, meteorology, and medicine. Natural science aimed to distill knowledge into simple general laws, as befitted a pursuit descended from logic-centered medieval philosophy and still called natural philosophy: its heritage echoed in Lester Ward's insistence in 1883 (quoted in Part I) that real truths are "demonstrable." The second model of knowledge was philology. It was embodied most influentially in classical philology and biblical criticism. Philology aimed at an interpretive kind of knowledge, as befitted a pursuit long linked with rhetorical training for public persuasion. The lines of division were rarely sharp; the two modes of knowledge often behaved more like allies than enemies; studies of nature and of language sometimes even reversed methodological roles.[6]

Still, two basic differences in approach were clear, and achievements of both physicists and philologists were loudly and separately celebrated. On the one hand, broadly speaking, the social or human sciences, at least as far back as the Scottish Enlightenment, modeled themselves on the law-seeking aspirations of Newtonian science, and as the nineteenth century wore on, this ideal of regular, general, predictive law conquered the rest of natural science, too.[7] On the other hand, the new studies called the humanities modeled themselves on philology, while the ancient but still flourishing textual scholarship also continued that tradition.

The children of nomothetic science retain high visibility today, but philology has faded so far from public view that many educated Americans do not even know what the word means. It helps to recall that philology, not natural science, was queen of *Wissenschaft* at the great German universities in the eighteenth century and first half of the nineteenth. And these universities provided for nineteenth-century Americans as much as for Europeans the august example of advanced academic knowledge. Put differently, philology, not natural science, presided over the institutional origins of modern academic knowledge. The point, however, is not to adjudicate claims to preeminence. It is, rather, to underline the influence of *both* philological and scientific epistemological ideals.

And this at last brings us back full circle to those two late-nineteenth-century innovations, specialization and the humanities. Disciplinary specialization grew from the physical sciences. Their much-admired practitioners, as the nineteenth century moved toward the twentieth, increasingly communicated with each other in arcane dialects, more and more mathematized or otherwise formalized, more and more inaccessible to outsiders. In this practice lay the origin of "disciplines," conceiving of knowledge as segmented into unconnected pieces. The humanities could—and after 1900 increasingly did—behave in disciplinary ways. But their true origins lay in philology—in its fascination with texts and contexts, in its interpretive animus.

These origins enabled the humanities to provide a tolerable substitute for the old unifying frame of knowledge embodied in moral philosophy, though one grounded very differently. This new form of integration was bottomed on two closely related assumptions of philology. The first was the principle that cultural context shaped every text, the second historicism.

The first axiom—looking to cultural context to decode the meanings of a text—was basic to philology centuries before the word *culture* meant anything other than growing plants.[8] (Indeed, the anthropological notion of culture ultimately derives from philology.) The reason lies in the paradigmatic philological problem. If a scholar wished to understand a document from another time and place, he needed to know the background that clarified the meanings of the writer's words. What, the philologist asked, were the possible translations of a particular Latin or Hebrew term? Which one made the best sense in the passage at hand? What political institutions or religious rituals or marriage customs or farming practices cast light on the shades of meaning? The greatest biblical philologist of the sixteenth century, Erasmus, "constantly" asked "who was writing a particular document, whom he was addressing, what he was really saying, and what were the surrounding circumstances that help explain what he said." He advised students of Scripture not merely to learn languages but to "study the history and geography of the Hebrew and Roman worlds."[9]

The same principle, grown more articulate and complex, underlay the researches three centuries later of early American academic philologists. Lecturing at Harvard in 1813 on biblical criticism, Andrews Norton stressed how language is embedded in culture. The nineteenth-century reader, he pointed out, with his "modern doctrines, prejudices, and associations," faced enormous barriers to understanding the "oriental style" of the New Testament. The writers of biblical times "embodie[d] intellectual & moral ideas" in "sensible images"; and such phrases a nineteenth-century reader would "certainly" misunderstand if interpreting them "according to the analogy of our common use of language." But problems of comprehension hardly ceased with the need to distinguish between "oriental" and modern Western styles. For, explained Norton, rarely does a word ever definitely and solely express "one certain idea, or series of ideas." Rather, the "circumstances in which it is used, are often a necessary commentary for defining its signification." So the critic had to learn, not only the style characteristic of a period, but the idiosyncrasies of a particular writer, the range of reference permitted by his social position and intellectual background, the conditions and outlook of the people to whom he directed his message, the historical circumstances under which he wrote, the social and economic institutions of his society, and so forth. For the philologist, language works as a web of meaning integral with the more extensive web of human social existence. Every ancient text thus expresses a historically distinct culture.[10]

From this axiom another followed easily: historicism. If the culture of nineteenth-century Boston differed from that of first-century Palestine, so, too, must first-century Palestine differ from Palestine a century before or after. All cultures were in flux; the careful scholar could discern patterns of change over time in every one. Already in the seventeenth century the leap was made from Renaissance philology to the idea that "historical facts" are not "self-evident" but "obtain significance only from the context in which they are embedded." From this grew historicism: the "tendency to view all knowledge and all forms of experience in a context of historical change."[11] Laws of nature might be timeless, but products of human beings—writings, paintings, buildings, mores, ways of making love and making war—were time-bound. Really to understand them, one needed to situate them in the flow of the history that shaped them.

The idea is powerful. Historians of religion have long appreciated the revolutionary effect of biblical philology within the churches, but historians of education have largely ignored the resonance of philology within American academe. Consider the most renowned paladin of the new humanities, Charles Eliot Norton. Norton, like his father, Andrews, the biblical critic, was a philologist, and the historicist principles deriving from philology shaped his teaching. But as any good philologist knows, every cultural practice takes specific local forms to suit local purposes, philology included. The younger Norton carried philology much further than his father had, into relatively uncharted academic domains.

Charles Norton's scholarship on Dante and Donne followed well-worn philological paths, but he also approached subjects like medieval cathedrals and Greek temples from a philological point of view.[12] That is, he treated the construction of the duomo of Siena or the temple of Zeus at Olympia as a philologist treated ancient texts. The meanings of these places of worship to their builders became clear only when a scholar set the buildings into a broad cultural context; conversely, as products of specific times and places, the structures and their building cast light on the worldviews of the societies that erected them. The context explained the "text"; the "text" illuminated its context—the philologist's hermeneutic circle. Norton made this the principle of his teaching as well as of his scholarship. Students in his courses heard him dwell on Athenian social organization and religious ideas as prolegomenon to the Parthenon, and then interpret the Parthenon as embodying and revealing the Athenian world view. Expanding the ideas of his own old teacher Cornelius Felton, Norton offered this sort of instruction under the name of "culture."[13]

*Culture* here acquired yet another meaning: shorthand for "cultivation of the imagination."[14] There were, Norton believed, "two superior sources of culture": the "history of what man has done" and "of what he has thought." The best culture of the imagination was immersion in great "poetry" (as Norton sweepingly defined poetry, to include architecture and the visual arts as well as all forms of literature); for through poetry "we may most easily quicken, and fully nourish our own feeble and undeveloped capacity of imaginative vision." Exposure to "poetry" produced this beneficent effect because the poet's own imagination "works more powerfully and consistently than in other men." At the same time, "without culture of the imagination we read poetry with a lack of appreciation."[15] The more one reflected on Shakespeare or Titian, the more one's imagination expanded; and the more one's imagination grew, the more susceptible it became of cultivation through literature and art. At least in structure this recursive upward spiral, this progressive dialectic of improvement, resembled the hermeneutic circle of philological scholarship: from text to context and back again, each move enriching understanding. On this level—and we shall consider others shortly—Norton's type of erudition underlay both his pedagogy in general and his ideal of culture in particular.[16]

And this essentially philological ideal inspired as well teachers and scholars of the humanities elsewhere. Like Norton, the majority of them believed that the proper approach to a text was to treat it as illuminating, and as being illuminated by, its culture (in the historian's sense of that last word). As Thomas Randolph Price told his students at the University of Virginia in 1881, the "true Literature of a nation is the collective result of its ideal energies, as seen in its intellectual productions," "the expression of a nation's ideas." The founding principle of Princeton's "School of Art" was that "works of art are the only trustworthy record of—not alone the history—but of the tastes, the mental character, and the manners and customs of various peoples in various ages": "To the student, the purpose and the persons for whom art objects were made, are of more importance than the artist." Nor did this notion inform only liberal arts colleges. Pennsylvania State College devoted itself to engineering and agriculture, but its students, in their required course in English literature, heard "each literary production" placed "into its proper contemporary setting in such a way as to bring out the circumstances that gave it birth and how it reflects, directly or indirectly, the spirit of its time."[17]

And further, most teachers believed this interpretive process the key to "culture" in its pedagogical sense. Thomas Apple told students at Franklin and Marshall College that "the literature of a people reveals to us their life," so that "un[con]ciously and imperceptibly the life grows on us" as we "commune" with them through their writings. Almost by definition courses acquired "culture value" for a student "by interpreting for him the institutions and ideals of the past." Even technical institutions now believed that "the narrowing influence of professional or special education should be counteracted by a preparatory drill in the general cultural subjects"; and a historical approach to literature and art provided the most potent antidote to narrowness; for history seemed "the most comprehensive of all the sciences." After all, the "subject of which it treats is the development of human life." Albert S. Cook of Yale in 1898 indeed described the "function of the philologist" as precisely

the endeavor to relive the life of the past; to enter by the imagination into the spiritual experiences of all the historic protagonists of civilization in a given period and area of culture; to think the thoughts, to feel the emotions, to partake the aspirations [sic], recorded in literature; to become one with humanity in the struggles of a given nation or race to perceive and attain the ideal of existence; and then to judge rightly these various disclosures of the human spirit, and to reveal to the world their true significance and relative importance.[18]

By the early twentieth century the hermeneutic circle of philology— context-text-context—had become a routine assumption of the now routine humanities. The 1913 Carleton College catalog rattled off a course description:

I. AMERICAN LITERATURE.—After a brief introductory study of the great political, social, industrial, and religious movements which form the background of the literature, many important writings are read, in chronological order, and studied intensively with reference to their revelation of the developing national life.

Indeed, so deeply had the informing assumption slipped into routine that probably few recognized it as philological in origin. Certainly amnesia had taken its toll within a decade or two, by which time textual philology had fallen into dusty disrepute.[19] But its historicist axiom had become thoughtless second nature for American academics in the humanities.

Yet how did an educational program of cultivation, inherited from philological historicism, enable the humanities to provide a new kind of coherence for college studies? Here the integrative impulse imbued in philology by its historicist practices was decisive. This is not to say that philology invariably took sweeping views of the human condition: mocking philologists for pointless pedantry and cramped outlook was already a popular sport in the Renaissance. But the animus of philology pushed toward making wider connections at least as powerfully as toward narrowing of focus. The ideal, after all, of philological scrutiny was to link a text with all cultural contexts that might illumine its meanings. And this integrative urge, however often eclipsed by the dust of scholarship, carried over into the teaching of the humanities in the late nineteenth century.

Again, Charles Norton, that most famous emblem of the humanities in their first generation, makes the point. In his own student days at Harvard in the 1840s he had experienced how moral philosophy infused coherence and sense of purpose into learning, starting from the axiom that one God had created a single universe and given his rational creatures the means to grasp it. Later as a professor Norton saw in Charles Eliot's elective system the breakdown of this intellectual cohesion.[20] And any nostalgia Norton may have felt for his old college studies (which was not much) could hardly disguise the stark fact that those old ways of integrating knowledge had lost plausibility. Specialization had already begun in practice to sap the assumption that intellectual life cohered, while God no longer commanded in theory universal assent as a unifying principle. The times demanded something novel. Norton provided it, though hardly by himself.

This new edition of liberal education had two key elements. The first was to acquaint students with beauty, especially as manifest in "poetry" broadly conceived. Because the point was to cultivate wide human sympathies, it made no sense for colleges to subdivide the humanities into bins divided by disciplinary specialization, as was happening in the sciences. The need for a "broad basis" of studies in order to cultivate extensive "sympathies" became a talisman of the humanities, even among scientifically minded philologists like William Gardner Hale of the University of Chicago. Thus, in Norton's seminar for advanced students, "the study of Dante" became "a study of literature, of poetry, of religion, of morals." But simple breadth, however effectual in widening sympathies, did not actually make knowledge more coherent; indeed, it might diffuse it.[21]

A second element thus entered the humanities: a stress on continuities linking the "poetry" of one era to that of succeeding periods and ultimately to our own. Such stretching became almost a defining mark of teachers of the humanities. Thomas Hume, lecturing on Homer in the 1880s at Norfolk College in Virginia, began by juxtaposing the *Iliad* to Virgil, Milton, and Dante; comparing "the religious system of Homer" with those of ancient Hebrews and modern Protestants; and discussing Homeric themes in poems of Tennyson and Paul Hamilton Hayne. The cultivated imagination needed to be dilated into sympathy with all human aspirations; it needed to be rooted in the long story of humanity. "For history deals with what is of peculiar interest to man,—the works of man, works of his brothers, with their passions and their emotions, and with their disappointments."[22]

Thus the notion of a continuous European civilization gained pedagogical importance. The concept descended from a common earlier idea of "universal civilization," which provided an organizing principle for some early history courses in American colleges. Princeton's Charles Woodruff Shields, for instance, learned from Guizot that there is "a course of destiny of the [human] race," and all "other facts" of history "merge in it, are condensed in it, and find their importance in it." But the newer theme stressed cultural distinctiveness and continuity. A common history had led the peoples of Europe (and their cultural descendants overseas) to share many beliefs and practices; these eventually made one modern civilization, the people of which, despite all differences dividing them, recognized themselves as distinct from the peoples of, say, Chinese or Egyptian civilization.[23]

The pedagogical effectiveness of "civilization" thus pivoted on the primacy of culture over nature. True, "civilization" often took on a racialist cast in the late-nineteenth-century atmosphere of imperialism and the White Man's Burden.[24] But far from central, this was actually damaging to the project; as Norton insisted, cultural history, not physical distinctions, separated "races" from each other, so it was culture that students should study. Nor did *civilization* necessarily have a normative sense; Norton meant by it merely the totality of a people's mental and material equipage "at a given time."[25]

The "given time" matters; ancient Greece, medieval Christendom, and modern Europe hardly comprised a single civilization.[26] Rather, a chain of influences ran from the ancient Mediterranean through Rome and medieval Europe to the present. R. H. Dabney of the University of Virginia stated the essential principle, the "great doctrine of the Unity of History": "the doctrine that (for example) the Roman Empire was the result of all the previous history of the Mediterranean lands, and the mother of all subsequent European states." Norton stressed how this continuity linked modern European literature, art, and architecture with very different earlier forms from which the later evolved. As early as "the arts" of ancient Egypt and Mesopotamia lay "the beginnings of our own civilization." Yet, he and most others believed, the Greeks had made the definitive breakthrough, initiating "a conscious study by man, of his own experience." Greek civilization was *not* our own, but it was "the first rudimentary stages of it." Thus, "with the Greeks our life begins."[27]

And because "our life" began with the Greeks and matured through their putative heirs, modern students could best apprehend their own civilization by studying the influences that made it, by learning of "the historic evolution of our civilization." "You cannot know yourselves unless you know history," Norton told the mob of students who annually jammed Fine Arts 3. Development here had a pedagogical specificity about it. It meant tracing in a classroom a continuous lineage of values and conceptions from Greece through the present. This did not imply that ideas passed through history essentially intact; such stasis would contradict the very principle of development (though most teachers of the humanities do seem to have believed in enduring basic human characteristics). Nor did it naively suggest that Dante or Shakespeare saw himself as part of a developing civilization. Neither, finally, did developmental continuity necessarily suggest progress; rather, knowledge of antiquity "provides us with standards by which to measure our own capacities and performances," while it "quickens our sympathies with the generations which have preceded us."[28]

This was, after all, the whole point. "Civilization" mattered not as a historic reality but as a historically based educational program. In this project, widening "sympathies" by rooting them in an ongoing story of humanity, the humanities gave students once again a way to integrate or at least to form a broad understanding of their education. Norton was not alone in seeing the humanities as counteracting the new specialized college studies that narrowed "intellectual vision." And thus the humanities helped to fill the vacuum in the curriculum left by the disintegration of the old moral philosophy.[29]

Yet, if parallel to the old way, the study of civilization opened a decidedly new road. The classical curriculum treasured discipline of the mind, and thus strengthening of intellectual grasp; "culture" valued development of imagination, and thus broadening of sympathetic reach. Moral philosophy acquainted students with a gamut of sciences, human and natural; the humanities with a "poetic" tradition constructed from literary, artistic, religious, and philosophical works. Moral philosophy provided a schema for linking all knowledge together; "civilization," an overview of the development of human works in the European sphere. Moral philosophy emphasized the (vertical) ties between God and creature; "civilization" replaced these with (horizontal) bonds between people. Philology had indeed transmuted itself into something scarcely recognizable.

Stressing the historic continuity of European civilization was hardly the only expedient for ensuring some coherence in knowledge. Occasionally a teacher assumed that the study of *any* great civilization could accomplish the "pedagogic" aim of "the true humanities"; for, in studying "one rounded civilization," the student could get "in touch with the active forces of all, and with the heart-beat of culture-history," could "learn the power of an ideal in human life," and so forth.[30] Many late-nineteenth-century professors apparently felt no need for any well-articulated integration of knowledge, content to fall back on the inherited faith that knowledge must in the end all hang together or on a vague philosophic idealism that served the same purpose. A few articulated that idealism more carefully. And for that matter, in many colleges an enfeebled version of moral philosophy struggled along until the end of the century.[31]

Yet the cultural and culturing agenda of the humanities exerted special appeal, for it had both resonance with the regnant idea of "liberal culture" and programmatic specificity. Even if developed in many different forms, the aims of the project—to broaden sympathies, to deepen understanding of the human condition, to infuse ideals, and thus to fill in a new way the old place of moral philosophy—seem to have inspired the humanities almost everywhere as the moral philosophy course faded from view. The "unity and independence of culture studies" was widely assumed. So was the animating axiom that the "ultimate aim" of the humanities "is to enrich the heart and mind of the student by leading him to live over in thought and feeling the complete spiritual unfolding of a great people by repeating in imagination the experience of their sensuous environment, of their religious sanctions, their social and political life, their poetry and formative art, their philosophy and science."[32]

Congregationalist Carleton College gave up moral philosophy before 1890: its reverend president promised instead "a broad, thorough, systematic culture." A few years later and a thousand miles south, the English professor at the Methodists' Polytechnic College near Fort Worth set students to

> study literature not in its merely external and adventitious aspects, but in its vital relation to permanent human interests, regarding it not as a part of history, but as the expression of all that is important and enduring in every period of history; indeed, conceiving of it as being the truest and most powerful interpretation of life itself.[33]

Maybe. The knowledge offered around 1900 in the humanities had a hard time qualifying as "real" knowledge, for it looked very different from the more disciplinary knowledge that "serious" scholars pursued. Even professors of literature or classics usually took a different, more disciplinary tack when they left the classroom for research. The cobbling together of general education programs—typically around the humanities, as in the Western Civilization curricula of the 1950s—has ever since proved both awkward and remarkably remote from the hard-core research concerns of the American university. Daniel Coit Gilman of Johns Hopkins saw the split clearly, and even if defining it obtusely, he suggests how the humanities tasted to an apostle of the new disciplinary knowledge, while echoing in his vocabulary the age-old distinction between philosophy/science and rhetoric/opinion:

> While the old line between the sciences and the humanities may be invisible as the equator, it has an existence as real. On the one side are cognitions which may be submitted to demonstrative proof; which do not depend upon opinion, preference, or authority; which are true everywhere and all the time; while on the other side are cognitions which depend upon our spiritual na-

tures, our aesthetic preferences, our intellectual traditions, our religious faith. Earth and man, nature and the supernatural, letters and science, the humanities and the realities, are the current terms of contrast between the two groups and there are no signs that these distinctions will ever vanish.[34]

Whether they ignored "the realities," the humanities did succeed in infusing college studies with a sense of breadth, even a sort of integration, otherwise lacking in the spreading elective system and utterly foreign to the new ideals of disciplinary specialization. When, during the first half of the twentieth century, wide latitude for students to choose their studies gradually became the rule in American colleges, and as academic knowledge increasingly hewed to the disciplinary model, some version of the approach to integrating studies pioneered in the humanities became the heart of general education. "We accordingly rejoice," wrote William Torrey Harris in 1898 with an almost audible sigh of relief, "in the fact of the increased popularity of the university in both of its functions—that of culture and that of specialization."[35]

# Chapter Seven

## FOR AND AGAINST SECULARIZATION

YET ENSURING SOME COHERENCE in learning met only half the problem. For disciplinary specialization threatened not just to crack the unity of learning, but also to cut the ties that bound knowledge to God.

Granted, the threat looked pretty remote in the late nineteenth century, when Protestant Christianity still ruled all but one or two limbs of the academic roost. Granted, too, most researchers who found themselves pursuing specialized work never imagined that their practices might have epistemological implications hostile to monotheism (most probably never imagined their work as having epistemological implications at all). In fact, modern academic specialization in the United States initially developed mostly within explicitly Christian institutions. Granted, further, from the pedagogical point of view, as distinct from epistemological, any problem seemed a merely theoretical one. Colleges and universities were mounting more and more Bible courses, and in general religion flourished in great good health on American campuses. The decades around the turn of the century were the golden age of college YMCAs and Christian Associations.

All this being conceded, a problem nonetheless remained. The protracted mortal illness of moral philosophy was gradually depriving American collegians of their once sturdy understanding of how the world embodied the will of God and how knowledge bodied forth a Christian view of reality. Its demise was also stranding students without the ethical meaning of knowledge, and the moral instruction that followed from it, once likewise provided by moral philosophy. Disciplinary specialization, though still infant, rode the rising tide; the actual fragmenting of academic knowledges made intellectually implausible any project to re-create in higher education an integrated Christian frame of knowledge closely equivalent to moral philosophy. (This is not to speak of other secularizing forces, tending to the same outcome.) In colleges where moral philosophy soldiered on and the faculty slumbered, the crisis might be postponed, but their number was dwindling.

Still, no sense of crisis prevailed, for ways of taming the problem were not in short supply. Key was the long association of Christianity and science in Anglo-American culture, explained in detail in Part I.[1] All truth was God's one truth, whether writ in the Book of Nature or the Book of Scripture; eventually it must all cohere, however dissonant science and Scripture might seem in the wake of the *Descent of Man* and the so-called Higher Criticism of the Bible. One did not have to be able to explain *how* all knowledge reflected a divine plan in order to believe that it *did*.

Meanwhile, the search for earthly truth remained as holy a vocation as proclamation of the revealed Word. President James Angell of the University of Michigan spoke to his graduating seniors in 1903: "Every scholar bears with him by his very calling a holy commission to push on to the uttermost the conquests of the scientific investigator. What is truth but the conformity of our conceptions to the facts of the universe as God has made it." Angell believed "all science" to be "in the proper sense, sacred." Angell was no philosopher, but in the philosophical climate of the fin de siècle, notions like his often came wrapped in German idealism. However articulated, the conviction was a widespread one, and it indicates how Protestant academics, and others anxious about spiritual and ethical dimensions of learning, subdued these concerns.[2]

Against this background the rocketing popularity of the humanities, and the particular and perhaps peculiar traits that they displayed in late Victorian America, become easier to comprehend. So, too, do some of the overtones that the humanities set ringing well into the twentieth century—and perhaps still do in certain quarters. For the humanities became a principal bearer, maybe the principal focus, of the spiritual and moral meanings of higher learning. Especially in the classroom, no other professors voiced the common ideals as persistently and loudly as those who professed the humanities. American colleges began in effect to transfer the pedagogical burden of explaining the world in "religious" terms from the explicitly Christian moral philosophy course to a more vaguely "spiritual" humanities curriculum. And by assuming the job, the humanities helped to reassure many university leaders that the essence of religion could survive the loss of an explicitly Christian framework of knowledge.

In this task philosophy still hefted a good deal more weight than it any longer could in ensuring the coherence of knowledge.[3] True, moral philosophy did not gasp its last in many colleges until 1900 or even slightly later. But its broad subject matter was fragmenting, spawning new disciplines—economics, political science, sociology—as detailed in Part I. Philosophy as such was shrinking into a much abridged edition of its former self, more professional and discipline-like. Probably few college philosophers wished literally to salvage its old mission; in general, especially in schools up to date, they seem to have taught their subject in the 1880s and 1890s more as analysis, less as inspiration, than in earlier decades.[4]

Yet it takes no sharp eye to ferret out thinly disguised religious concerns in philosophy classrooms. These were manifest in the idealist metaphysics prominent in philosophy departments around the turn of the century: a bulwark against the threat of materialist scientism.[5] And for their part, students flocked to philosophy teachers of an ethical, even explicitly religious stripe, men like Charles E. Garman at Amherst, George Herbert Palmer at Harvard, and Henry Horace Williams at the University of North Carolina.[6]

Williams, like many other college philosophers in his generation, actually studied for a ministerial career, at Yale Divinity School in the mid-1880s.[7] But in New Haven he drifted toward Hegel, then went on to sit under William James and Josiah Royce at Harvard and to dip his toes directly in German philosophy at Heidelberg.[8] Harvard taught him that "Religion is the feeling towards a supernatural presence manifesting itself chiefly in truth goodness & Beauty"—a trio we shall meet again shortly—and introduced him to Asian religions. In 1890 he returned to North Carolina, his alma mater, as professor of philosophy. In that role he meant to show students "how a man can be perfectly modern and yet a good Christian."[9]

A man (perhaps even a woman) could do so by dividing religion from knowledge. Knowledge had its original motive in religious impulses, and knowledge in turn "stimulates the growth of Religion," as "a shower" does "a flower." Yet religion differs radically from its irrigant. It concerns solely "the inner life," and it is "deeper" than and—significantly —"independent of Knowledge." Religion is about conduct, not metaphysics, and the "true man will be both Greek and Hebrew," "interested both in knowledge & religion." The other shoe dropped near the end of the course when Williams quoted approvingly the principle of Matthew Arnold's vaguely quasi-theistic religion: "There is a power not ourselves, that makes for righteousness."[10]

That Williams succeeded in salvaging a place for religion in student minds is clear from the cult that flourished around him for decades. (He is probably the only American philosopher to have an airport named after him—the one in Chapel Hill). That the religion he rescued corresponded to Christianity is less obvious. Williams himself detached his "Christianity" from all Christian doctrine and—concerned to free his alma mater from the iron talons of southern evangelical orthodoxy—declared that he "would teach Christian philosophy if the professor of mathematics would teach Christian math."[11] Williams's decisive severing of religion from knowledge would have appalled James McCosh, and he instilled "Christianity" by meandering for a year through a grand historical narrative of the major world religions, whose development he explicated in naturalistic terms, reaching Christ in April. Labeled *philosophy*, the course might more accurately have been called comparative religions, an academic study which in fact Williams prefigured. Indeed, in sweep and narrative cogency, his teaching resembled Norton's culture courses at Harvard, and it achieved the same effect of restoring some coherence to an increasingly elective curriculum.

Charles Garman's legendary teaching at Amherst College had a more orthodox tinge, both in its resemblance to the traditional structure of the moral philosophy course and in its proximity to Christianity. Yet in important respects Garman's work, like Williams's, provided a bridge to a less sectarian, less doctrinal idea of religion. Like Williams and the older moral philosophers, Garman sought deliberately to shore up the Christian beliefs of his students. Like Williams but unlike the older moral philosophers, he did so by urging them to cast off "obedience to authority" in matters of religion and assume "self-direction." He expounded "the laws of the unfolding of the life of the individual and of the community" to make his students learn "that the great question of human history is not so much where we are as whither we are drifting." Annually the students first grew "almost as frightened as some horses are when the blinders are taken off," but they eventually learned to follow not authority but "simple honesty to one's self." Garman, again like Williams, was a brilliant teacher who neglected publication and "chose to write on living men's hearts." It seems apt that his students spoke of him "with perfect reverence."[12]

This revealingly religious phrase provides a clue worth following in the other humanities, for this characteristic fin de siècle college philosophy seems in some ways to have served as propadeutic to their teaching. By blurring formerly clear distinctions among creedal Christianity, liberal non-Christian theism, and completely untheistic "spirituality," teachers like Williams and Garman promoted a new curricular religion of individual "inner life" and high ideals—enunciating in the classroom the same sort of vaguely idealistic, much diluted Christianity that presidents like Angell were fond of proclaiming in their public orations. This provided an intellectual background against which art and literature, the avatars of beauty, could take on a new pedagogical function, offering a sort of catechesis in the Ideal.

Indeed, in the end these humanities—the ones rooted in philology—probably mattered more in instilling a new religious meaning into the curriculum broadly, for they were the heart of the new "liberal culture." And liberal culture subordinated the old collegiate goal of "mental discipline" to the "higher" purpose of "cultivating" youth through humanistic study: a cultivation understood as moral or even spiritual in nature. "The culture-historical function operates by humanizing and is essentially ethical, the linguistic-logical function operates by disciplining the practical powers of the mind and is essentially intellectual and subsidiary to the high ethical aim of the humanities." By preserving a "subsidiary" place for mental discipline, the humanities could recognize the importance of the "rational and scientific" side of literary and language study—the impressive *wissenschaftlich* work of philology—while subordinating it to a "broad, humanistic spirit" and quasi-religious aim.[13]

The philological humanities could assume this leading role in the religious repristination of collegiate learning because of their interpretive bent. And this methodological bias derived in turn from one of the defining marks of philology: its hermeneutic method of handling texts. Extracting meanings from texts was, after all, a principal goal of philology. When elaborated in a new voice, this philological striving gave the humanities distinctive power to restore to the curriculum religious import, even though of a drastically new variety.

The humanities inherited from philology the habit of scrutinizing texts in order to draw out their meanings. These meanings could be very literal ones—and in the teaching of *Piers Plowman* or the *Canterbury Tales* often were. But biblical philology, especially, had a penchant for searching out deeper, more metaphysical meanings. This inclination reappeared in the humanities. According to Carleton College's English professor the "chief study" of literature was its "living spirit," not its "material body."[14]

Mere elucidation of phrases and contexts did not sufficiently illuminate a poem, for its significance lay deeper than its signification. The professor's task became inspiration as much as information. Cornell's Hiram Corson, author of one of the most widely used literature textbooks, tried to specify the elusive "aims of literary study." The "acquisition of knowledge" was, he conceded, "a good thing." So was "sharpening of the intellect" and "the cultivation of science and philosophy." *But* "there is something of infinitely more importance than all these—it is, the rectification, the adjustment, through that mysterious operation we call sympathy, of the unconscious personality, the hidden soul, which coöperates with the active powers, with the conscious intellect, for righteousness or unrighteousness."[15] If the search for meanings hidden in a text owed much to philology, the discovery of the "hidden soul" there owed nothing to philology—but a lot to the same foggy idealism that enveloped contemporaneous commencement addresses.

Though Corson almost deprecated the historically oriented "civilization" courses, preferring to bring the "spiritual faculties" of students directly "into sympathetic relationship with the permanent and the eternal," his approach nonetheless resonated with the purpose of such courses, for they likewise depended for success on the "mysterious operation we call sympathy." The teacher of past cultures aimed to inculcate the right "spiritual habits" in his or her young charges by working "to habituate" them to "noble, social ideals." Greek history had a "great lesson," according to Charles Norton: that every man should seek his own ideal development, should strive to "shape himself into the best that the material he possesses within himself, will allow." There was no better "corrective," he added, for American tendencies to dismiss "the ideal."[16]

Norton's son half-jokingly characterized his father's Harvard courses as "Lectures on Modern Morals as illustrated by the Art of the Ancients," and the students who packed his lecture hall understood what young Norton meant. His father, inheriting the ethical didacticism of the old-time moral philosophy professor, utterly transformed it. Fifty years later one student remembered how under Norton's tutelage "Beauty became not aesthetic satisfaction merely but took her place high among Moralities." And somehow morality elided into a kind of godless spirituality, for Norton "never divorced the spiritual from the beautiful." He began Fine Arts 3 in 1897 by telling his students, "The great danger and difficulty in college life today is the substitution of the lower interests for the higher interests of life,—the substitution of material interests for spiritual interests." The humanities, he said elsewhere, provided "the strongest forces in the never-ending contest against the degrading influences of the spirit of materialism," hence "the knowledge most useful for the invigoration and elevation of character."[17]

Norton hardly concocted this Gospel of the Ideal on his own, though he was its greatest American prophet. His closest friend, James Russell Lowell, one of America's earliest teachers of the humanities, believed that imaginative writers were in essence moral teachers, that therefore immersion in great literature made readers more ethical. Lowell had imbibed something of the Emersonian idea of the poet as seer, and he translated the poetic function of moral illumination onto an almost transcendental, quasi-religious plane. He spoke as readily of the "mysterious and pervasive essence always in itself beautiful" as he did of the etymology of a Provençal noun.[18]

So did many other teachers of the humanities. Not every one: the heavy perfume of Victorian moralism could turn a stomach. And in practice a lot of courses in subjects like English literature largely comprised a running compendium of plots and characters, enriched by occasional critical remarks. Yet even teachers who stressed beauty rather than ethics thought the character-building effect of literature important if indirect. And amid summaries of Elizabethan plays something higher was aimed at. When Arthur Richmond Marsh became America's first professor of comparative literature, he proposed to use that post to encourage "the renascence of the intellectual and spiritual man"; for he wished his work to subserve "the imaginative and spiritual life of man."

This strain echoed more and more in the humanities as the century neared its end. George Woodberry, at Columbia, infused a spirit of "natural piety" into the teaching of literature, while at Yale "words of enchantment" issued from the lips of Charlton Miner Lewis.[19]

Why should reading George Eliot or gazing at Giotto have seemed a spiritual experience? How did the humanities come to exude religious influence? For one thing, these classroom prophets were only repeating Romantic themes that had echoed for decades in Victorian culture. Slightly more specifically, they enunciated a well-worn urge to link Art with The World Beyond. John Henry Newman had not a speck of Transcendentalism in his background, but he did love to play the violin; and he "wondered whether 'musical sounds and their combinations,' although 'momentary,' were 'not some momentary opening and closing of the Veil which hangs between the worlds of spirit and sense.' "[20] For the agnostic Norton, a consistent positivist in epistemology, no veil divided "the worlds of spirit and sense"; he located "spirit" entirely in human ideals. Yet religious unbelief did not inhibit him from, so to speak, taking the Veil—nor from elevating a Romantic commonplace into a major purpose of education.

Yet he was able to do so because the links between art and spirit, between beauty and morality, were already forged in higher education. The connection did not arise merely from the rhetorical habits of college presidents, nor from the generic platitude that "objects that surround the spirit in the years especially of college life, work upon it continually with a plastic force, the impressions of which can never afterwards be lost" because they "stamp their image on the very constitution of the soul."[21] Doubtless this nurturing environment mattered.

But more precisely and philosophically, American colleges inherited "that splendid revelation of ancient philosophy that perfect goodness and perfect beauty are the same." Usually antique conviction spoke in the modern voice of Scottish moral philosophy, sometimes inflected in New England by the Neoplatonism for which Puritans had had an affinity. But it could even adopt a Teutonic accent, as at Franklin and Marshall College with its Pennsylvania German heritage. Regardless, the essential message was the same. Lyman Atwater described "Truth, beauty, and goodness" to his Princeton students in 1858 as the triple "offspring of God," flowing from His "changeless perfections." In 1911 the distinguished classical scholar Francis W. Kelsey was still declaring "the beautiful" to be "inseparably associated" with "the good and the true."[22]

The practical point at the core of this aesthetic was "the development of character." Art could promote moral and spiritual growth because the "three primordial ideas, the good, the beautiful and the true" are "one in their objective constitution, that is they are different phases of a common principle." Art and literature might even teach moral and spiritual ideals more effectively than could sermons and exhortations. For "the beautiful," though having "the same substance with the true and the good," is differently achieved. The true and the good work straightforwardly on the intellect or the will. But the beautiful necessarily presents itself to the intuition, grasps the imagination; "the power [of inspiration] runs through the whole process by which the ideal is brought to pass." "The most important thoughts of a man are not those of purpose and logical invention, but such as come upon him he knows not how."[23]

The broad appeal of this sort of intuitionism in American colleges (though not its specific ground in every case) owes much to the hegemony of Scottish philosophy.[24] More precisely, two related Scottish teachings were nearly ubiquitous in American moral philosophy: that of the moral sense (à la Francis Hutcheson) and that of self-evident truths (per Thomas Reid). In American hands these doctrines could prove remarkably pliable. At Princeton Lyman Atwater mixed Reid's "self-evident truths" with Coleridge's misunderstanding of Kant to provide his students with an iron-clad guarantee of their capacity to perceive "intuitive supersensual truths." Atwater did warn the boys not to go hog-wild with it, but only an unusually heavy sleeper could have sat through the course without growing confident that under proper conditions his mind could immediately intuit the good, the true, and the beautiful.[25]

The humanities came quickly to be understood in this mode. Given proper education in recognizing and appreciating beauty, students could apprehend it through immediate simple intuitions, in the process conforming themselves closer and closer to truth and goodness. Cornell's Hiram Corson stressed "those spiritual instincts and spiritual susceptibilities" that enabled one to "know, *without* thought, some of the highest truths—truths which are beyond the reach of the discourse of reason." By bypassing the rational faculties and going straight to the imagination, the humanities sent a kind of continuous electrical pulse of beauty through their students, inspiring them almost helplessly to truth and goodness. (The analogy to divine grace is, so to speak, irresistible.) Mockery and dullness, those ancient forms of student interference, might short the circuit. But otherwise, connecting with Shakespeare would "stimulate and nourish motive and feeling, not by turning the dry light of reason alone on their secret working, but by setting them aglow and quickening them into healthful activity under the genial warmth of imagination." In imagination "conscience finds its mightiest reinforcements."[26]

Thomas Hume told the young ladies of Norfolk College about "the essential connection between the true and the beautiful":

What is wrong morally cannot be made to appear—before a rightly consti-tuted mind—really beautiful. The feeling of a just relation to the ideal stan-dard of truth and goodness creates within us the same emotion as our con-sciousness that a physical type is conformed to the ideal of beauty.

When we see any "gross and sensual treatment of a subject," our "sense of proportion is outraged, the necessity of 'the fitness of things' is vio-lated." The happy conclusion: "Imagination & Faith are Allies dealing with that which is unseen and eternally true," and from this alliance the "value of true poetry" followed "then as a study."[27]

The greater the beauty, the more powerful the effect of association with it. "A man in sympathy with a sublime man is lifted out of his own selfish sphere." Thus the humanities should emphasize "the best which has been thought and said in the world"—Homer in preference to Vir-gil, Michelangelo rather than Cimabue, Goethe instead of Schiller, George Eliot not Mark Twain. This was why the historical approach was so important; the teacher trolled through European civilization, se-lecting only the finest catches from his creel. By giving students "'an association with all that is noblest and best in the literatures of the past,'" the humanities nurtured "'the widening of our sympathies and the vivifying of our imagination,'" thus aiding "the development of the higher nature." Even the seamier side in literature had its worth. Con-fronting "sin and its consequences" in past cultures helped to lay "the foundations of correct moral judgment," just as "contact with the high-est ideals" gave "inspiration to right conduct."[28]

The humanities had no monopoly at all on the familiar notions they propagated, but the humanities did have a virtual classroom monopoly on beauty—which left them with at least oligopolistic control of good-ness, even if they did have to share truth with the scientists. Routine Latin courses (if taught as literature) could exert "an effective influence" on "the formation of personal character." All the humanities shared this moral purpose. "Officially I am a teacher of English literature," wrote Vernon L. Parrington in 1908,

> but in reality my business in life is to wage war on the crude and selfish materialism that is biting so deeply into our national life and character, and I do it by teaching whomever I can lay my hands on that the worship of materi-alism can never make a people either noble or great. . . . Whatever gifts are mine are devoted to teaching the need of a high civic and personal morality: And I mean by morality that integrity of purpose that keeps one upright and just and honorable, and that endeavors to enlarge the realm of sanity and justice and honor in this world.

Thus the "fruitage" of "culture," according to Carleton's president, was "Christian manhood."[29]

The word *Christian* here may sound wishfully specific, but it rolled off the tongues of more presidents than Carleton's. Morality elided into spirituality, and the elusory hybrid offered a kind of quasi transcendence if not pseudoreligion. In this way professors of the humanities in their first half century helped to warrant that the classroom remained safe for tender young Christians, even as it began to shed its Christian presuppositions. Many faculty members no longer taught an explicitly Christian worldview; some were no longer even Christians; but they did teach high ideals and moral character. In 1875 the Harvard Board of Overseers had nearly balked at appointing an agnostic as professor, even so distinguished a one as Charles Norton. When Norton died in 1908 an orthodox Protestant magazine published its obituary under the headline "A Christian Gentleman." Despite his inconvenient relation to Christianity, the editors deemed Norton "none the less a follower of Christ."[30]

This was utter poppycock, but poppycock had its point. The humanities helped to make higher education comfortable for more than Protestants. The religious diversification of American society in the later nineteenth century produced, as nineteenth turned into twentieth, a broadening of the American college population. Most southern universities and a lot of smaller colleges everywhere remained Protestant enclaves. But on many campuses Catholics, Jews, and even nonbelievers strolled halls lately populated almost exclusively by Protestants. The aggressively nonsectarian, often nontheistic "religion" of the humanities helped college leaders to adapt to these new demographic realities without abandoning their traditional duty to guide students in paths of righteousness.

Recall Horace Williams's inspiring lectures on the evolution of the great world religions. The story Williams told had an ecumenical inclusiveness. (Indeed, at a southern university Williams was, demographically speaking, several decades ahead of his time.) Not only could the adherents of every major faith find their place in the narrative, but his lectures could be heard in a range of voices. Fairly orthodox Christians, given moderately selective attention and only slightly modernist bent, could perceive Williams's historical approach as showing the providential workings of God in history, as the "inner life" of the race evolved from foreshadowings of truth among Buddhists, Parsis, and Greeks to its full revelation in Christ. (This fitted well the immanentism of much late-nineteenth-century American theology, discussed in Part I.) Non-Christians could hear the same lectures as displaying the natural origins of humanity's nobler impulses, even as providing empirical reassurance of the universality of moral principles. Everyone could see the humanities as cultivating morality and "spirituality," in the sense of high ideals—a least common denominator of "religious" instruction acceptable to all.

The fading of Protestant Christianity in academic knowledge thus ultimately nurtured within the humanities a new, broader purpose of college education. In 1850 colleges aimed to make good Christians; today they hope to sensitize students to ethical values (a mission foreign to European higher education). The head of the Harvard Board of Preachers in the 1920s declared "the fundamental religion" of his university to be

> the sincerity, the enthusiasm, the self-sacrificing devotion with which the men in it pursue every kind of truth and every kind of good. What are called services of religion are no substitute for this. They are, at most, means and aids to this real religion of the place.[31]

At the end of the twentieth century Harvard still included moral reasoning among its general education requirements.

From the wreckage of Christian knowledge, a liberal Protestant might well have said, the humanities had helped to rescue the essential religious purpose of higher education, had remodeled for an ecumenical America the old Protestant mission of her colleges. Indeed, as late as 1927 the well-informed authors of a study of New England colleges could easily assume that these institutions hewed faithfully to their original "exalted purpose" of "bind[ing] education to religion."[32] Was a devout Protestant like Michigan's President Angell perhaps justified in feeling that in the end Christianity had won the laurels?

If so, he really did not have the humanities to thank. Over the course of several decades academic knowledge in the United States crept away from a resilient traditional ideal of knowledge cohering under a Christian worldview toward an attractive new ideal of specialized disciplinary learning. This transition profoundly shaped the humanities, and the humanities in turn offered a resolution to its dilemmas, but a resolution that in the end must be judged deceptive. Placing the humanities at the heart of liberal education when moral philosophy fizzled helped colleges and universities to ease concerns about specialization and the spread of electives. Faculties then became freer, in research and in other teaching fields, to manipulate knowledge without regard to its larger interrelationships, following the dictates of disciplinary specialization. The consequences may have been good, bad, or, as is usually the case, mixed; and certainly the humanities were only one among many actors in the long shift toward disciplinarity. But there is no point in mystifying their role. In the end efforts like Norton's, far from ensuring a "broad culture," actually smoothed the road to the disciplinary model that people like him despised.

For what is here called *philological historicism* lay at the heart of the humanities, and in its basic axiom this kind of historicism militated against any cogent epistemological holism. The working assumption of philological historicism was that every human phenomenon was determined by its own distinct, unique, and ultimately contingent history. But if this were the case, if no overarching law of progress or evolution existed but only history as an undirected collection of events, then no larger pattern could link all cultural histories into a whole. To be sure, a grand schema, even a Christian meaning, might be imposed by *positing* the unity of all human history; and among conservative Protestants at the turn of the century, this was not uncommon.[33]

But historicism neither fostered nor welcomed this sort of imposition, because any such general direction in history undermined the historicist principle that a unique and contingent set of cultural circumstances determined every human system of belief. True, philological historicism did repudiate the extremes of disciplinary specialization, but it did so only to replace disciplinary knowledges with knowledges that were in the end equally incommensurable, because bound within traditions textual or cultural in nature rather than disciplinary. True, "civilization" gave breadth and meaning to college studies, but it did so at the implicit cost of denying the possibility of a single unified knowledge, because every human knowledge was necessarily the product of its own distinct, unique pattern of civilizational development. From this historicist viewpoint, Chinese science cannot be compatible with Western science, any more than Confucian values fit with Christian ones.

Without this philologically grounded idea of distinct cultures, each with its own way of conceiving the world, it is hard to imagine an antifoundationalist, communitarian epistemology such as Richard Rorty's as being widely credible. In this sense—without denying other, specifically philosophical antecedents—postmodern antifoundationalism is the natural child of philological historicism, bred up by the humanities. Making this point is simply a dramatic way of making a larger one: whatever else the humanities may have done for academic knowledge, they certainly did not save the unity of knowledge when moral philosophy decayed but, by disguising the collapse, only made it easier to accept.

In a parallel pattern, by soothing the anxiety of orthodox Protestants the humanities helped to lull them into letting their ideal of Christian knowledge slip away. For as should be abundantly clear in the foregoing history, there was in fact nothing specifically Christian, nothing essentially theistic, in the humanities.[34] Teachers of the humanities were instead apt to espouse such tenets as "the incalculable effect produced by noble passion and perfect expression." What exactly did this amount to? According to the author, the University of Chicago classicist William Gardner Hale, the "incalculable effect" belonged "to the finest issues of human life"—and from there drifted into a fog. Such a "matter of spiritual and aesthetic perception," Hale frankly confessed, "cannot be defined." He was certainly right that it could not in any sense comprehensible in terms of American higher education's Protestant past.[35]

Worse from this particular Christian point of view, the humanities emerged in the long run as more than passive abettors in the deconstruction of the religious framework of knowledge; ironically, they proved to be active undercover agents, a fox welcomed into the henhouse. For historicism eventually had the effect of sapping Christianity, indeed undermining any conviction of objective truth transcending human beings.

This is an old and well-known problem. Unpacking the idea of historicism uncovers an implication troubling to belief in absolute or objective truths that transcend specific human cultures. If our knowledge and beliefs are formed by the historical circumstances under which they happened to take shape, then how can they claim either objective reality or transcendent validity? Making everything depend radically on its historical setting undermines every stable norm. This is the "crisis of historicism" first fully described by Ernst Troeltsch in his classic *Der Historismus und seine Probleme* (1922).

The dilemma is sometimes put in more general terms by students of secularization: "The immanence of meaning in the world necessarily denies any independent, external meaning to the world as a whole."[36] But this phrasing merely states a tautology. The question is *why* meaning should have become "immanent in the world." In the American academic context (and there were of course other contexts), there were two agents of change: philological historicism, as outlined here, and methodological naturalism, as explained in the first part of this book. Identifying these two forces does not exclude the possibility that some deeper cultural trait in turn explains the appeal of philology and of naturalism, but if such exists, it can hardly be "secularization"—overused by historians as an explanatory principle—unless the effect can serve as the cause.

More specifically, once the humanities had carried historicism into the heart of academic knowledge, belief in the Christian God or religious doctrines could hardly remain a plausible framework for that knowledge. So devout a Christian scholar as Andrews Norton insisted in 1812 that "the scriptures, both Jewish and Christian, are to be understood only through the same means of elucidation, as are applied to all other writings of similar or great antiquity."[37] By the late nineteenth century, no other principle of interpretation seemed compatible with the canons of academic knowledge—and the "means of elucidation" had come to be historicist in nature. In this light, why should Christian beliefs not prove as transient a product of history as belief in Athena or animal sacrifice? Historicism posed an especially sensitive problem for Christianity precisely because Christians claimed to find transcendent truths incarnated in historical events and stated in historical documents.[38]

For obvious reasons philology struck nearest to the heart of Christianity in the form of biblical criticism, and this wound began really to fester in the nineteenth century. No *logical* contradiction obtains between a weak, partial version of historicism and a belief in transcendent truth. Andrews Norton accepted that human beings see religious truth through a glass darkly, that cultural circumstances always mediate and limit human comprehension of truth; yet, he also believed that people can and do grasp, shakily but sufficiently, real truths that transcend particular experiences and cultures. Indeed, Norton believed, human comprehension of truth actually grows through historical progress. But a *psychological* problem did exist, especially once belief in Christian teachings began to weaken for other reasons, and it became easier to conceive of Christianity as only one more product of the human imagination. Then philological historicism began to bite, especially since it had helped to sap these doctrines in the first place.[39] Norton's student Theodore Parker, abandoning the conservative Harvard scholarly tradition for the radical German philologist D. F. Strauss, took philological principles almost far enough to abolish religion. After separating "the Transient" from the "Permanent in Christianity," Parker eventually had left only a vague theism grounded in an equally fuzzy intuition of the divine.[40]

The humanities drank this potentially toxic historicism from their own philological sources. The old college presidents held up before students the tenets of divine law; the humanities stressed "high ideals, noble ambitions, and the indescribable qualities that constitute character." Moral philosophy had wished students to know God and His creation; "Know thyself" the humanities set before them as "the wisest and the most comprehensive maxim for the guidance of life that man has attained." These were Charles Norton's words, and probably relatively few of the early professors of the humanities were agnostics like Norton. There is indeed good reason to think most of them Christian, given the biases of college presidents in hiring faculty.[41]

Yet the methodological principles of the humanities rooted in philology (that is, excluding philosophy), anthropocentric as they were, encouraged professors of the humanities to exclude transcendental beliefs from their lectures and writings. It is perhaps doubtful that most such faculty members were even conscious of this implication of their teaching and research; regardless, the persistence of God-talk in their classrooms reflected ingrained habit or personal conviction, not academic consistency.

What, after all, did the humanities strive to do but "to understand man himself, as he has shown himself in history, and above all, as he

has shown himself in that more intimate history which is called literature"? The "inner life of the people"—their "spirit and genius"—were
"embodied" in literature, said the devoutly, if perhaps not soundly, Presbyterian catalog of Austin College in Texas. And if literature was solely
a historical outgrowth of a human society, then Christian or other religious beliefs likewise made intellectual sense only as themselves products
of human history. Any "historical phenomenon," a Christian professor
pointed out to his students in 1906, referring specifically to religion,
"can only be explained by its history." Norton called morality itself "the
result and expression of the secular experience of mankind"—a claim
not only congruent with but bottomed on his philological historicism.[42]

The shift in intellectual axioms, and sometimes its rapidity, was star-
tling. In 1892 the president of Austin College described its curriculum
in these words:

> After the student has been carefully trained in language and mathematics, and
> has obtained a fair knowledge of the works of creation through the natural
> sciences, he is ready to take up the study of man[,] the crowning work of
> creation, considered intellectually and morally.

Less than a decade later a new president rephrased the statement:

> After the student has been carefully trained in the Languages, Mathematics,
> and Bible Studies, and has a fair knowledge of History and the Natural Sci-
> ences, he is prepared to take up the more abstract as well as the more practical
> subjects taught in this department [philosophy].

God had vanished, except for a lurking presence in Bible Studies. Both
presidents were Presbyterian ministers.[43]

To attribute the dissolution of the old Protestant mode of learning
chiefly to the new humanities would be bizarre; to exaggerate its speed,
erroneous. The reasons for academic secularization were too manifold
to grasp; its pace was meandering. At the same time, it would be blind
to ignore the roles of philology in softening Christian axioms and of the
humanities as principal carrier of philology's corrosive historicism into
colleges and universities throughout the United States. Taking over from
moral philosophy the curricular duty of understanding the "inner life"
and "spirit" of the human person, the humanities tended (on methodological principle) to reduce "spirit" to historical contingency. If disciplinary specialization was one chief manifestation of epistemological secularization, the humanities reinforced the other, naturalism. And where
specialization tended only to exclude religious belief from knowledge (as
in the sciences), historicism actually tended to explain it away.

Was it coincidence that church-related institutions began to advertise heavily their commitment to "Christian education" simultaneously with the rise of the humanities?[44] Such rhetoric served no purpose until Protestant assumptions departed general academic knowledge; and the humanities played a complex role, and not a negligible one, in helping knowledge to shed its Christian chrysalis. Conversely, that historic task left its lasting mark on the humanities.

# NOTES

## CHAPTER ONE
## RELIGION, SCIENCE, AND HIGHER EDUCATION

1. For expressions of this general view, see, for example, George M. Marsden, *The Soul of the American University: From Protestant Establishment to Established Nonbelief* (New York, 1994); Julie A. Reuben, *The Making of the Modern University: Intellectual Transformation and the Marginalization of Morality* (Chicago, 1996); Laurence R. Veysey, *The Emergence of the American University* (Chicago, 1965); Burton J. Bledstein, *The Culture of Professionalism: The Middle Class and the Development of Higher Education in America* (New York, 1976); Daniel J. Wilson, *Science, Community, and the Transformation of American Philosophy, 1860–1930* (Chicago, 1990), 3; Larry Owens, "Pure and Sound Government: Laboratories, Gymnasia, and Playing Fields in the Nineteenth-Century Search for Order," *Isis* 76 (1985): 182; Richard Hofstadter and C. DeWitt Hardy, *The Development and Scope of Higher Education in the United States* (New York, 1952), 3.

2. Marsden, *Soul of the American University,* 31.

3. It is not easy to draw confident inferences about what students were actually taught in classrooms, for while student notes often record effectively enough the subject matter described in the course titles, they had a practical orientation that was ill calculated to reproduce often offhand material relating to a faculty member's underlying philosophy, theology, and methodology. This makes it difficult to ascertain the extent to which professors' published work on issues relating to ontological, epistemological, methodological, and theological concerns reflected positions that they articulated within the classroom. Still, it seems unlikely that this work radically dissented from perspectives and methodological approaches presented in the classroom. Accordingly, the discussion of the natural and human sciences in this book draws heavily, though not exclusively, on published sources.

4. Henry P. Tappan [1851], cited in *American Higher Education: A Documentary History,* ed. Richard Hofstadter and Wilson Smith, 2 vols. (Chicago, 1961), 2: 506–507 (quotation on 506); Winton U. Solberg, "The Conflict between Religion and Secularism at the University of Illinois, 1867–1894," *American Quarterly* 18 (1966): 186–189. For the relationship between churches and higher education, see the often-differing perspectives presented by William C. Ringenberg, "The Old-Time College, 1800–1865," in *Making Higher Education Christian: The History and Mission of Evangelical Colleges in America,* ed. Joel A. Carpenter and Kenneth W. Shipps (Grand Rapids, Mich., 1987), 77–97; Mark A. Noll, "The Revolution, the Enlightenment, and Christian Higher Education in the Early Republic," in ibid., 56–76; Mark A. Noll, "Christian Colleges, Christian Worldviews, and an Invitation to Research," in William C. Ringenberg, *The Christian College: A History of Protestant Higher Education in America* (Grand Rapids, Mich., 1984), 1–36; Howard Miller, *The Revolutionary College: American Presbyterian Higher Education 1707–1837* (New

York, 1976); Douglas Sloan, "Harmony, Chaos, and Consensus: The American College Curriculum," *Teachers College Record* 73 (1971): 221–251; Natalie A. Naylor, "The Ante-Bellum College Movement: A Reappraisal of Tewksbury's Founding of American Colleges and Universities," *History of Education Quarterly* 13 (1973): 261–274; David B. Potts, "American Colleges in the Nineteenth Century: From Localism to Denominationalism," *History of Education Quarterly* 11 (1971): 363–380.

5. Anonymous, "Original Papers in Relation to a Course of Liberal Education," *American Journal of Science and Arts* 15 (1829): 300. See also Ringenberg, "The Old-Time College," 84; Conrad Cherry, "The Study of Religion and the Rise of the American University," in *Religious Studies, Theological Studies and the University-Divinity School,* ed. Joseph Mitsuo Kitagawa (Atlanta, 1992), 117; Naylor, "Ante-Bellum College Movement," 269–270; Louise L. Stevenson, *Scholarly Means to Evangelical Ends: The New Haven Scholars and the Transformation of Higher Learning in America, 1830–1890* (Baltimore, 1986), 56; Sloan, "Harmony, Chaos, and Consensus," 246; Noll, "Christian Colleges," 19–20.

Of the numerous discussions of the role of faculty psychology in shaping the emphasis on mental discipline in antebellum education, see, for example, Veysey, *Emergence,* 22–23; Sloan, "Harmony, Chaos, and Consensus," 244; Stanley M. Guralnick, "The American Scientist in Higher Education, 1820–1910," in *The Sciences in the American Context: New Perspectives,* ed. Nathan Reingold (Washington, D.C., 1979), 105–106.

For the importance of the Yale report, see Alan Creutz, "From College Teacher to University Scholar: The Evolution and Professionalization of Academics at the University of Michigan, 1841–1900," 2 vols., Ph.D. diss., University of Michigan, 1981, 1: 21–22; Reuben, *Making of the Modern University,* 26.

6. Noll, "Christian Colleges," 20–23; Marsden, *Soul of the American University,* 99; Frederick Rudolph, *The American College and University: A History* (New York, 1962), 140.

Useful discussions of moral philosophy include D. H. Meyer, *The Instructed Conscience: The Shaping of the American National Ethic* (Philadelphia, 1972); Wilson Smith, *Professors and Public Ethics: Studies of Northern Moral Philosophers before the Civil War* (Ithaca, N.Y., 1956); Daniel Walker Howe, *The Unitarian Conscience: Harvard Moral Philosophy, 1805–1861* (Cambridge, Mass., 1970); Allen C. Guelzo, "'The Science of Duty': Moral Philosophy and the Epistemology of Science in Nineteenth-Century America," in *Evangelicals and Science in Historical Perspective,* ed. David N. Livingstone et al. (New York, 1999), 267–289; Reuben, *Making of the Modern University,* 19, 22–23; Noll, "Christian Colleges," 18–20. The discussion of moral philosophy in both the above passage and subsequent passages in Part I is indebted to these works.

7. Theodore Hornberger, *Scientific Thought in the American Colleges, 1638–1800* (Austin, Tex., 1946); Stanley M. Guralnick, *Science and the Ante-Bellum American College* (Philadelphia, 1975), 4–46; Robert V. Bruce, *The Launching of Modern American Science 1846–1876* (Ithaca, N.Y., 1987), 84,

passim; Guralnick, "American Scientist," 102–105; George H. Daniels, *American Science in the Age of Jackson* (New York, 1968); Hamilton Cravens, "American Science Comes of Age: An Institutional Perspective, 1850–1930," *American Studies* 17 (Fall 1976): 49–51.

8. Frederick A. P. Barnard, quoted in Bruce, *Launching,* 128–134 (quotation on 128). See also Denison Olmsted, *Outlines of a Course of Lectures on Astronomy, Addressed to the Senior Class in Yale College* (New York, 1852), 4; William H. Allen, "An Address before the Cuvierian Society of the Wesleyan University, Middletown, Conn., July 31, 1838," *Methodist Magazine* 20 (1838): 435; James D. Dana, "Science and Scientific Schools," *American Journal of Education* 2 (1856): 357; Guralnick, *Science and the Ante-Bellum American College,* 125.

9. C. S. Henry [1836], quoted in Guralnick, *Science and the Ante-Bellum American College,* 147–148. See also Daniels, *American Science in the Age of Jackson,* 20–27, 48; Veysey, *Emergence,* 59–60.

10. Rudolph, *American College and University,* 228–233. For a good discussion of the University of Wisconsin's efforts to develop a "Department of the Practical Applications of Science," see Merle Curti and Vernon Carstensen, *The University of Wisconsin, 1848–1925: A History,* 2 vols. (Madison, Wis., 1949), 1: 75–77.

11. Edward Everett, "The Uses of Astronomy," *American Journal of Education* 2 (1856): 623; Joseph LeConte, "Morphology and Its Connection with Fine Art," *Southern Presbyterian Review* 12 (1859): 109; Rudolph, *American College and University,* 225–226 (quotation from Albert Hopkins on 226). See also Allen, "An Address before the Cuvierian Society," 434.

12. Edward Hitchcock, "The Relations and Consequent Mutual Duties between the Philosopher and the Theologian," *Bibliotheca Sacra and American Biblical Repository* 10 (1853): 177. See also Everett, "Uses of Astronomy," 623; Jon H. Roberts, *Darwinism and the Divine in America: Protestant Intellectuals and Organic Evolution, 1859–1900* (Madison, Wis., 1988), 9–10; James Turner, *Without God, Without Creed: The Origins of Unbelief in America* (Baltimore, 1985), passim; George H. Daniels, "The Process of Professionalization in American Science: The Emergent Period 1820–1860," *Isis* 58 (1967): 163, 163n; Guralnick, *Science and the Ante-Bellum American College,* 154–156.

For some suggestive, albeit incomplete, statistics concerning the incidence of clergy among the presidents and faculties of antebellum colleges, see Richard Hofstadter and Walter P. Metzger, *The Development of Academic Freedom in the United States* (New York, 1955), 297.

A valuable discussion of the important role of religious interpretations of science in shaping geology and university reform at Oxford and Cambridge can be found in Nicolaas A. Rupke, *The Great Chain of History: William Buckland and the English School of Geology (1814–1849)* (Oxford, 1983), esp. 233–240.

13. [Orville Dewey], "Diffusion of Knowledge," *North American Review* 30 (1830): 312; Walter Minto [1788], quoted in Thomas Jefferson Wertenbaker, *Princeton 1746–1896* (Princeton, 1946), 95; Charles W. Eliot [1854], quoted in Henry James, *Charles W. Eliot: President of Harvard University 1869–1909,* 2

vols. (Boston, 1930), 1: 64; Louis Agassiz, *Contributions to the Natural History of the United States,* 4 vols. (Boston, 1857–1862), 1: 135. See also Dana, "Science and Scientific Schools," 363–364; LeConte, "Morphology and Its Connection," 114; Ormsby M. Mitchel, quoted in Philip S. Shoemaker, "Stellar Impact: Ormsby MacKnight Mitchel and Astronomy in Antebellum America," Ph.D. diss., University of Wisconsin–Madison, 1991, 199; Henry Morton Bullock, *A History of Emory University* (Nashville, 1936), 143; Allen P. Tankersley, *College Life at Old Oglethorpe* (Athens, Ga., 1951), 79–80; Miller, *Revolutionary College,* 167–168; Mark A. Noll, "Common Sense Traditions and American Evangelical Thought," *American Quarterly* 37 (1985): 216–238, esp. 220–225; Noll, "Christian Colleges," 13.

14. Theodore Dwight Bozeman, *Protestants in an Age of Science: The Baconian Ideal and Antebellum American Religious Thought* (Chapel Hill, 1977), 71–100, esp. 80–81; Edward Hitchcock [1866], quoted in Clifford Harold Peterson, "The Incorporation of the Basic Evolutionary Concepts of Charles Darwin in Selected American College Biology Programs in the Nineteenth Century," Ed.D. diss., Columbia University, 1970, 52. See also Frederick A. P. Barnard, "Inaugural Address," *Proceedings at the Inauguration of Frederick A. P. Barnard, S.T.D., LL.D., as President of Columbia College, on Monday, October 3, 1864* (New York, 1865), 61–62; [Benjamin Peirce], "Address of Professor Benjamin Peirce, President of the American Association for the Year 1853, on Retiring from the Duties of President," American Association for the Advancement of Science, *Proceedings* 8 (1854): 14; George I. Chace, "Of the Existence and Natural Attributes of the Divine Being," *Bibliotheca Sacra and Theological Review* 7 (1850): 334; Anonymous, Review of *The Indications of the Creator . . . ,* by George Taylor, *Biblical Repertory and Princeton Review* 24 (1852): 142; Gary Lee Schoepflin, "Denison Olmsted (1791–1859), Scientist, Teacher, Christian: A Biographical Study of the Connection of Science with Religion in Antebellum America," Ph.D. diss., Oregon State University, 1977, 30, 305, 350–351; Daniels, *American Science in the Age of Jackson,* 53; David B. Potts, *Wesleyan University 1831–1910: Collegiate Enterprise in New England* (New Haven, 1992), 38; Sloan, "Harmony, Chaos, and Consensus," 236, 238.

15. Martin Brewer Anderson [1856], quoted in Guralnick, *Science and the Ante-Bellum American College,* 154–155. See also Dana, "Science and Scientific Schools," 353, 357.

16. Guralnick, *Science and the Ante-Bellum American College,* 154; Guralnick, "American Scientist," 108; Schoepflin, "Denison Olmsted," 30–31; Hofstadter and Metzger, *Development of Academic Freedom,* 289; James D. Dana, "Science and the Bible. Number II. With Further Remarks on 'The Six Days of Creation' of Prof. Tayler Lewis," *Bibliotheca Sacra* 13 (1856): 643; Bruce, *Launching,* 119; Bozeman, *Protestants in an Age of Science,* 77; Clark Albert Elliott, "The American Scientist, 1800–1863; His Origins, Career, and Interests," Ph.D. diss., Case Western Reserve University, 1970, 97–98.

17. Asa Gray, *Introduction to Structural and Systematic Botany, and Vegetable Physiology, Being a Fifth and Revised Edition of the Botanical Text-book* (New York, 1857), 367; Josiah Parsons Cooke, *Religion and Chemistry* (1864;

New York, 1880), 329. See also [James D. Dana], "Address of Professor James D. Dana, President of the American Association for the Year 1854, on Retiring from the Duties of President," American Association for the Advancement of Science, *Proceedings* 9 (1855): 2; [Francis Bowen], "Chalmer's Natural Theology," *North American Review* 54 (1842): 359.

The importance of natural theology in the United States is discussed in a variety of works, including Bozeman, *Protestants in an Age of Science,* passim; E. Brooks Holifield, *The Gentlemen Theologians: American Theology in Southern Culture, 1795–1860* (Durham, N.C., 1978), 72–85; Ronald L. Numbers, *Creation by Natural Law: Laplace's Nebular Hypothesis in American Thought* (Seattle, 1977), 77–87; Daniels, "Process of Professionalization," 163; Roberts, *Darwinism and the Divine,* 8–13; Turner, *Without God,* 96–101.

18. Sloan, "Harmony, Chaos, and Consensus," 238; Reuben, *Making of the Modern University,* 20. Even pious scientists such as James Dana refused to allow prevailing biblical interpretations to influence interpretation of the history of life and the earth. James R. Moore, "Geologists and Interpreters of Genesis in the Nineteenth Century," in *God and Nature: Historical Essays on the Encounter between Christianity and Science,* ed. David C. Lindberg and Ronald L. Numbers (Berkeley and Los Angeles, 1986), 322–350; Conrad Wright, "The Religion of Geology," *New England Quarterly* 14 (1941): 335–353; John H. Giltner, "Genesis and Geology: The Stuart-Silliman-Hitchcock Debate," *Journal of Religious Thought* 23 (1966–1967): 3–13; Numbers, *Creation by Natural Law,* 95–100.

19. Archibald Alexander, quoted in Miller, *Revolutionary College,* 275.

20. Numbers, *Creation by Natural Law;* Francis C. Haber, *The Age of the World: Moses to Darwin* (Baltimore, 1959); Charles Coulston Gillispie, *Genesis and Geology: The Impact of Scientific Discoveries upon Religious Beliefs in the Decades before Darwin* (Cambridge, Mass., 1951); Rupke, *Great Chain of History;* A. Bowdoin Van Riper, *Men among the Mammoths: Victorian Science and the Discovery of Human Prehistory* (Chicago, 1993); David N. Livingstone, "The Preadamite Theory and the Marriage of Science and Religion," *Transactions of the American Philosophical Society,* 82, Part 3 (1992); Rodney L. Stiling, "Scriptural Geology in America," in *Evangelicals and Science in Historical Perspective,* 177–192; Bruce, *Launching,* 120; R[ufus] P. S[tebbins], "The Religion of Geology," *Christian Examiner and Religious Miscellany,* 4th ser., 18 (1852): 59; Edward Hitchcock, *The Religion of Geology and Its Connected Sciences* (Boston, 1851), 2–5; Roberts, *Darwinism and the Divine,* 21–26.

21. Daniel C. Gilman, "Education in America, 1776–1876," *North American Review* 122 (1876): 224.

22. David Duncan Wallace, *History of Wofford College 1854–1949* (Nashville, 1951), 56–57; Morgan B. Sherwood, "Genesis, Evolution, and Geology in America before Darwin: The Dana-Lewis Controversy, 1856–1857," in *Toward a History of Geology,* ed. Cecil J. Schneer (Cambridge, Mass., 1967), 305–316. See also Hitchcock, "Relations and Consequent Mutual Duties," 191–192; Joseph Henry, "On the Importance of the Cultivation of Science," *Popular Science Monthly* 2 (1873): 468–469.

23. Edward Hitchcock, "Special Divine Interpositions in Nature," *Bibliotheca Sacra and American Biblical Repository* 11 (1854): 796. See also Barnard, "Inaugural Address," 61; Bozeman, *Protestants in an Age of Science*, 61; Roberts, *Darwinism and the Divine*, 8.

24. Bledstein, *Culture of Professionalism*, 269. See also Noll, "University Arrives in America," 101; Wilson, *Science, Community*, 13; Cravens, "American Science," 54; Guralnick, "American Scientist," 115, 127.

25. Cravens, "American Science," 50–51; Daniels, "Process of Professionalization," 152–154; Daniels, *American Science in the Age of Jackson*, 35; John Higham, "The Matrix of Specialization," in *The Organization of Knowledge in Modern America, 1860–1920*, ed. Alexandra Oleson and John Voss (Baltimore, 1979), 4; Veysey, *Emergence*, 142.The literature on the importance of Baconianism in America is enormous. For a good, brief description of the major tenets of the "classical" Baconian position in American science, see Daniels, *American Science in the Age of Jackson*, 65.

26. Charles Darwin, *On the Origin of Species by Means of Natural Selection, or the Preservation of Favoured Races in the Struggle for Life* (1859; facsimile ed., Cambridge, Mass., 1964), 488 and the epigraphs opposite the title page; William North Rice, "The Darwinian Theory of the Origin of Species," *New Englander* 26 (1867): 608. See also ibid., 618; George F. Wright, "Recent Works Bearing on the Relation of Science to Religion. No. II—The Divine Method of Producing Living Species," *Bibliotheca Sacra* 33 (1876): 480; [Francis Ellingwood Abbot], "Philosophical Biology," *North American Review* 107 (1868): 379–380; Asa Gray, *Darwiniana: Essays and Reviews Pertaining to Darwinism*, ed. A Hunter Dupree (1876; Cambridge, Mass., 1963), 78–79; Asa Gray, *Natural Science and Religion: Two Lectures Delivered to the Theological School of Yale College* (New York, 1880), 77; Simon Newcomb, "Modern Scientific Materialism. 2: Correlation of Mental and Material Phenomena," *Independent* 32 (December 23, 1880): 1; David Starr Jordan, "Science and the Colleges," *Popular Science Monthly* 42 (1893): 733; Gray, *Darwiniana*, 204; Gray, *Natural Science and Religion*, 77; Simon Newcomb, in Simon Newcomb, Noah Porter, Joseph Cook, James Freeman Clarke, and James McCosh, "Law and Design in Nature," *North American Review* 128 (1879): 540; S. R. Calthrop, "Religion and Evolution," *Religious Magazine and Monthly Review* 50 (1873): 205; David L. Hull, *Darwin and His Critics: The Reception of Darwin's Theory of Evolution by the Scientific Community* (Cambridge, Mass., 1973), 74–75. For useful discussions that parallel the point that I am making, see Turner, *Without God*, 184–187; Neal C. Gillespie, *Charles Darwin and the Problem of Creation* (Chicago, 1979), 13.

In 1979 Neal C. Gillespie suggested that "miraculous creation was much more accepted among American naturalists than English." Gillespie, *Charles Darwin*, 162, n. 15. Somewhat later, however, in a study of Anglo-American conchology he asserted that "by the time Darwin made his celebrated attack on design in 1859, natural theology of any kind, despite its strong grip on men's minds as a worldview, had virtually ceased to be a significant part of the day-to-day practical explanatory structure of natural history." Neal C. Gillespie, "Preparing for

Darwin: Conchology and Natural Theology in Anglo-American Natural History," *Studies in History of Biology* 7 (1984): 93–135 (quotation on 95). The evidence suggests that this latter assertion is true in only a narrow sense. Most often natural historians did focus their energies on trying to arrive at explanations using natural, "secondary" causes. Only when they failed to achieve that goal did they invoke supernatural agency. Nevertheless, they commonly drew the explicit inference that the design their investigations had disclosed required the existence of a divine Designer. In addition, they rarely appear to have hesitated to attribute phenomena for which they had no scientific explanations to supernatural activity. In this context, it seems appropriate to note that Gillespie has acknowledged that "there was, of course, no sudden abandonment of either creationism or the analytical formulae of natural theology. American conchologists particularly were insistent on them." Ibid., 124, 129–133.

Useful discussions of important scientific formulations appearing prior to Darwin's work that expressed the operation of natural phenomena in terms of the work of intelligible secondary agencies include Gillispie, *Charles Darwin*, 32–33; Numbers, *Creation by Natural Law*; Frank Miller Turner, *Between Science and Religion: The Reaction to Scientific Naturalism in Late Victorian England* (New Haven, 1974), 24–29; Ronald E. Martin, *American Literature and the Universe of Force* (Durham, N.C., 1981), xii, 6–31.

27. [Louis Agassiz], "Prof. Agassiz on the Origin of Species," *American Journal of Science and Arts*, 2nd ser., 30 (1860): 146. See also Thorstein Veblen, "The Evolution of the Scientific Point of View," *University of California Chronicle* 10 (1908): 397–400; J. Mark Baldwin, "The Influence of Darwin on Theory of Knowledge and Philosophy," *Psychological Review*, n.s., 16 (1909): 213; [Abbot], "Philosophical Biology," 390; W J [*sic*] McGee, "Fifty Years of American Science," *Atlantic Monthly* 82 (1898): 317–318; Gillespie, *Charles Darwin*, 146–147; Roberts, *Darwinism and the Divine*, 82–83; Ronald L. Numbers, "Darwinism and the Dogma of Separate Creations: The Response of American Naturalists to Evolution," in *Darwinism Comes to America* (Cambridge, Mass., 1998), 47–48.

We have been unable to locate the origin of the term *methodological naturalism*, but it nicely captures the phenomenon at issue. George Marsden has used the term "methodological secularization" to similar effect. Marsden, *Soul of the American University*, 156. See also Turner, *Without God*, 179; Gillespie, "Preparing for Darwin," 93–145, esp. 96. An excellent survey of the history of methodological naturalism can be found in Ronald L. Numbers, "Science without God: Natural Laws and Christian Beliefs," in *Christianity and Science: Twelve Case Histories*, ed. David C. Lindberg and Ronald L. Numbers (Chicago, forthcoming).

28. J. Mark Baldwin, "Sketch of the History of Psychology," *Psychological Review* 12 (1905): 153. See also Newcomb, "Modern Scientific Materialism," 1; Edwin Grant Conklin, "Science and the Faith of the Modern," *Scribner's Magazine* 78 (1925): 453; Henry S. Pritchett, *What Is Religion? And Other Student Questions: Talks to College Students* (Boston, 1906), 39–40, 67.

29. Simon Newcomb, "Evolution and Theology. A Rejoinder," *North Ameri-*

*can Review* 128 (1879): 660–661. See also Josiah Parsons Cooke, *The Credentials of Science the Warrant of Faith* (New York, 1888), 245; John Hedley Brooke, *Science and Religion: Some Historical Perspectives* (Cambridge, UK, 1991), 270–271; [Henry Ware Holland], "Gray's *Darwiniana,*" *Nation* 23 (December 14, 1876): 358; Karl E. Guthe, "The Religious and Character Value of the Physical Sciences," *Religious Education* 6 (1911): 381; Edwin Diller Starbuck, *The Psychology of Religion: An Empirical Study of the Growth of Religious Consciousness,* with a Preface by William James (New York, 1900), 2.

As late as 1888 Union Theological Seminary invited the Harvard chemist Josiah Parsons Cooke to present a series of lectures discussing the relationship between science and natural theology. Cooke's lectures, published as *The Credentials of Science the Warrant of Faith,* constituted a kind of updated exposition of natural theology. Cooke's work, however, was becoming quite unusual within the scientific community. We suspect that there is a generational issue involved, but more research needs to be done before one can assert this confidently. For a more modest espousal of the idea that science "proved" God's existence, see Ira Remsen, "Is Science Bankrupt? An Address delivered at the Graduating Exercises of the Class of '97 of Case School of Applied Science," unpaginated reprint, Ira Remsen Papers, Ms. 39, Box 11, Milton S. Eisenhower Library, The Johns Hopkins University.

For psychologists' use of the promise to reinforce theism in promoting their discipline, see John M. O'Donnell, *The Origins of Behaviorism: American Psychology, 1870–1920* (New York, 1985), 54, 58–65, 108, 116–120; Hugh Hawkins, *Pioneer: A History of The Johns Hopkins University, 1874–1889* (Ithaca, N.Y., 1960), 202. Most discussion of psychology has been deferred until Chapter 2.

30. George Malcolm Stratton, *Psychology of the Religious Life* (London, 1911), 360–361; Paul Jerome Croce, *Science and Religion in the Era of William James: Volume 1, Eclipse of Certainty, 1820–1880* (Chapel Hill, 1995), 4; John M. Coulter, "The Cooperation of Evolution and Religion" [undated. Accompanying sheet says piece was written for *Presbyterian Banner*], John M. Coulter Papers, Box III, Folder 12, Department of Special Collections, the University of Chicago Library, 6–7; Anonymous, "The Nebular Hypothesis," *Southern Quarterly Review* 28 (1856): 115–116; F. W. Clarke, "Scientific Dabblers," *Popular Science Monthly* 1 (1872): 596–597; Joseph Henry, "On the Importance of the Cultivation of Science," *Popular Science Monthly* 2 (1872–1873): 648–649; Benjamin Peirce, "The Conflict between Science and Religion: A Sermon," *Unitarian Review and Religious Magazine* 7 (1877): 665; David Starr Jordan, "The Church and Modern Thought," *Overland Monthly* 18 (1891): 392; Conklin, "Science and the Faith," 457; Ira Remsen, "The Science vs. the Art of Chemistry," *Popular Science Monthly* 10 (1877): 691–692; Guthe, "Religious and Character Value," 382–383; Donald Fleming, *John William Draper and the Religion of Science* (Philadelphia, 1950), 45–46.

Ronald L. Numbers has shown that most of the some eighty American natural historians elected to the National Academy of Sciences between 1863 and 1900 for whom evidence is available remained members of Christian churches. Numbers, "Darwinism and the Dogma of Separate Creations," 40–43.

The relative indifference and often antagonism of scientists to positivism is one reason why Charles Cashdollar's claim that positivism was "the central issue of the previous century" is somewhat misleading. Charles D. Cashdollar, *The Transformation of Theology, 1830–1890: Positivism and Protestant Thought in Britain and America* (Princeton, 1989), 446.

31. G. Stanley Hall, "Research the Vital Spirit of Teaching," *Forum* 17 (1894): 569; G. S. Hall, "The University Idea," *Pedagogical Seminary* 15 (1908): 99; Peirce, "Conflict between Science and Religion," 660–661; William James, *The Principles of Psychology,* 2 vols. (New York, 1890), 1: vi; George Trumbull Ladd, "Is Psychology a Science?" *Psychological Review* 1 (1894): 392; Starbuck, *Psychology of Religion,* 10; James Bissett Pratt, *The Religious Consciousness: A Psychological Study* (1920; New York, 1930), 25; Roberts, *Darwinism and the Divine,* 138–139; Thomas C. Chamberlin, "Change in the Concept of Cosmogony" [Aug. 29, 1916], Thomas Chrowder Chamberlin Papers, Addenda, Box VII, Folder C, Department of Special Collections, the University of Chicago Library, 2–3; Thomas C. Chamberlin, "The Moral Functions of Modern Scholarship" [undated fragment], Thomas Chrowder Chamberlin Papers, Box VII, Folder 2, Department of Special Collections, the University of Chicago Library, 17–19; Thomas C. Chamberlin, "The Importance of a Belief in the Divine Immanence at the Present Crisis of Intellectual Development" [undated], Thomas Chrowder Chamberlin Papers, Box VII, Folder 11, Department of Special Collections, the University of Chicago Library, passim.

32. Conklin, "Science and the Faith," 457; David Starr Jordan, "The Stability of Truth," *Popular Science Monthly* 50 (1897): 648–649; Daniel Greenleaf Thompson, "Science in Religious Education," *Popular Science Monthly* 30 (1886–1887): 45; G. Wallace Chessman, *Denison: The Story of an Ohio College* (Granville, Ohio, 1957), 145–146.

33. Gray, *Natural Science and Religion,* 69; Anonymous, "The Nebular Hypothesis," 115–116; Rice, "Darwinian Theory," 608–609; Newcomb, "Evolution and Theology," 657; Starbuck, *Psychology of Religion,* 1; McGee, "Fifty Years of American Science," 317–318; [Holland], "Gray's *Darwiniana,*" 358; Pratt, *Religious Consciousness,* 445–446; S. R. Calthrop, "Religion and Science," *Unitarian Review and Religious Magazine* 2 (1874): 323; R. S. Woodward, "The Progress of Science," *Popular Science Monthly* 59 (1901): 517–518; Edwin G. Conklin, "The World's Debt to Darwin," *Proceedings of the American Philosophical Society* 48 (1909): xxxviii.

34. G. Stanley Hall, *Life and Confessions of a Psychologist* (New York, 1923), 359. See also Baldwin, "Sketch of the History of Psychology," 158–159; Cooke, *Credentials of Science,* 251–252; H. Newell Martin, "The Study and Teaching of Biology," *Popular Science Monthly* 10 (1877): 299–300; G. S. Hall, "Confessions of a Psychologist," *Pedagogical Seminary* 8 (1901): 111; [Daniel Coit] Gilman, "Prospects of Science in the United States at the Beginning of the Twentieth Century," [Presented at the 46th Convocation at the University of Chicago] *University Record* 8 (July 1903): 30–31. Our discussion of this issue

is a close paraphrase of Roberts, *Darwinism and the Divine*, 82–83. See also Numbers, "Darwinism and the Dogma of Separate Creations," 47–48; Veysey, *Emergence*, 144.

35. James D. Whelpley, "Second Letter on Philosopohical Analogy," *American Journal of Science and Arts*, 2nd ser., 5 (1848): 330–331. See also [Asa Gray], "Review of Darwin's Theory on the Origin of Species, by Means of Natural Selection," *American Journal of Science and Arts*, 2nd ser., 29 (1860): 180–184; [Chauncey Wright], "The Philosophy of Herbert Spencer," *North American Review* 100 (1865): 428; Newcomb, "Evolution and Theology," 654; Peirce, "Conflict between Science and Religion," 660–661; George A. Coe, *The Spiritual Life: Studies in the Science of Religion* (New York, 1900), 15–16.

36. John Bascom, "The Natural Theology of Social Science," *Bibliotheca Sacra* 25 (1868): 270. See also Anonymous, Review of *The Epoch of Creation*, by Eleazar Lord, *Biblical Repertory and Princeton Review* 23 (1851): 696. See also Anonymous, "Nebular Hypothesis," 115–116; Edward Hitchcock, "The Historical and Geological Deluges Compared," *American Biblical Repository* 11 (1838): 22; Borden P. Bowne, *Studies in Theism* (New York, 1879), 148; Joseph Le Conte, "Science and Mental Improvement," *Popular Science Monthly* 13 (1878): 100; Roberts, *Darwinism and the Divine*, 136–140, passim; Borden P. Bowne, "Gains for Religious Thought in the Last Generation," *Hibbert Journal* 8 (1910): 891; Charles Woodruff Shields, *The Final Philosophy, or System of Perfectible Knowledge Issuing from the Harmony of Science and Religion* (New York, 1877), 10; Noah Porter, *Two Sermons: I. "On Leaving the Old Chapel." II. "On Entering the New"* (New Haven, 1876), 25; Noah Porter, "The American Colleges and the American Public," *New Englander* 28 (1869): 761–763; J[ohn] B[razer], "Evidences of Christianity," *Christian Examiner and Religious Miscellany*, 4th ser., 1 (1844): 372.

37. For Princeton, see Cashdollar, *Transformation of Theology*, 334–338. For Bowdoin, see George T. Little, ed., *Memorial: Alpheus Spring Packard, 1798–1884* (Brunswick, Maine, 1886), 6. We are indebted to Ronald L. Numbers for passing along his notes on this work. For Columbia, see T. Watson Street, "The Evolution Controversy in the Southern Presbyterian Church with Attention to the Theological and Ecclesiastical Issues Raised," *Journal of the Presbyterian Historical Society* 37 (1959): 232–250; Clement Eaton, "Professor James Woodrow and the Freedom of Teaching in the South," *Journal of Southern History* 28 (1962): 3–17; Ernest Trice Thompson, *Presbyterians in the South* (Richmond, Va., 1973), 2: 457–490; Ronald L. Numbers (and Lester D. Stephens), "Darwinism in the American South: From the Early 1860s to the Late 1920s," in *Darwinism Comes to America*, 58–75. A listing of the dates for the institution of many of these professorships can be found in Moore, "Geologists and Interpreters," 349–350, n. 31. For Franklin and Marshall, see W. Bruce Leslie, *Gentlemen and Scholars: College and Community in the "Age of the University," 1865–1917* (University Park, Pa., 1992), 81. Continued efforts at Wesleyan in the 1890s to provide a doxological approach to science are discussed in Potts, *Wesleyan*, 148–149.

38. Potts, *Wesleyan*, 158; Thomas C. Chamberlin, "Secular Theology, An

Appropriate Field of Public Instruction" [undated], Thomas Chrowder Chamberlin Papers, Box VII [Appendix: Papers and Addresses], Folder 9, Department of Special Collections, the University of Chicago Library, 8; John M. Coulter, "The Case for Religion" [undated], John M. Coulter Papers, Box III, Folder 10, Department of Special Collections, the University of Chicago Library, 4–5; George Trumbull Ladd, "Modern Theism," *Methodist Review Quarterly* 68 (1919): 388–389; Pratt, *Religious Consciousness,* 20; William James, *The Varieties of Religious Experience: A Study in Human Nature* (1902; New York, 1914), 491–493. See also Turner, *Without God,* 186–187; Reuben, *Making of the Modern University,* 35; Peterson "Incorporation of the Basic Evolutionary Concepts," 102.

Robert Young has described the process of the detachment of science from theology in Great Britain as the "fragmentation of a common context." Robert M. Young, "Natural Theology, Victorian Periodicals, and the Fragmentation of a Common Context," in *Darwin's Metaphor: Nature's Place in Victorian Culture* (Cambridge, UK, 1985), 126–161. Young's reasoning and arguments, with certain modifications, are also applicable to the United States.

39. Roberts, *Darwinism and the Divine,* 120–126; Reuben, *Making of the Modern University,* 88–89.

For the relevance of neo-Kantianism to the science-religion question, see especially George Marsden, "The Collapse of American Evangelical Academia," in *Faith and Rationality: Reason and Belief in God,* ed. Alvin Plantinga and Nicholas Wolterstorff (Notre Dame, 1983), 245–246; Bruce Kuklick, *Churchmen and Philosophers: From Jonathan Edwards to John Dewey* (New Haven, 1985), 193–195. The fact that neo-Kantianism became popular in the United States *after* efforts of science made by scientists to limit their discourse to the evidence of the senses suggests that philosophy was responding to science, not vice versa, although there was doubtless interaction between the two.

William James presented a memorable statement of the disdain that at least some thinkers not unfriendly to religion held toward natural theology in *Varieties of Religious Experience,* 492–493.

40. Joland Ethel Mohr has noted that the role model for the eminent college presidents in the last half of the nineteenth century was the clergymen-presidents of their youth. Joland Ethel Mohr, "Higher Education and the Development of Professionalism in Post–Civil War America: A Content Analysis of Inaugural Addresses Given by Selected Land-Grant College and University Presidents, 1867–1911," 2 vols., Ph.D. diss., University of Minnesota, 1984, 1: 39. This made lobbying by scientists for the importance and autonomy of their disciplines especially important. See also Gillespie, *Charles Darwin,* 153.

41. The estimate of the number of scientists in American higher education as of 1870 is drawn from Nathan Reingold, "Definitions and Speculations: The Professionalization of Science in America in the Nineteenth Century," in *The Pursuit of Knowledge in the Early American Republic: American Scientific and Learned Societies from Colonial Times to the Civil War,* ed. Alexandra Oleson and Sanborn Brown (Baltimore, 1976), 58. Although it is impossible to quantify the number of nonscientists who helped scientists in attempting to privilege sci-

entific inquiry, it seems reasonable to assume that they comprised a sizable number of the some two thousand people who, in an important study of the American scientific community, were termed "cultivators" of science. Daniel J. Kevles, Jeffrey L. Sturchio, and P. Thomas Carroll, "The Sciences in America, Circa 1880," *Science* 209 (July 4, 1980): 27. See also Robert E. Kohler, "The Ph.D. Machine: Building on the Collegiate Base," *Isis* 81 (1990): 641; Daniel Kevles, "The Physics, Mathematics, and Chemistry Communities: A Comparative Analysis," in *The Organization of Knowledge in Modern America*, 153; Edward Shils, "The Order of Learning in the United States: The Ascendancy of the University," in ibid., 31–32; Alfred Goldsborough Mayer, "Our Universities and Research," *Science* 32 (1910): 257–258; Ira Remsen, "Scientific Investigation and Progress," *Popular Science Monthly,* 64 (1903–1904): 302; Jordan, "Science and the Colleges," 731; Wilson, *Science, Community,* 6–7.

42. David A. Hollinger, "Justification by Verification: The Scientific Challenge to the Moral Authority of Christianity in Modern America," in *Religion and Twentieth-Century American Intellectual Life,* ed. Michael J. Lacey (Cambridge, UK, 1989), 117. See also David A. Hollinger, "Inquiry and Uplift: Late Nineteenth-Century American Academics and the Moral Efficacy of Scientific Practice," in *The Authority of Experts: Studies in History and Theory,* ed. Thomas L. Haskell (Bloomington, Ind., 1985), 143; Veysey, *Emergence,* 149–150; Fleming, *John William Draper,* 129–134; Lorraine Daston and Peter Galison, "The Image of Objectivity," *Representations* 40 (Fall 1992): 121–122; Charles E. Rosenberg, *No Other Gods: On Science and American Social Thought* (Baltimore, 1976), 12, 138–139; Shils, "Order of Learning," 31; Remsen, "Scientific Investigation," 300; Guthe, "Religious and Character Value," 379.

43. C. Darwin to W. Graham, July 3, 1881, in *The Life and Letters of Charles Darwin, Including an Autobiographical Chapter,* ed. Francis Darwin (London, 1887), 1: 316. See also Marsden, "Collapse," 228; Thomas C. Chamberlin, *The Ethical Functions of Scientific Study: An Address Delivered at the Annual Commencement of the University of Michigan, June 28, 1888* (Ann Arbor, 1888), 5, 7–8, 22; Cooke, *Credentials of Science,* 6–8; Anonymous, "An Illustration of an Abuse," *Science* 1 (1883): 502; Henry A. Rowland, "The Physical Laboratory in Modern Education," *Johns Hopkins University Circulars 5* (1885–1886): 104–105; Edwin G. Conklin, "Biology and Human Life," *Science* 68 (November 16, 1928): 469; [Wright], "Philosophy of Herbert Spencer," 431; David Starr Jordan, "Comrades in Zeal," *Popular Science Monthly* 64 (1904): 306; Guthe, "Religious and Character Value," 375; Pritchett, *What Is Religion?* 7–8; John Dewey, "Reconstruction" [1894], *The Early Works, 1882–1898,* ed. Jo Ann Boydston (Carbondale, Ill., 1969), 4: 102; Veysey, *Emergence,* 147; and Hawkins, *Pioneer,* 293.

44. Thomas Chrowder Chamberlin, "The Mission of the Scientific Spirit," *Quarterly Calendar,* University of Chicago, 2 (May 1893): 15, 20–21; Coulter, "Case for Religion," 7; Floyd Davis, "Science as a Means of Human Culture," *Popular Science Monthly* 45 (1894): 672; Jordan, "Stability of Truth," 642, 643, 646–647; William Forbes Cooley, "Can Science Speak the Decisive Word

in Theology?" *Journal of Philosophy, Psychology, and Scientific Methods* 10 (May 22, 1913): 298; Remsen, "Scientific Investigation," 300; Edwin G. Conklin, "Biology and Religion: Must We Continue the Age-Old Conflict?" *Princeton Alumni Weekly* 25 (March 18, 1925): 549; Max Weber, "Science as a Vocation" [1918], *Daedalus* 87 (1958): 116; David A. Hollinger, "The Knower and the Artificer," *American Quarterly* 39 (1987): 42.

James Turner's discussion of considerations prompting some individuals to become agnostics applies with equal force to concerns voiced by apologists for science: "Epistemological doubts bred moral repugnance. If doctrines rested on shaky evidence, then belief in them meant bowing to the yoke of authority—the authority of tradition, the authority of the Bible, the authority of the church—rather than investigating for oneself." Turner, *Without God,* 159.

45. Cooke, *Credentials of Science,* 42; Jordan, "Comrades in Zeal," 306–307, 314; Pritchett, *What Is Religion?* 7–8. See also Josiah P. Cooke, Jr., "Scientific Culture," *Popular Science Monthly* 7 (1875): 513–514; Thomas C. Chamberlin, "The Scientific and the Non-Scientific" [undated], Thomas Chrowder Chamberlin Papers, Box VII [Appendix: Papers and Addresses], Folder 16, Department of Special Collections, the University of Chicago Library, 4–5, 8; Henry Hudson, "Veracity," *Popular Science Monthly* 53 (1898): 204–205; David Starr Jordan, "Correspondence—The Moral of the 'Sympsychograph,'" *Popular Science Monthly* 50 (1896): 265; Chamberlin, *Ethical Functions,* 5; Remsen, "Scientific Investigation," 301; Henry A. Rowland, "The Physical Laboratory in Modern Education," [1886], mss., Daniel C. Gilman Papers, Gilman Correspondence, Ms. 1, File Henry A. Rowland, Milton S. Eisenhower Library, The Johns Hopkins University, 12–13, 24–25; John L. Le Conte, "Modern Biological Inquiry," *Popular Science Monthly* 8 (1875–1876): 291; Chamberlin, "Mission of the Scientific Spirit," 15; Rowland, "Physical Laboratory" [*Circulars*], 104; Ira Remsen, undated mss. Address on the Scientific or Laboratory Method, Remsen Papers, Ms. 39, Box 12, Milton S. Eisenhower Library, The Johns Hopkins University, 20; Thomas C. Chamberlin, "Life after Death from the Point of View of Science" [March 14, 1897], Thomas Chrowder Chamberlin Papers, Box III [Misc. Papers and Addresses], Folder 21, Department of Special Collections, the University of Chicago Library, 3–4; Wilson, *Science, Community,* 6; Frank Miller Turner, *Between Science and Religion: The Reaction to Scientific Naturalism in Late Victorian England* (New Haven, 1974), 19–20; Reuben, *Making of the Modern University,* 46–47; Hawkins, *Pioneer,* 294; Owens, "Pure and Sound Government," 182.

46. John Dewey, "Science as Subject-Matter and as Method" [1910], *The Middle Works, 1899–1924,* ed. Jo Ann Boydston (Carbondale, Ill., 1978), 6: 78; John Dewey, "Reconstruction," 102; C. S. Peirce, "Illustrations of the Logic of Science—First Paper.—The Fixation of Belief," *Popular Science Monthly,* 12 (1877): 11–12. See also Robert B. Westbrook, *John Dewey and American Democracy* (Ithaca, N.Y., 1991), 141–142.

47. Thomas C. Chamberlin, "The Cosmos, The Psychos, the Monotos. The Reinterpretation of Evolution. Evolution in the Re-making" [February 13, 1927], Thomas Chrowder Chamberlin Papers, Addenda, Box 7, Folder C, De-

partment of Special Collections, the University of Chicago Library, 4–5. See also Simon Newcomb, "Exact Science in America," *North American Review* 119 (1874): 293–294; Henry, "On the Importance," 648–649; Chamberlin, *Ethical Functions,* 8–9; Cooke, "Scientific Culture," 525; Chamberlin, "Mission of the Scientific Spirit," 15, 17; John M. Coulter, *Mission of Science in Education: An Addresss Delivered at the Annual Commencement of the University of Michigan, June 21, 1900* (Ann Arbor, 1900), 19, 27; Jordan, "Stability of Truth," 646–647; Cooke, *Credentials of Science,* 54–55; David Starr Jordan, "The Religion of the Sensible American," *Hibbert Journal* 6 (1908): 855; Conway MacMillan, "The Scientific Method and Modern Intellectual Life," *Science,* n.s., 1 (1895): 539–540; Woodward, "Progress of Science," 517–518; Reuben, *Making of the Modern University,* 5; Merriley Borell, Deborah J. Coon, H. Hughes Evans, and Gail A. Hornstein, "Selective Importation of the 'Exact Method': Experimental Physiology and Psychology in the United States, 1860–1910," unpub. paper, *British Society for the History of Science and the History of Science Society, Program, Papers, and Abstracts for the Joint Conference, Manchester England, 11–15 July 1988,* organized by Ronald L. Numbers and John V. Pickstone (Madison, Wis., [1988]), 190.

G. Stanley Hall thus promised Daniel Coit Gilman to work on "problems for the solution of which the technical means & methods at our disposal will prove adequate." G. Stanley Hall to Gilman, October 9, 1882, quoted in Philip J. Pauly, "G. Stanley Hall and His Successors: A History of the First Half-Century of Psychology at Johns Hopkins," in *One-Hundred Years of Psychological Research in America: G. Stanley Hall and the Johns Hopkins Tradition,* ed. Stewart H. Hulse and Bert F. Green, Jr. (Baltimore, 1986), 28. Philip J. Pauly has argued that it was this kind of pledge that ultimately led Gilman to appoint Hall rather than the more speculative George Sylvester Morris as professor of philosophy. Ibid. See also Dorothy Ross, "The Development of the Social Sciences," in *The Organization of Knowledge in Modern America,* 122.

Several historians have pointed to the role of considerations of professional advancement and institutional contraints in fostering the emphasis on answerable questions. See, for example, Bledstein, *Culture of Professionalism,* 328; Kohler, "Ph.D. Machine," 658–659. Although these considerations undoubtedly played a role, the role of more purely intellectual considerations, especially in light of the previous salience of philosophical and religious considerations, deserves greater attention.

In the late nineteenth century *objectivity,* like the scientific method, was an ambiguous, often contested, term, and historians are only beginning to unpack its multifarious meanings. See, for example, Daston and Galison, "Image of Objectivity," 81–128; the essays in Allan Megill, ed., *Rethinking Objectivity* (Durham, N.C., 1994); Theodore M. Porter, *Trust in Numbers: The Pursuit of Objectivity in Science and Public Life* (Princeton, 1995).

48. John Dewey, "The Influence of Darwinism on Philosophy," in *The Influence of Darwin on Philosophy* (New York, 1910), 1–19; Veblen, "Evolution of the Scientific Point of View," 400; Newcomb, "Exact Science," 293–294; Hudson, "Moral Standard," 206–207.

The insistence of scientists on selecting "doable" problems was one of the considerations that led William James to complain that psychologists left much of reality out of their investigations. Mark R. Schwehn, "Making the World: William James and the Life of the Mind," *Harvard Library Bulletin* 30 (1982): 451.

49. John Merle Coulter, "Science and Religion. I. The Methods and Results of Science," *Biblical World*, n.s., 54 (1920): 347. See also Peirce, "Fixation of Belief," 2; Hudson, "The Moral Standard," 204–205; Cooke, "Scientific Culture," 525; Ira Remsen, undated mss. of an address on the opening of a science building at Vanderbilt University, Ira Remsen Papers, Ms. 39, Box 12, Milton S. Eisenhower Library, The Johns Hopkins University, 24–25; Chamberlin, *Ethical Functions*, 7–8; Conklin, "Biology and Religion," 549; John M. Coulter, "The Role of Science in Modern Civilization" [undated typed mss.], John M. Coulter Papers, Box III, Folder 23, Department of Special Collections, the University of Chicago Library, 19; Cooke, *Credentials of Science*, 182–183; Chamberlin, "Mission of the Scientific Spirit," 15; Veysey, *Emergence*, 135–136; Kevles, "Physics, Mathematics, and Chemistry Communities," 146–147; Higham, "Matrix of Specialization," 8; Shils, "Order of Learning," 33.

For institutional and educational imperatives fostering an emphasis on fact gathering, see Kohler, "Ph.D. Machine," 659–660.

50. Gray, *Natural Science and Religion*, 61–62 (quotation on 61). See also Cooke, *Credentials of Science*, 209; Theodore Gill, "The Doctrine of Darwin," *Proceedings of the Biological Society of Washington, with the Addresses. Read on the Occasion of the Darwin Memorial Meeting, May 12, 1882,* 1: November 19, 1880, to May 26, 1882 (Washington, D.C., 1882), 68–69; Cooke, "Scientific Culture," 523, 526; William James, "The Hidden Self," *Scribner's* 7 (1890): 361; Hudson, "Moral Standard," 12–13; Edwin G. Conklin, "The Aims in General Biology at Princeton," *School and Society* 21 (1925): 3; Irving King, *The Development of Religion: A Study in Anthropology and Social Psychology* (New York, 1910), 9–10; Thorstein Veblen, "The Place of Science in Modern Education," *American Journal of Sociology* 11 (1906): 595–596, 598; Veblen, "Evolution of the Scientific Point of View," 395–400; Jordan, "Comrades in Zeal," 308–310; Baldwin, "Sketch of the History of Psychology," 164; Veysey, *Emergence,* 136; Wilson, *Science, Community,* 13; Noll, "Christian Colleges," 27.

51. Jordan, "Comrades in Zeal," 309; Henry, "On the Importance," 645; Remsen, "Science vs. the Art of Chemistry," 691–692; Jordan, "Stability of Truth," 642; Hudson, "Moral Standard," 12–13; Bledstein, *Culture of Professionalism,* 326.

In emphasizing the hermeneutic advantages of science, we do not wish to deny the role that more mundane, technologically oriented payoffs played in the apologetic constructed by the architects of scientific culture. It is easy, however, to overestimate the significance of such "practical" appeals. As David Hollinger has noted, "The sense of the growing autonomy of scientists was often accompanied by a perception that scientific work was becoming less 'practical.'" Hollinger, "Inquiry and Uplift," 148. Few academic scientists made heroic efforts to try to alter that perception. After all, many proponents of the culture of science within higher education were intent on arguing for pure rather than applied science. See, for example, Newcomb, "Exact Science," 293–294; Josiah P. Cooke, Jr., "The Nobility of Knowledge," *Popular Science Monthly* 5 (1874): 618. Although they occasionally accompanied this argument with an emphasis that pure science often ultimately proved practically beneficial, they often coupled that with the caveat that it was frequently difficult to ascertain which aspects of scientists' research agenda would ultimately bear such fruit. See, for example, Charles W. Eliot to M. A. Mikkelsen, February 27, 1897, Presidents' Papers, Charles W. Eliot, Letterbook, Harvard University Archives, Box 91, n.p (Courtesy of the Harvard University Archives). Moreover, until the beginning of the twentieth century, business and industry had little use for science—or at least made little use of it. Kevles, "Physics, Mathematics, and Chemistry Communities," 141, 143.

52. Hudson, "Veracity," 198–200; Charles William Eliot, "On the Education of Ministers" [1883], *Educational Reform: Essays and Addresses* (New York, 1898), 69–70; Peirce, "Fixation of Belief," 14. For later expressions of the same view, see Conklin, "Science and the Faith of the Modern," 453; Chamberlin, *Ethical Functions,* 8. For a discussion of this point in a somewhat different context, see Hollinger, "Inquiry and Upflift," 148–149.

53. Charles W. Eliot, in L. Emmett Holt et al., "The Formal Opening of the Laboratory of the Rockefeller Institute for Medical Research," *Science,* n.s., 24 (July 6, 1906): 14; Cooke, *Credentials of Science,* 111–113; Jordan, "Stability of Truth," 752; Chamberlin, "Cosmos, Psychos, Monotos," 4; Hollinger, "Inquiry and Uplift," 149–150; Reuben, *Making of the Modern University,* 41–44.

Prior to 1870 the belief that science produced certainty was one of the sources of its prestige. Even after 1870, nonscientists were often inclined to equate science with certainty. See, for example, Parke Godwin, "Correspondence—The Sphere and Limits of Science," *Popular Science Monthly* 3 (1873): 106.

54. Charles Peirce, quoted in Wilson, *Science, Community,* 72; E. D. Cope, *The Origin of the Fittest: Essays on Evolution* (1886; New York, 1887), 3. See also Cooke, *Credentials of Science,* 6–8; Woodward, "Progress of Science," 518; Gray, *Natural Science and Religion,* 61–62, 69; Charles Otis Whitman, "The Problem of the Origin of Species," in *Congress of Arts and Science: Universal Exposition, St. Louis, 1904,* ed. Howard J. Rodgers, 8 vols. (Boston, 1906), 5: 41–42; Martin, "Study and Teaching," 300–301; A. E. Dolbear, "On the Increased Importance of a Knowledge of Science," *The Academy* 4 (1890): 545; Peirce, "Marriage of Religion and Science," 3559; Nicholas Murray Butler, "The Progress of Psychical Research," *Popular Science Monthly* 29 (1886): 482; Rowland, "Physical Laboratory" [*Circulars*], 105; Veblen, "Evolution of the Scientific Point of View," 395–396; William James, *The Meaning of Truth: A Sequel to 'Pragmatism'* (1909; Cambridge, Mass., 1975), 40; Gill, "Doctrine of Darwin," 68–69; Cooke, *Credentials of Science,* 209; Guthe, "Religious and Character Value," 375, 378; Rowland, "Physical Laboratory" [Gilman Papers], 6–7; Wilson, *Science, Community,* 37; N. Rashevsky, "Is the Concept of an Organism as a Machine a Useful One?" in *The Validation of Scientific Theories,*

ed. Philipp G. Frank (Boston, 1956), 151; Reuben, *Making of the Modern University,* 43–44.

The classic expression of the idea that scientists would ascertain truth "in the long run" was presented by Charles Peirce. For a valuable discussion of Peirce's view, see R. Jackson Wilson, *In Quest of Community: Social Philosophy in the United States, 1860–1920* (New York, 1968), 32–59.

Apparently, theories played a more important role in shaping research in some fields than in others. Physicists in the United States, for example, were somewhat belated in organizing their research around key theoretical problems. Kohler, "Ph.D. Machine," 659.

55. John Merle Coulter, "The International Mission of Universities," *University Record* 10 (1924): 265–267; Remsen, "Scientific Investigation and Progress," 293; Remsen, "The Science vs. the Art of Chemistry," 694–695; Guthe, "Religious and Character Value," 381; Rowland, "Physical Laboratory" [*Circulars*], 103; Jordan, "Correspondence," 265; Reuben, *Making of the Modern University,* 44; Veysey, *Emergence,* 135; Croce, *Science and Religion,* 5.

56. R. H. Chittenden, in Thomas Dwight et al., "The Position that Universities Should Take in Regard to Investigation," *Science,* n.s., 11 (1900): 54; Hall, *Life and Confessions,* 338. See also Joseph Henry, "On the Importance," 647. See also Cooke, "Scientific Culture," 522–523; Remsen, "Scientific Investigation," 301–302; T. C. Chamberlin, "The State University and Research" [June 9, 1904], Thomas Chrowder Chamberlin Papers, Box III [Misc. Papers and Addresses], Folder 12, Department of Special Collections, the University of Chicago Library, 4; Edward Scribner Ames, *Beyond Theology: The Autobiography of Edward Scribner Ames,* ed. Van Meter Ames (Chicago, 1959), 57; Bruce, *Launching,* 335.

57. Shils, "Order of Learning," 21; R. S. Woodward, "Academic Ideals," *Columbia University Quarterly* 7 (1904): 13–14; E. L. Thorndike, "The University and Vocational Guidance," in *Readings in Vocational Guidance,* ed. Meyer Bloomfield (Boston, 1915), 100; Martin, "Study and Teaching," 300–301; Charles W. Eliot to his mother, March 16, 1854, quoted in James, *Charles W. Eliot,* 1: 62; Chessman, *Denison,* 128–130; Charles Henry Rammelkamp, *Illinois College: A Centennial History 1829–1929* (New Haven, 1928), 386; Louis G. Geiger, *University of the Northern Plains: A History of the University of North Dakota 1883–1958* (Grand Forks, N.D., 1958), 72–73; Lucy Lilian Notestein, *Wooster of the Middle West* (New Haven, 1937), 184–186; Veysey, *Emergence,* 141; Higham, "Matrix of Specialization," 10; Kohler, "Ph.D. Machine," 643–648; Kevles, "Physics, Mathematics, and Chemistry Communities," 147–148, 154.

The role of scholarship as a "refuge of unselfishness" is briefly discussed, albeit in a different context, in Donald Fleming, "Social Darwinism," in *Paths of American Thought,* ed. Arthur M. Schlesinger, Jr., and Morton White (Boston, 1963), 136–137.

58. H. A. Rowland, "A Plea for Pure Science," *Popular Science Monthly* 24 (1883–1884): 34; William T. Sedgwick, "Educational Value of the Methods of Science," *Educational Review* 5 (1893): 250. See also Henry, "On the Impor-

tance," 646; Macmillan, "Scientific Method," 537–538; Chamberlin, "Scientific and the Non-Scientific," 8; Mark Beach, "Professional versus Professorial Control of Higher Education," *Educational Record* 49 (1968): 264.

For the view that in the popular mind, "science" was equated with natural science, see Chamberlin, *Ethical Functions*, 4–5. See also Veysey, *Emergence*, 127; Noll, "Christian Colleges," 26; Mark Beach, "Professional versus Professorial Control of Higher Education," *Educational Record* 49 (1968): 266; Conrad Cherry, *Hurrying toward Zion: Universities, Divinity Schools, and American Protestantism* (Bloomington, Ind., 1995), 91–92.

59. Eliot, "On the Education of Ministers," 71; Josiah Royce, "Present Ideals of American University Life," *Scribner's Magazine* 10 (1891): 378; Guralnick, "American Scientist," 119–120, 134; Bruce, *Launching*, 327.

CHAPTER TWO
THE EMERGENCE OF THE HUMAN SCIENCES

1. Richard J. Bernstein, *The Restructuring of Social and Political Theory* (New York, 1976), 52.

2. Throughout this book, the terms *human sciences* and *social sciences* will be used as synonyms.

Discussions of efforts by practitioners of the social sciences to describe their work in terms of science include Dorothy Ross, *The Origins of American Social Science* (New York, 1991), xiii, 59–60, 62, 290–295, passim; Mary O. Furner, *Advocacy and Objectivity: A Crisis in the Professionalization of American Social Science, 1865–1905* (Lexington, Ky., 1975), 1; George W. Stocking, Jr., "Lamarckianism in American Social Science, 1890–1915," in *Race, Culture, and Evolution: Essays in the History of Anthropology* (New York, 1968), 238.

3. Robert L. Church, "The Economists Study Society: Sociology at Harvard, 1891–1902," *Social Sciences at Harvard 1860–1920: From Inculcation to the Open Mind,* ed. Paul Buck (Cambridge, Mass., 1965), 24–25. A. W. Coats, "The Educational Revolution and the Professionalization of American Economics," in *Breaking the Academic Mould: Economists and American Higher Learning in the Nineteenth Century* (Middletown, Conn., 1988), 349–350; Robert L. Church, "Economists as Experts: The Rise of an Academic Profession in the United States, 1870–1920," in *The University in Society,* ed. Lawrence Stone, 2 vols. (Princeton, 1974), 2: 574; A. W. Coats, "The First Two Decades of the American Economic Association," *American Economic Review* 50 (1960): 561; Bruce Kuklick, "The Emergence of the Humanities," *South Atlantic Quarterly* 89 (1990): 202; Anna Haddow, *Political Science in American Colleges and Universities 1636–1900* (New York, 1939), 231.

In addition to the above, useful discussions of how subjects that later became the social sciences were taught in the period prior to 1870 include Haddow, *Political Science*; Michael J. L. O'Connor, *Origins of Academic Economics in the United States* (1944; New York, 1974).

For the relationship between moral philosophy and the social sciences in the United States, see Gladys Bryson, "The Emergence of the Social Sciences from Moral Philosophy," *International Journal of Ethics* 42 (1932): 304–323; Gladys

Bryson, "Sociology Considered as Moral Philosophy," *Sociological Review* 24 (1932): 26–36; Gladys Bryson, "The Comparable Interest of the Old Moral Philosophy and the Modern Social Sciences," *Social Forces* 11 (1932): 19–27; Ross, *Origins of American Social Science,* esp. 53–97.

The emergence of the social sciences within institutions of higher education after the Civil War is discussed in ibid.; Haddow, *Political Science*; Thomas L. Haskell, *The Emergence of Professional Social Science: The American Social Science Association and the Nineteenth-Century Crisis of Authority* (Urbana, Ill., 1977); Furner, *Advocacy and Objectivity.*

The issue of whether history should be considered a social science is a highly controverted one. Although there are good reasons for considering history a branch of humanistic inquiry, history is included also in discussions of the development of the social sciences, both because it deals with the behavior of human beings within society and because social scientists in the late nineteenth and early twentieth centuries often included history within the rubric of the social sciences. See Church, "Economists as Experts," 575, n. 7; Haskell, *Emergence of Professional Social Science,* 25.

4. W. W. Willoughby [1904], quoted in Albion W. Small, "Fifty Years of Sociology in the United States (1865–1915)," *American Journal of Sociology* 21 (1916): 783; [E. L. Youmans], "The Social Science Association," *Popular Science Monthly* 5 (1874): 368. See also William Stanton, "The Scientific Approach to the Study of Man in America," *Journal of World History* 8 (1965): 779–780; Roger L. Geiger, *To Advance Knowledge: The Growth of American Research Universities, 1900–1940* (New York, 1986), 27.

As in the case of the natural sciences, apologists for a social *science* were not limited to social scientists. In fact, one of the noteworthy characteristics of the American Social Science Association, the organization founded in 1865 as an umbrella institution for the social sciences, was the sizable number of natural scientists in it. Indeed, the first president was the eminent geologist William Barton Rogers. Haskell, *Emergence of Professional Social Science,* 90. However, in contrast to discussions of the natural sciences, which were frequently carried on by people who were not themselves practicing scientists, much of the discussion of the nature and scope of the social sciences was conducted by the practitioners themselves.

5. A useful account of the decline of moral philosophy that stresses the criticism that as philosophy, the subject was too "theological" is Reuben, *Making of the Modern University,* esp. 89–90. The decline of moral philosophy will be discussed more extensively in Part II of this book.

6. Richard T. Ely, *Ground under Our Feet: An Autobiography* (New York, 1938), 40. See also Edward A. Ross, *Seventy Years of It: An Autobiography* (1936; New York, 1977), 30–31; Jurgen Herbst, *The German Historical School in American Scholarship: A Study in the Transfer of Culture* (Ithaca, N.Y., 1965), esp. 8, 103–104, 124, 130–131, 203; Ross, *Origins of American Social Science,* 55.

7. Peter Novick, *That Noble Dream: The "Objectivity Question" and the American Historical Profession* (Cambridge, UK, 1988), 24–25, 31, 33, 40

(quotation on 33). For the quoted references from Adams and Turner, the allusion to Rhodes, and an excellent discussion of the relationship between natural science and history, see W. Stull Holt, "The Idea of Scientific History in America," *Journal of the History of Ideas* 1 (1940): 352–362 (quotations are on 353–355). See also Herbert Baxter Adams, "Methods of Historical Study," *Johns Hopkins University Studies in Historical and Political Science,* 2nd ser., 1–2 (1884): 64, 103; Herbert B. Adams, "Seminary Libraries and University Extension," *Johns Hopkins University Studies in Historical and Political Science,* 5th ser., 11 (1887): 454–455; Frank H. Foster, *The Seminary Method of Original Study in the Historical Sciences* (New York, 1888), 7; William Coleman, "Science and Symbol in the Turner Frontier Hypothesis," *American Historical Review* 72 (1966): 22–49.

8. Charles F. Dunbar [1886], quoted in Church, "Economists as Experts," 593–594; Charles F. Dunbar [1891], quoted in Church, "Economists Study Society," 31; Richard T. Ely, "The Past and the Present of Political Economy," *Johns Hopkins University Studies in Historical and Political Science,* 2nd ser., 3 (1884): 44–46. See also Furner, *Advocacy and Objectivity,* 36, 48; Herbst, *German Historical School,* 105–106; Benjamin G. Rader, *The Academic Mind and Reform: The Influence of Richard T. Ely in American Life* (Lexington, Ky., 1966), 45–50; Church, "Economists Study Society," 22. Among the American Economic Association's priorities were "the encouragement of research" and "the publication of economic monographs." Coats, "Educational Revolution," 356.

9. John W. Burgess, "Political Science and History," *American Historical Review* 2 (1896–1897): 407; Henry Jones Ford [1905 and 1915], cited in Ross, *Origins of American Social Science,* 289. See also Dwight Waldo, "Political Science: Tradition, Discipline, Profession, Science, Enterprise," in *Political Science: Scope and Theory,* ed. Fred I. Greenstein and Nelson W. Polsby (Reading, Mass., 1975), 28–30, 38; Ross, *Origins,* 282–288.

10. Ulysses G. Weatherly, in James Q. Dealey et al., "Lester Frank Ward," *American Journal of Sociology* 19 (1913–1914): 69; William Graham Sumner, "The Scientific Attitude of Mind," [1905] in *Essays of William Graham Sumner,* ed. Albert Galloway Keller and Maurice R. Davie, 2 vols. (New Haven, 1934), 1: 46; William G. Sumner, "Sociology," *Princeton Review,* n.s., 8 (1881): 308; Franklin H. Giddings, "The Theory of Sociology," *Supplement to the Annals of the American Academy of Political and Social Science* 7 (July 1894): 71.

11. [William James], "The Teaching of Philosophy in Our Colleges," *Nation* 23 (September 21, 1876): 178; William James, "A Plea for Psychology as a 'Natural Science,'" *Philosophical Review* 1 (1892): 146–153; John B. Watson, "Psychology as the Behaviorist Views It," *Psychological Review* 20 (1913): 158–177. See also Wilson, *Science, Community,* 76–120; O'Donnell, *Origins of Behaviorism,* 67, 92, passim.

A significant portion of this paragraph is a very close paraphrase of Jon H. Roberts, "The Human Mind and Personality," *Encyclopedia of the United States in the Twentieth Century,* ed. Stanley I. Kutler, 4 vols. (New York, 1996), 2: 87.

12. Church, "Economists as Experts," 574.

13. Historians have rarely explicitly dealt with the decline of theological categories in social science and the significance of that important change. One recent student of the role of the social sciences in higher education, for example, has asserted that "as they began to forge distinct identities during the 1870s and 1880s, the social sciences retained their religious and moral orientation." D. G. Hart, "American Learning and the Problem of Religious Studies," in *The Secularization of the Academy,* ed. George M. Marsden and Bradley J. Longfield (New York, 1992), 201–202. Although the idea that the social sciences retained at least some of the traditional moral perspective is true enough, the notion that the social sciences retained the religious perspective is at best a half-truth. The role of God had clearly changed, and to ignore that change is to ignore a crucial element in the relationship between religion and the social sciences.

For discussions of the religious backgrounds and proclivities of social scientists in the late nineteenth century see, for example, Susan E. Henking, "Sociological Christianity and Christian Sociology: The Paradox of Early American Sociology," *Religion and American Culture* 3 (1993): 49–67; Roscoe C. Hinkle, Jr., and Gisela J. Hinkle, *The Development of Modern Sociology* (New York, 1954), 3; Mark C. Smith, *Social Science in the Crucible: The American Debate over Objectivity and Purpose, 1918–1941* (Durham, N.C., 1994), 20; Cecil E. Greek, *The Religious Roots of American Sociology* (New York, 1992), 72.

14. Guelzo, "'Science of Duty,'" 273–275; Meyer, *Instructed Conscience,* 27; Andrew C. McLaughlin, "The Force of Christianity in United States History," in Martin L. D'Ooge et al., *Religious Thought at the University of Michigan: Being Addresses Delivered at the Sunday Morning Services of the Students' Christian Association* (Ann Arbor, 1893), 25–27. The will of God, McLaughlin asserted, was simply "manifesting itself through men." Ibid. See also J. B. Clark, "The Nature and Progress of True Socialism," *New Englander* 38 (1879): 572, 577. For more on John Bates Clark's providentialism during the early stages of his career, see John Rutherford Everett, *Religion in Economics: A Study of John Bates Clark, Richard T. Ely, Simon N. Patten* (New York, 1946), 51, 56–57, 71, 154, n. 90. In view of the fact that when Clark discussed the mechanisms of economic interaction and the nature of economic processes he confined himself to natural agencies, Everett's emphasis on Clark's providentialism seems overdrawn, at least insofar as it relates to the issue of God's role within society. Moreover, in Clark's later career, references to God are virtually nonexistent.

15. Amasa Walker [1866], quoted in Everett, *Religion in Economics,* 32. See also Charles D. Cashdollar, "The Social Implications of the Doctrine of Divine Providence: A Nineteenth-Century Debate in American Theology," *Harvard Theological Review* 71 (1978): 267–278; Meyer, *Instructed Conscience,* 24–25; Smith, *Professors and Public Ethics,* esp. 30, 36. For the ways in which providentialism affected political economy prior to the late nineteenth century, see Ross, *Origins of Social Science,* 42–50.

As late as 1880, an influential English political economist cited "the conspicuousness of a theological element" as one of the characteristics of American discussions of his discipline. T. E. C. Leslie, "Political Economy in the United States," *Fortnightly Review,* n.s., 28 (1880): 496–497.

144 NOTES TO CHAPTER TWO

16. Thomas L. Haskell has made a similar point with regard to human agency. See Haskell, *Emergence of Professional Social Science,* 165, passim.

17. Lester F. Ward, *Dynamic Sociology: Or Applied Social Science as Based upon Statical Sociology and the Less Complex Sciences,* 2 vols., 2nd ed. (1897; New York, 1968), 1: 65–66, 70; Lester F. Ward, *Pure Sociology: A Treatise on the Origin and Spontaneous Development of Society* (New York, 1903), 56–57. Useful treatments of Ward's thought and his role in American sociology include Small, "Fifty Years of Sociology," 754–758; Harp, *Positivist Republic,* esp. 109–154; Robert C. Bannister, *Sociology and Scientism: The American Quest for Objectivity, 1880–1940* (Chapel Hill, 1987), 13–31. A number of eminent sociologists testified to Ward's influence. See, for example, Dealey et al., "Lester Frank Ward," 61–78; Albion W. Small, "The Evolution of a Social Standard," *American Journal of Sociology* 20 (1914–1915): 10; Harp, *Positivist Republic,* 159–160; Julius Weinberg, *Edward Alsworth Ross and the Sociology of Progressivism* (Madison, Wis., 1972), 31.

18. Giddings, "Theory of Sociology," 71–72; Albion Small, in Dealey et al., "Lester Frank Ward," 76–77; Albion W. Small, *Origins of Sociology* (Chicago, 1924), 337. See also Henking, "Sociological Christianity and Christian Sociology," 51–52; Ross, *Origins of American Social Science,* 123.

19. Ross, *Seventy Years of It,* 32; Edward Alsworth Ross, *Foundations of Sociology* (New York, 1905), 54, 185, 17. See also Sumner, "Sociology," 303; and Harp, *Positivist Republic,* 174–177.

20. Ephraim Emerton, "The Study of Church History," *Unitarian Review and Religious Magazine* 19 (1883): 7; Morris Jastrow, *The Study of Religion* (New York, 1902), 20. See also Preserved Smith, "Luther's Early Development in the Light of Psycho-Analysis," *American Journal of Psychology* 24 (1913): 360. For a suggestive discussion of the decline of providentialism and its impact on thinking about history, see Dorothy Ross, "Historical Consciousness in Nineteenth Century America," *American Historical Review* 89 (1984): 909–928.

21. Arthur Latham Perry, *Elements of Political Economy* (1865; New York, 1869), 1, 39; Arthur Latham Perry, *Principles of Political Economy* (1890; New York, 1891), 14–15, 26, 29–30, 85–87, 143–144, 154, 540–541 (quotation on 26); Thorstein Veblen, "Why Is Economics Not an Evolutionary Science?" *Quarterly Journal of Economics* 12 (1897–1898): 376–378, 380–381, 396–397 (quotations on 378, 380, 381). See also Edwin R. A. Seligman to H. C. Adams, November 30, 1882, quoted in Furner, *Advocacy and Objectivity,* 109; Francis Walker [1884], quoted in Ross, *Origins of American Social Science,* 79.

22. John Burgess, *Political Science and Comparative Constitutional Law,* 2 vols. (1890; Boston, 1900), 1: 59–64. See also Waldo, "Political Science," 27; Ross, *Origins of American Social Science,* 68.

23. G. Stanley Hall, "The New Psychology," *Andover Review* 3 (1885): 120–135, 239–248 (quotation on 247); J. Mark Baldwin, "Psychology Past and Present," *Psychological Review* 1 (1894): 373–374; James, *Principles of Psychology,* 1: 182; James, "Plea for Psychology," 147–150 (quotation on 149); James H. Leuba, "The Field and the Problems of the Psychology of Religion," *American Journal of Religious Psychology and Education* 1 (1904): 166. See also Deborah

J. Coon, "Testing the Limits of Sense and Science: American Experimental Psychologists Combat Spiritualism, 1880–1920," *American Psychologist* 47 (1992): 143–151, esp. 149; John Dewey, "The New Psychology," *Andover Review* 2 (1884): 284; George Trumbull Ladd, "Influence of Modern Psychology upon Theological Opinion," *Andover Review* 14 (1890): 557–578; O'Donnell, *Origins of Behaviorism,* 62–63.

24. Sumner, "Sociology," 303; W. J. McGee, "Man's Place in Nature" [1901], in *Readings in the History of Anthropology,* ed. Regna Darnell (New York, 1974), 243. See also Hamilton Cravens, "History of the Social Sciences," *Osiris,* 2nd ser., 1 (1985): 195–196.

25. Sumner, "Sociology," 303. In the quoted statement, Sumner was referring to sociology, although it is apparent from the context that his suggestion would have included all of the social sciences.

26. Murray G. Murphey, "On the Scientific Study of Religion in the United States, 1870–1980," in *Religion and Twentieth-Century American Intellectual Life,* 136–171; R. Laurence Moore, "Secularization: Religion and the Social Sciences," in *Between the Times: The Travail of the Protestant Establishment in America, 1900–1960,* ed. William R. Hutchison (New York, 1989), 233–252; Reuben, *Making of the Modern University,* 101–113; Turner, *Without God,* 174.

27. Ross, *Origins of American Social Science,* 106; Morton White, *Social Thought in America: The Revolt against Formalism,* 2nd ed. (Boston, 1957), 12; Haskell, *Emergence of Professional Social Science,* 10–12; Ross, "Historical Consciousness," passim; Dorothy Ross, "Modernist Social Science in the Land of the New/Old," in *Modernist Impulses in the Human Sciences 1870–1930,* ed. Dorothy Ross (Baltimore, 1994), 172; Dorothy Ross, "An Historian's View of American Social Science," *Journal of the Behaviorial Sciences* 29 (1993): 100. For representative primary sources, see, for example, Small, "Fifty Years," 792–795; Ross, *Foundations of Sociology,* 13.

28. Ross, *Foundations of Sociology,* 65–66; Haskell, *Emergence of Professional Social Science,* 251.

29. Ross, "Modernist Social Science," 173, 175; Ross, "Historical Consciousness," esp. 910, 915–916, 924. For the religious interests of social scientists, see, in addition to the citations in fn. 13, Church, "Economists as Experts," 584–585; Bernhard J. Stern, "The Letters of Albion W. Small to Lester F. Ward," *Social Forces* 12 (1933): 163.

30. James Harvey Robinson, *The Humanizing of Knowledge,* rev. ed. (New York, 1923), 31–32; Ross, *Origins of American Social Science,* 65–66; Novick, *That Noble Dream,* 33–35. The focus on "unlawlike" particulars is one of the elements that has historically made it difficult to determine whether history is a social science or one of the humanities.

31. Ely, "Past and the Present," 47; Ross, *Foundations of Sociology,* 54, 90–91. See also Furner, *Advocacy and Objectivity,* 14.

32. Small, "Fifty Years of Sociology," 769; Ely, "Past and the Present," 47. See also William Graham Sumner [1873], quoted in Donald C. Bellomy, "The Molding of an Iconoclast: William Graham Sumner, 1840–1880," Ph.D. diss.,

Harvard University, 1980, 251; Franklin H. Giddings, quoted in L. L. Bernard, "The Teaching of Sociology in the United States," *American Journal of Sociology* 15 (1909): 196; Adams, "Methods of Historical Study," 25–26; Herbst, *German Historical School*, 38; Furner, *Advocacy and Objectivity*, 14–16; Church, "Economists as Experts," 587–588.

Edward A. Ross was representative of social scientists in coupling confidence that a "science of society" could be created with awareness of how little he or anyone else knew about such a science. Ross, *Seventy Years of It*, 57. Similarly, one of the principles in the American Economic Association's "Statement of Principles" was that "political economy as a science is still in an early stage of its development." American Economic Association, "Statement of Principles," quoted in Small, "Fifty Years of Sociology," 782. See also Ely [1885], quoted in ibid., 780–781. For Ely's criticism of economists for being too quick to posit mechanistic laws, see Rader, *Academic Mind*, 37, 41.

33. Small, "Fifty Years of Sociology," 833–834; Albion Small to the editor of the *Boston Herald*, August 11, 1894, University Presidents' Papers, 1889–1925, Box LX, Folder 28, Department of Special Collections, the University of Chicago Library. See also Franklin H. Giddings, quoted in Bernard, "Teaching of Sociology," 196; C. A. Ellwood, "The Social Function of Religion," *American Journal of Sociology* 19 (1913): 290–291.

34. Small, "Fifty Years of Sociology," 832; Sumner, "Scientific Attitude," 44, 50. See also Small, "Fifty Years of Sociology," 769–770, 797; Albion W. Small and George E. Vincent, *An Introduction to the Study of Society* (New York, 1894), 31–32; Adams, "Methods of Historical Study," 22. Ely conceived of the kind of scientific enterprise that economists were engaged in as "a progressive unfolding of truth." Ely, quoted in Everett, *Religion in Economics*, 97.

35. John Dewey, "Psychology and Social Practice" [1900], *The Middle Works, 1899–1924*, ed. Jo Ann Boydston (Carbondale, Ill., 1976), 1: 149–150. See also Ward, *Dynamic Sociology*, 2: 2; Smith, *Social Science in the Crucible*, 17, 20; Veysey, *Emergence*, 73–79, passim.

36. Charles H. Cooley, quoted in Bernard, "Teaching of Sociology," 204; [Albion W. Small], "Scholarship and Social Agitation," *American Journal of Sociology* 1 (1895–1896): 564; Weinberg, *Edward Alsworth Ross*, 68; Richard T. Ely, *Social Aspects of Christianity and Other Essays*, rev. ed. (New York, 1889), 122–123, passim; Richard T. Ely, "Ethics and Economics," *Science* 7 (1886): 532; Burgess, "Political Science and History," 407–408; Coats, "Educational Revolution," 358; Church, "Economists as Experts," 583–587; Furner, *Advocacy and Objectivity*, esp. 49–54, 70; Jean B. Quandt, "Religion and Social Thought: The Secularization of Postmillennialism," *American Quarterly* 25 (1973): 390–409; Henking, "Sociological Christianity," 51–54, 59; Veysey, *Emergence*, 80; Rader, *Academic Mind*, 22–23, 60–66; Everett, *Religion in Economics*, passim; Greek, *Religious Roots*, 73; Reuben, *Making of the Modern University*, esp. 137, 143–167; Haskell, *Emergence of Professional Social Science*, 184; Bannister, *Sociology and Scientism*.

The special relationship that existed between sociology and social reform is rooted in the fact that sociology began its career in higher education as a hodgepodge of courses dealing with contemporary social problems, philanthropy, and vocational training in social service occupations. Anthony Oberschall, "The Institutionalization of American Sociology," in *The Establishment of Empirical Sociology: Studies in Continuity, Discontinuity, and Institutionalization,* ed. Anthony Oberschall (New York, 1972), 210–213. This continued to be the case in small colleges during the first decade of the twentieth century. See Bernard, "Teaching of Sociology," 195–210. Prior to the 1890s the field was dominated by social reformers and clergymen. Ross, *Origins of American Social Science,* 122. The presence of the clergy in some departments persisted after 1890. At Harvard, for example, sociology in the 1890s was taught by Edward Cummings, a clergyman who left the institution in 1900 to become an associate pastor at Boston's Unitarian South Church. Church, "Economists Study Society," 37. This prompted Albion Small to observe that the birth of the discipline was due "more directly to the appeal of sympathy than to that of science." [Albion Small], "A Comtean Centenary," *American Journal of Sociology* 27 (1921–1922): 512.

37. H. C. Adams, "Christianity as a Social Force," in D'Ooge *et al., Religious Thought at the University of Michigan,* 54–58; Everett, *Religion in Economics,* 97; Ely to Gilman [1885], quoted in Haskell, *Emergence of Professional Social Science,* 182. See also Coats, "Henry Carter Adams," 179–195, esp. 182, 188; Albion Small, "My Religion" [an undated 1-p. document], University Presidents' Papers, 1889–1925, Box LX, Folder 28, Department of Special Collections, the University of Chicago Library. The absence of concrete theological content in the work of social scientists probably accounts for why, as Julie A. Reuben has noted, "in the universities of the late nineteenth and early twentieth centuries there was no sharp division between educators who saw science as a support for religious morality and those who advocated independent secular moral education." Reuben, *Making of the Modern University,* 173.

Within divinity schools and seminaries sociology continued to be taught from a Christian perspective, but even there social science was frequently accorded preeminence in establishing the nature of the social order. For a good discussion of Graham Taylor's work at Chicago Theological Seminary, see Henking, "Sociological Christianity," 54–60.

For discussion of the contrast between ideals and knowledge within the humanities, see James Turner, *The Liberal Education of Charles Eliot Norton* (Baltimore, 1999).

38. Small and Vincent, *An Introduction to the Study of Society,* 19, 32; [Albion W. Small], "The Limits of 'Christian Sociology,'" *American Journal of Sociology* 1 (1895–1896): 510–511 (quotations on 511); Albion W. Small, Review of *Towards a Christian Sociology,* by Arthur J. Penty, *American Journal of Sociology* 30 (1924): 226. See also [Albion W. Small], "Christian Sociology," *American Journal of Sociology* 1 (1895–1896): 216; Vernon K. Dibble, *The Legacy of Albion Small* (Chicago, 1975), 60–62; Henking, "Sociological Christianity," 52–54; Reuben, *Making of the Modern University,* 172–173. Lester F. Ward took the same position as did Small. Ward [1895], quoted in Bernhard J.

Stern, "The Letters of Albion W. Small to Lester F. Ward," *Social Forces* 12 (1933): 171.

39. Ross, *Origins of American Social Science,* 79; Haskell, *Emergence of Professional Social Science,* 187, n. 48; William Graham Sumner, "Liberty and Responsibility" [c. 1887–1889], in *Earth-Hunger and Other Essays* (1913; New Brunswick, N.J., 1980), 203; S. Newcomb, "Aspects of the Economic Discussion," *Science* 7 (1886): 539; Small and Vincent, *Introduction to the Study of Society,* 19; Albion W. Small, "The Methodology of the Social Problem. Division I. The Sources and Uses of Material," *American Journal of Sociology* 4 (1898–1899): 113–114; [Albion W. Small], "The Era of Sociology," *American Journal of Sociology* 1 (1895–1896): 7. For a succinct statement of objectivist social science from this later period, see, for example, William F. Ogburn, "Folkways of a Scientific Sociology," *Publications of the American Sociological Society* 24, Part 2 (1930): 1–11. Useful studies of that period include Bannister, *Sociology and Scientism;* Smith, *Social Science in the Crucible.*

40. Wells, quoted in Bernard, "Teaching of Sociology," 196. See also Small, "Fifty Years of Sociology," 773, 854; Church, "Economists as Experts," 571, 573; Haskell, *Emergence of Professional Social Science,* 162–164.

41. Small, "Fifty Years of Sociology," 861–862; Church, "Economists Study Society," 23, 19. See also Reuben, *Making of the Modern University,* 145–175; Smith, *Social Science in the Crucible,* 23. The changing views of Daniel Coit Gilman concerning the compatibility of "agitation" and "investigation" are discussed in Haskell, *Emergence of Professional Social Science,* 160–161.

42. Daniel Coit Gilman [1880], quoted in Stanton, "Scientific Approach to the Study of Man in America," 780. See also Haskell, *Emergence of Professional Social Science,* 156–157; Small, "Fifty Years of Sociology," 729–730, 802; Dorothy Ross, "American Social Science and the Idea of Progress," in *The Authority of Experts: Studies in History and Theory,* ed. Thomas L. Haskell (Bloomington, Ind., 1985), 157; Smith, *Social Science in the Crucible,* 4; Hamilton Cravens, "The Abandonment of Evolutionary Social Theory in America: The Impact of Academic Professionalization upon American Sociological Theory, 1890–1920," *American Studies* 12 (Fall 1971): 8; Ross, *Origins of American Social Science,* 131; Fernando Sanford, *The Scientific Method and Its Limitations* (Palo Alto, Calif., 1899), 12–13, 21–22; Ross, *Social Foundations,* 66; Church, "Economists as Experts," 574–575.

43. Jordan, "Science and the Colleges," 721. See also Gilman, "Prospects of Science," 303. The close relationship between philosophy and science during the late nineteenth and early twentieth centuries has received able treatment in Wilson, *Science, Community.* For other fields, see Jordan, "Science and the Colleges," 733; John Harley Warner, "Ideals of Science and Their Discontents in Late Nineteenth-Century American Medicine," *Isis* 82 (1991): 477; Kenneth M. Ludmerer, *Learning to Heal: The Development of American Medical Education* (New York, 1985), 48–51, 66–67; William R. Johnson, *Schooled Lawyers: A Study in the Clash of Professional Cultures* (New York, 1978), xv; Cherry, *Hurrying Toward Zion,* 87–123.

CHAPTER THREE
KNOWLEDGE AND INQUIRY IN THE ASCENDANT

1. Charles E. Rosenberg, *No Other Gods: On Science and American Social Thought* (Baltimore, 1976), 14.

2. W. T. Hewett, "University Administration," *Atlantic Monthly* 50 (1882): 513; Eliot, "On the Education of Ministers," 69–70; Veysey, *Emergence,* 176–177; Guralnick, "American Scientist," 115–116; Geiger, *To Advance Knowledge,* 35–39; Kevles, "Physics, Mathematics, and Chemistry Communities," 144.

3. Shils, "Order of Learning," 30; Kohler, "Ph.D. Machine," 655, 659; Geiger, *To Advance Knowledge,* 1–93; Douglas Sloan, "Science in New York City, 1867–1907," *Isis* 71 (1980): 67; Kevles, "Physics, Mathematics, and Chemistry Communities," 144–145; Veysey, *Emergence,* 158; President's [McCosh's] Report [to the Trustees], November 11, 1880, Princeton University President Report, Department of Rare Books & Special Collections, Seeley G. Mudd Manuscript Library, Princeton University; Daniel Coit Gilman, "The Johns Hopkins University in Its Beginning: An Inaugural Address" [1876], in *University Problems in the United States* (New York, 1898), 17–20; Davis, "Science as a Means of Human Culture," 672; Owens, "Pure and Sound Government," 193.

It is a telling commentary on the support that colleges and universities gave scientific research that even as late as 1891, endowments for medical schools were only about $500,000, while endowments for American theological schools were about $18 million. Richard H. Shryock, *American Medical Research Past and Present* (New York, 1947), 49. We are indebted to Ronald L. Numbers for bringing this source to our attention.

The centrality of teaching within higher education and the relationship between character and the curriculum will be further explored in Part II of this volume.

4. Rowland, "Physical Laboratory" [*Circular*], 104; David Starr Jordan, "Science in the High School," *Popular Science Monthly* 36 (1890): 721; Davis, "Science as a Means of Human Culture," 662; Joseph Le Conte, "Science and Mental Improvement," *Popular Science Monthly* 13 (1878): 97; Chamberlin, "The Scientific and the Non-Scientific," 1; Cooke, "Scientific Culture," 528–529; Hall, "Research the Vital Spirit of Teaching," 566; Charles W. Eliot, in Charles W. Eliot et al., *Addresses at the Inauguration of Charles William Eliot as President of Harvard College, Tuesday, October 19, 1869* (Cambridge, Mass., 1869), 35–36; Pritchett, *What Is Religion?* 18–19; Remsen, "Scientific Investigation and Progress," 301; Thomas C. Chamberlin, "The Ethical Nature of True Scientific Study" [Lawrence University, June 20, 1899], Thomas Chrowder Chamberlin Papers, Box III [Misc. Papers and Addresses], Folder 24, Department of Special Collections, the University of Chicago Library, 3; Edwin Grant Conklin, "The Christian College in the Modern World," address at Ohio Wesleyan University, undated mss., Edwin G. Conklin Papers, C0322, Carton 14, Manuscript Division, Department of Rare Books & Special Collections, Princeton University Library, 2, 6; Guthe, "Religious and Character Value," 379–380. See also Hollinger, "Justification by Verification," 122; Bledstein, *The*

*Culture of Professionalism,* 146–147; Kohler, "Ph.D. Machine," 640; Pauly, "G. Stanley Hall and His Successors," 24; Reuben, *Making of the Modern University,* 135–136.

Historians have tended to underestimate the continuing significance of the idea of mental discipline in the late nineteenth century. For an example, see Owens, "Pure and Sound Government," 184–185. Actually, although the metaphorical underpinnings of the concept changed—later nineteenth-century proponents of mental discipline no longer thought of the brain as a muscle needing exercise—belief in the need for mental discipline continued to be widespread.

5. Foster, *Seminary Method,* 3; James B. Angell, "The Old College and the New University," *University* [of Chicago] *Record* 4 (July 1899): 79. See also Herbst, *German Historical School,* 34–39; Reuben, *Making of the Modern University,* 64–66.

6. Jordan, "Comrades in Zeal," 306; John M. Coulter, "The Religious and Character Value of the Curriculum. Biology," *Religious Education* 6 (1911–1912): 365; Jordan, "Science in the High School," 722; Remsen, "Scientific Investigation," 300–301.

7. Shils, "Order of Learning," 28; James Turner and Paul Bernard, "The Prussian Road to University? German Models and the University of Michigan, 1837–c. 1895," University of Michigan, *Rackham Reports,* n.v. (1988–1989): 12.

8. Thompson, "Science in Religious Education," 452; Hitchcock, "Relations and Consequent Mutual Duties," 192. See also Pritchett, *What Is Religion?* 26, 70; Henry, "On the Importance," 648–649; Woodward, "Progress of Science," 518; Hudson, "Veracity," 206–207.

One manifestation of hostility to views not predicated on scientific inquiry was the complaints advanced by a number of scientists at the University of Chicago that the classical curriculum rested on undue respect for tradition. See Richard J. Storr, *Harper's University: The Beginnings* (Chicago, 1966), 117–128.

For discussion of Draper's work, see Fleming, *John William Draper,* 122–135. Useful discussions of Andrew Dickson White's work include James R. Moore, *The Post-Darwinian Controversies: A Study of the Protestant Struggle to Come to Terms with Darwin in Great Britain and America 1870–1900* (New York, 1979), 29–49; Marsden, *Soul of the American University,* 113–120.

For expressions of the older view, see Benjamin Peirce, "On the Constitution of Saturn's Ring," *Astronomical Journal* 2 (June 16, 1851): 19; Miller, *Revolutionary College,* 271–279.

9. Moore, *Post-Darwinian Controversies,* 1–122; David C. Lindberg and Ronald L. Numbers, "Beyond War and Peace: A Reappraisal of the Encounter between Christianity and Science," *Church History* 55 (1986): 338–354. It should probably be said that while the "warfare" thesis is incorrect, this does not mean that the relationship between science and religion has always been free of tension and even conflict.

The Alexander Winchell case and James Woodrow cases are relevant here, but they hardly demonstrate strong or widespread challenges to the hegemony of academic science. The difficulties that scientists did experience were customarily handled without serious jeopardy to their professional lives. The Methodist Book Concern refused to publish a book on evolution that it had originally commissioned from William North Rice of Wesleyan, for example, because Rice denied "the historicity of the first eleven chapters of Genesis." Nevertheless, Rice succeeded in getting his book, *Christian Faith in an Age of Science,* published by the commercial publisher A. C. Armstrong. Potts, *Wesleyan,* 159–160, 317, n. 100 (quotation on 159).

10. William Watts Folwell, "Inaugural Address" [1869], in *University Addresses* (Minneapolis, 1909), 18; Charles W. Eliot, in C. W. Eliot and O. C. Marsh, "Addresses of Eliot and Marsh, At the Opening of the American Museum of Natural History," *Popular Science Monthly* 12 (1877–1878): 473–474. See also Charles William Eliot, "Address at the Inauguration of Daniel C. Gilman" [Feburary 22, 1876], *Educational Reform,* 42–43; Charles W. Eliot, "Is a Classical Education a Practical Education?" [Typescript of Speech before the Liberal Club, Buffalo, March 16, 1894], Charles W. Eliot, Presidents' Papers, Harvard University Archives, Box 335, Folder 52, 12 (Courtesy of the Harvard University Archives); Guralnick, "American Scientist," 114; Bruce, *Launching,* 326.

11. Daniel Coit Gilman, "Higher Education in the United States" [1893], in *University Problems,* 298; Andrew Dickson White, "Inaugural Address" [1868], in *Builders of American Universities: Inaugural Addresses,* ed. David Andrew Weaver, 2 vols. (Alton, Ill., 1950), 1: 259. See also Gilman, "Prospects of Science," 36; W. R. Harper, "Shall the Theological Curriculum Be Modified, and How?" *American Journal of Theology* 3 (1899): 49; Eliot, "On the Education of Ministers," 69–71; Charles William Eliot, "More Harvard Graduates for the Ministry," in George Angier Gordon et al., *The Ministry as a Profession: Three Addressses Delivered Before the Divinity Club of the Harvard Divinity School* (Cambridge, Mass., 1907), 29; Nicholas Murray Butler, in Holt et al., "The Formal Opening of the Laboratory," 12; Davis, "Science as a Means of Human Culture," 672; Pauly, "G. Stanley Hall and His Successors," 24; Daniel C. Gilman, *The Sheffield Scientific School of Yale University: A Semi-Centennial Historical Discourse, October 28, 1897* (New Haven, 1897), 11.

12. David Starr Jordan, *The Foundation Ideals of Stanford University* (Stanford, 1915), 8; Eliot, "More Harvard Graduates for the Ministry," 24–25, 29; Daniel Coit Gilman, "The Characteristics of a University: An Address before the Phi Beta Kappa Society of Harvard University" [1886], in *University Problems,* 87; James Burrill Angell, *The Old and the New Ideal of Scholars: A Baccalaureate Address Delivered June 18, 1905* (Ann Arbor, 1905), 3. See also Jordan, "Science and the Colleges," 726; Charles William Eliot, "The Aims of the Higher Education" [1891], *Educational Reform: Essays and Addresses* (New York, 1898), 226–227, 231; D. C. Gilman, "The Christian Resources of Our Country," [speech before the Evangelical Alliance in Washington, D.C., Dec. 1887], Daniel C. Gilman Papers, Ms. 1, Series 5, Box 5.3, Milton S. Eisenhower Library, The Johns Hopkins University, 278, 281; James B. Angell, "The Old

College and the New University," *University* [of Chicago] *Record* 4 (July 1899): 81; Reuben, *Making of the Modern University,* 67–69.

This view of higher education is not intended to deny the importance of professionalism, but it does make that process only one of a number of factors that helped shape colleges and universities in the late nineteenth and early twentieth centuries. For doubts about the sufficiency of professionalization as an explanation for the changes in higher education in the late nineteenth century, see, for example, Higham, "Matrix of Specialization," 3; Turner and Bernard, "Prussian Road," 37, n. 7.

13. Porter, *Two Sermons,* 31, 37, 27. See also Porter, "American Colleges," 81, 76; Julius Seelye [1876], quoted in Thomas Le Duc, *Piety and Intellect at Amherst College 1865–1912* (New York, 1946), 45.

14. Porter, "American Colleges," 761–763; President's [McCosh's] Report [to the Trustees], December 22, 1875, Princeton University President Report, Department of Rare Books & Special Collections, Seeley G. Mudd Manuscript Library, Princeton University; President's [McCosh's] Report [to the Trustees], June 16, 1884, Princeton University President Report, Department of Rare Books & Special Collections, Seeley G. Mudd Manuscript Library, Princeton University. See also Charles A. Blanchard, "The Purpose of Higher Education" [1891, Proofsheets of a paper that Blanchard said in a letter of April 14, 1891, to Eliot that he had read at the parlor conference on the subject of higher education held in the home of C. H. Case, 201 Ashland Ave., Chicago], Charles W. Eliot, Presidents' Papers, Harvard University Archives, Box 80, Folder 1891 Bi-By, 4–5 (Courtesy of the Harvard University Archives); George E. Peterson, *The New England College in the Age of the University* (Amherst, 1964), 59–60; Veysey, *Emergence,* 76–77, passim.

15. Daniel Coit Gilman, *The Launching of a University and Other Papers: A Sheaf of Remembrances* (New York, 1906), 20–23; James B. Angell, "The Expanding Power of Christianity," in D'Ooge et al., *Religious Thought at the University of Michigan,* 146; Gilman, "The Christian Resources of Our Country," 282, 288; Jordan, "Comrades in Zeal," 315; Andrew D. White, "The Warfare of Science," *Popular Science Monthly* 8 (1876): 568–569; Charles W. Eliot, "What Place Should Religion Have in a College" [typescript of speech before the XIX Century Club of New York, February 3, 1886], Charles W. Eliot, Presidents' Papers, Harvard University Archives, Box 334, Folder 36, 14–15 (Courtesy of the Harvard University Archives). For the religiously inspired resistance to Andrew Dickson White's efforts to make Cornell nonsectarian and his plan to give "scientific studies the same weight as classical studies," see Ronald L. Numbers, "Science and Religion," *Osiris,* 2nd ser., 1 (1985): 59–60.

16. Beach, "Professional versus Professorial Control," 264. Angell apparently agreed with Gilman. He later expressed similar sentiments. See Angell [1891], quoted in Reuben, *Making of the Modern University,* 90. See also Hall, *Life and Confessions,* 245; Turner, *Liberal Education of Charles Eliot Norton,* 354.

Not everyone was as sanguine as Gilman about imposing religious restrictions on faculty hiring. See, for example, John Bascom, "Atheism in Colleges," *North American Review* 132 (1881): 35.

17. Gilman, *Launching of a University,* 133. See also Angell, "Expanding Power of Christianity," 142–143; Charles W. Eliot, "Is a Classical Education a Practical Education?" [typescript of speech before the Liberal Club, Buffalo, March 16, 1894], Charles W. Eliot, Presidents' Papers, Harvard University Archives, Box 335, Folder 52, 12 (Courtesy of the Harvard University Archives); Daniel C. Gilman, "The Benefits Which Society Derives from Universities: The Annual Address before the Johns Hopkins University, Delivered in Baltimore, February 23, 1885," *Johns Hopkins University Circulars,* 4, No. 37 [March 1885] (1885): 47; Daniel Coit Gilman, "The University of California in Its Infancy" [1872], in *University Problems,* 170–171; Hawkins, *Pioneer,* 297; Daniel C. Gilman to A. D. White [draft], April 1896, Daniel C. Gilman Papers, Gilman Correspondence, Ms. 1, File Andrew D. White, Milton S. Eisenhower Library, The Johns Hopkins University, n.p.

Gilman embraced a division of labor in which religion interpreted the Bible and science other phenomena. Daniel Coit Gilman, "The Johns Hopkins University in Its Beginning: An Inaugural Address" [1876], in *University Problems,* 18.

18. Eliot, in Eliot and Marsh, "Addresses of Eliot and Marsh," 474–475. See also Eliot, "What Place Should Religion Have in a College," 14–15. See also Gilman, "Benefits Which Society Derives from Universities," 47; Gilman, "Prospects of Science," 36; Gilman, *Address before the Phi Beta Kappa Society,* 22–23.

For Ritschlianism, see Hugh Ross Mackintosh, *Types of Modern Theology: Schleiermacher to Barth* (New York [1937]), 138–180. Its importance within American liberal theology is briefly discussed in William R. Hutchison, *The Modernist Impulse in American Protestantism* (Cambridge, Mass., 1976), 112–113, 122–132. For liberal Protestants' use of scientific analysis in the cause of social reform, see Quandt, "Religion and Social Thought," 390–409. It is a commonplace that not all liberal Protestants adhered to the "social gospel." Nevertheless, there was a good deal of overlap. For recognizable similarities between the themes of "social Christianity" and Protestant liberalism, see William M. King, "An Enthusiasm for Humanity: The Social Emphasis in Religion and Its Accommodation in Protestant Theology," in *Religion and Twentieth-Century American Intellectual Life,* 49–77. For the popularity of immanentism in the late nineteenth century, see Roberts, *Darwinism and the Divine,* 137–142.

19. Marsden, *Soul of the American University,* 85.

20. Shils, "Order of Learning," 32, 46; Croce, *Science and Religion,* 4.

21. William Graham Sumner captured the feelings of many when he lamented in 1872, "Not two or three, nor a score, but a hundred claimants wrangle for the faith of men." William Graham Sumner, "Farewell Discourse" [sermon of Sept. 6, 1872], William Graham Sumner Papers, Group No. 291, Ser. II, Box 61, Folder 1418, Manuscripts and Archives, Yale University Library, n.p.

22. Hollinger, "Inquiry and Uplift," 152; Veblen, "Place of Science," 585–586 (quotation on 585). See also McGee, "Fifty Years," 320; Marsden, *Soul of the American University,* 202; Kohler, "Ph.D. Machine," 645–646.

23. Roberts, *Darwinism and the Divine in America,* 238–240.

24. John W. Burgess, *Reminiscences of an American Scholar: The Beginnings*

*of Columbia University* (New York, 1934), 147–148; Charles W. Eliot, in Eliot et al., *Addresses at the Inauguration of Charles William Eliot,* 35. See also Angell, *Old and the New Ideal,* 3–4. See also Albion W. Small, "Research Ideals," *University Record* 10 (1905): 87; Sumner, "Scientific Attitude," 50–52.

25. Chamberlin, "Ethical Nature of True Scientific Study," 5. See also Chamberlin, "Scientific and the Non-Scientific," 5; William Rainey Harper, *Religion and the Higher Life: Talks to Students* (Chicago, 1904), 134; Coulter, "Religious and Character Value," 365–366; Coulter, "Science and Religion," 343–344; Rowland, "Physical Laboratory" [*Circulars*], 103–104; Thorstein Veblen, *The Higher Learning in America* (New York, 1918), 181; John M. Coulter, "The Personal Faith of a Scientist" [undated], John M. Coulter Papers, Box III, Folder 21, Department of Special Collections, the University of Chicago Library, 18.

The best historically oriented discussion of the relationship between trust and scientific conceptions of truth is Steven Shapin, *A Social History of Truth: Civility and Science in Seventeenth-Century England* (Chicago, 1994).

26. Hall, "University Idea," 104; L. L. Bernard, "Religion and Theology," *Monist* 32 (1922): 79; Bruce A. Kimball, *The "True Professional Ideal" in America: A History* (Cambridge, UK, 1992), 212.

CHAPTER FOUR
THE TRIUMPH OF THE HUMANITIES

1. A word may be in order about the larger context within which we need to understand change in our colleges and universities. It is wrong to see American colleges as inheriting a solidly fixed "traditional" curriculum from Europe. There were certain constants from medieval times onward—chiefly Latin and philosophy—but their weight was shifting and the other components of the curriculum were in flux, even as the first colleges were being founded in British North America. Instability remained the rule until, by 1900, even Latin and philosophy had lost their fixed presence. The story of higher education in the United States is not the two-stage one recounted in some older histories—in which "the old-time classical college" was replaced by the modern university and liberal arts college—but, as historians of the subject have now long recognized, a tale of persisting change, varying only in intensity. This pretty obvious historical fact perhaps gets masked by the tendency of each generation (professors no less than others) to see its educational experience as a traditionary norm.

2. Both the natural and the social sciences had long been a part of higher education in the United States. American colleges had taught a bit of natural science from their seventeenth-century beginnings. Its place, as Part I reminds us, increased considerably after 1820, so that by 1850 the average college student spent more hours learning natural science than he (or by then she) would half a century later—or does today. The social sciences entered the curriculum at the turn of the eighteenth century, smuggled in via the moral philosophy course imported from Scotland. They pretty much remained embedded in that course through the 1860s, though political economy achieved an independent existence much earlier. But much that late-nineteenth-century academics would

call political science or sociology was taught under the rubric of moral philosophy (or moral science, as the subject was also called). A good example is Francis Wayland, *The Elements of Moral Science,* ed. Joseph Blau (1837; Cambridge, Mass., 1963), the best-selling moral philosophy textbook.

3. *Oxford English Dictionary,* s.v. *humanity.*

4. It is usually hard to tell precisely what a writer included under "humanities," but probably the word also encompassed English rhetoric after that subject began to be widely taught in American colleges.

5. *Catalogue of the College of New Jersey,* 1872–1873, 45–46; Nora Campbell Chaffin, *Trinity College, 1839–1892: The Beginnings of Duke University* (Durham, N.C., 1950), 297 (quoting the 1873–1874 Trinity College catalog).

Though nominally published, nineteenth-century college and university catalogs usually survive only as archival material, and all those cited below were consulted in the archives of the respective institutions, except where noted. Titles of an institution's catalogs often varied slightly from year to year; rather than pedantically reproducing every minor variant, the following notes, after an initial full citation, give a short form of that title, unless a major change occurred, such as Princeton's adopting its present cognomen in lieu of the original "College of New Jersey."

6. The term *classical studies* had not been unusual earlier (though simple *Greek, Latin,* or collective *ancient languages* seems to have been commoner), but the substitution of noun for adjective and the addition of the definite article seems to have signaled a new conception of the meanings of these old subjects. On the transformation of classical studies into one of the new humanities, the essential work is Caroline Winterer, "The Classics and Culture in the Transformation of American Higher Education, 1830–1890" (Ph.D. diss., University of Michigan, 1996).

7. George M. Marsden, *The Soul of the American University: From Protestant Establishment to Established Unbelief* (New York, 1994). On the phenomenon of secularization more generally, see (theoretically) David A. Martin, *A General Theory of Secularization* (New York, 1978), and (for its intellectual history) Owen Chadwick, *The Secularization of the European Mind in the Nineteenth Century* (Cambridge, 1975). On the sweep of secularization in the nineteenth-century United States, see James Turner, *Without God, Without Creed: The Origins of Unbelief in America* (Baltimore, 1985), pp. 116–126.

8. "Difficulties of the *university*" but "consequences for *higher education*" is a deliberate phrasing. For the transformation of knowledge resulted specifically from refitting learning to the new universities, while the results of this transformation befell liberal arts colleges and universities alike.

9. This account goes into some detail only about the early study of literature, because confusion prevails on that subject in much secondary literature.

10. On this earliest form, see especially Norman Fiering, *Moral Philosophy at Seventeenth-Century Harvard: A Discipline in Transition* (Chapel Hill, 1981). More generally, the first colleges were founded in the British colonies at a time of academic transition, when the educational program of Renaissance hu-

manism was waging a fairly successful guerrilla war against a philosophically based university curriculum inherited from medieval Scholasticism. This (along with other factors, such as the influence of Reformed Protestant academies) helps to explain not only the relatively reduced place of philosophy in the curriculum vis-à-vis ancient languages, but also the instability of its form. See generally Bruce A. Kimball, *Orators and Philosophers: A History of the Idea of Liberal Education*, 2d ed. (New York, 1995), and more specifically and controversially Anthony Grafton and Lisa Jardine, *From Humanism to the Humanities: Education and the Liberal Arts in Fifteenth- and Sixteenth-Century Europe* (Cambridge, Mass., 1986), a book that seems to us persuasive, especially since the well-known and ironic fate of Humboldt's *Bildungsidee* in nineteenth-century Germany so clearly parallels Grafton and Jardine's argument (see, e.g., Hans Steffen, ed., *Bildung und Gesellschaft: Zum Bildungsbegriff von Humboldt bis zur Gegenwart* [Göttingen, 1972]).

11. Antebellum colleges commonly required logic and "mental philosophy" in addition to moral philosophy. See, for example, *Catalogue of the Officers and Students of the College of New Jersey for 1830 and 1831* (Princeton, 1831), 10–11; *Catalogue of the Officers and Students of Marshall College for 1850–'51* (Troy, N.Y., 1851), 19–20. ("Mental philosophy" was more or less psychology, in its preexperimental, philosophical mode. Sometimes the course was actually labeled "Psychology," as in *Catalogue of Marshall College*, 1850–1851, 19–20.) Even Harvard's experiment in the 1840s with a largely elective curriculum still required logic and two further years of philosophy. *A Catalogue of the Officers and Students of Harvard University for the Academical Year 1845–46* (Cambridge, Mass., 1845).

12. Winterer, "Classics and Culture." In many schools, courses appeared in the late nineteenth century on "classics in translation," which actually did treat Greek and Latin texts as literature; for most students who continued to study them in the original tongues, one suspects that matters of syntax and prosody still overwhelmed the literary aspect.

13. Samuel Eliot Morison, *Three Centuries of Harvard, 1636–1936* (Cambridge, Mass., 1936), pp. 228–230, 238, 263–264; David Tyack, *George Ticknor and the Boston Brahmins* (Cambridge, Mass., 1967); Martin Duberman, *James Russell Lowell* (Boston, 1966). Gerald Graff and Michael Warner assert in *The Origins of Literary Studies in America: A Documentary Anthology* (New York, 1989) that these three men were "rhetoric-and-oratory" professors who held the Boylston chair of rhetoric (famously occupied in this period by Edward Channing and Francis J. Child); this elementary error of fact both compounds and helps to explain Graff's earlier profound misunderstandings of Lowell in *Professing Literature: An Institutional History* (Chicago, 1987).

14. Marshall College in 1850 (and possibly earlier; the catalogs are lost) did offer "Lectures in German, on subjects connected with History or Poetry" for juniors and seniors "who may understand the Language." *Catalogue of Marshall College*, 1850–1851, p. 20. But this seems to have been a special concession to community worries about sustaining German culture in an English-speaking land, rather than the reflection of a pedagogical principle.

15. Oral public presentations by students had always figured in colleges (and continued through much of the nineteenth century). But distinct courses in rhetoric began to enter the curriculum of American colleges in the later eighteenth century: Frederick Rudolph, *Curriculum: A History of the American Undergraduate Course of Study since 1636* (San Francisco, 1977), 38–39. The rhetoric courses seem first to have emphasized public speaking but gradually to have shifted the stress to writing.

The question of what constitutes "literature" and a "literary" approach is eschewed here because we merely repeat a classification taken for granted in the nineteenth century. To the extent that the meanings of this category need to be spelled out, they will be when necessary.

16. Wallace E. Caldwell, "The Humanities at the University of North Carolina, 1795–1945, A Historical Survey," in *A State University Surveys the Humanities,* ed. Loren C. MacKinney et al. (Chapel Hill, 1945), 4–5, 15–17; *Catalogue of College of New Jersey,* 1830–1831. The turn to studying literature as Art did not squelch the use of literary works to teach rhetoric. A statement at the head of the listing of English courses in the *University of North Carolina Catalogue, 1893–'94* (Chapel Hill, 1894), 38, declares that work in English "begins with the theory and practice of rhetoric" but goes on to say, "Enough literature is read from the first to serve as models and sources of inspiration."

17. Thomas Jefferson Wertenbaker, *Princeton, 1746–1896* (Princeton, 1946), 236; Matthew Boyd Hope, "Lectures on Belles Lettres" (1847, manuscript notes by David E. Smith, Seeley G. Mudd Library, Princeton University); Chaffin, *Trinity College, 1839–1892,* 150. (Seeley G. Mudd Library is hereafter cited as Mudd.) Wertenbaker's implication that Hope taught what we might call English literature appears to be pure fancy. The fledgling University of Michigan likewise offered a freshman course in "English Language and Lit'ture" in 1852–1853: *Catalogue of the Officers and Students of the University of Michigan: 1852–53* (Ann Arbor, 1853), 24. But precedent breeds the strong suspicion that this, too, was a typical "freshman composition" course.

18. So at least concluded Frederick Rudolph, who has perhaps read more college catalogs than any other historian: *Curriculum: A History of the American Undergraduate Course of Study since 1636* (San Francisco, 1977), 140. Even March, however, still taught "the masterpieces of literature" with an emphasis on examination of vocabulary and etymology "line by line and word by word." Francis A. March, "English at Lafayette College," in William Morton Payne, ed., *English in American Universities* (Boston, 1895), 76–77.

19. *Catalogue of University of Michigan,* 1857–1858, 39; Charles H. Grandgent, "The Modern Languages, 1869–1929," in Samuel Eliot Morison, ed., *The Development of Harvard University since the Inauguration of President Eliot, 1869–1929* (Cambridge, Mass., 1930), 66–67; Rudolph, *Curriculum,* 134, 140; George Wilson Pierson, *Yale College: An Educational History, 1871–1921* (New Haven, 1952), 52; *Catalogue of the Agricultural College of Pennsylvania, 1872* (Philadelphia, 1872), 27; *Catalogue of Austin College, Sherman, Texas, for the Session of 1878–79* (St. Louis, 1879), 9–10. At first White taught literature as an addition to the sophomore rhetoric course, but he severed literature

entirely from rhetoric in 1861. *Catalogue of University of Michigan, 1860–1861*, 43–44. Grandgent noted in a similar vein that "English" did not appear as a distinct field of study in the Harvard catalog until 1868–1869. Even proudly classical Yale College found "a little" English literature creeping into the rhetoric course by 1875, and within a few years elective courses for upperclassmen in English literature began to appear. Pierson, *Yale College*, 70, 75.

20. *Catalogue of North Texas Female College and Conservatory of Music. Sherman, Texas, 1892–1893* (n.p., [1893]), 24–25; *The Polytechnic College of the Methodist Episcopal Church, South* [catalogue for 1892–1893] (Fort Worth, 1893), 12–14; Winton U. Solberg, *The University of Illinois, 1867–1894: An Intellectual and Cultural History* (Urbana, 1968), 109, 266–267; Pierson, *Yale College*, 299. Pierson notes (pp. 85–86) that in the mid-1880s Yale began to require sophomores to study Shakespeare's plays and in 1892 required of freshman "a survey of English literature and Shakespeare's plays." (Catalogs of the Polytechnic College are in the archives of Texas Wesleyan University, its successor institution. The North Texas Female College, later Kidd Key College, no longer exists; for its catalogs, see records of North Texas Female College/Kidd Key College, DeGolyer Library, Southern Methodist University. Illinois Industrial University was the original name of the University of Illinois.)

21. Corporation Records, 30 January 1874, Harvard University Archives, and E. W. Gurney to Norton, 11 February 1874, box 16, Miscellaneous Papers, Charles Eliot Norton Papers, Houghton Library, Harvard University. (Harvard University Archives is hereafter cited as HUA, Houghton Library as Houghton, the Charles Eliot Norton Papers as NP.)

22. The "Fine Arts" lecturer was the Rev. William Armstrong Dod, whose lectures appear in 1855 and vanish in 1860. *Catalogue of the College of New Jersey, 1855–1856*, 19, and *1859–1860*, 5, 20. It is unclear whether Dod's lectures stressed art history or matters of technique—more likely the latter, given other early offerings in art; in any case they stood apart from the regular curriculum, in a lecture series open to nonstudents. This was also the case for the earlier courses of lectures in the history of architecture, offered first by the physicist Joseph Henry, then by the mathematician Albert B. Dod. These seem to have been technical rather than cultural in focus. See Marilyn Aronberg Lavin, *The Eye of the Tiger: The Founding and Development of the Department of Art and Archaeology, 1883–1923, Princeton University* (Princeton, 1983), 7–8. (Lavin seems not to grasp the extracurricular status of all these lectures.)

Henry P. Tappan, president of the University of Michigan, had meant to include "The Arts of Design" in his stillborn "University Course" in the 1850s. James Turner and Paul Bernard, "The 'German Model' and the Graduate School: The University of Michigan and the Origin Myth of the American University," *History of Higher Education Annual* 13 (1993): 75. Yale in 1869 and Syracuse in 1873 had actually opened schools of art; these, however, devoted themselves to studio art rather than art history. John Ferguson Weir, *The Recollections of John Ferguson Weir, Director of the Yale School of the Fine Arts*, ed. Theodore Sizer (New York and New Haven, 1957), 69–88; W. Freeman Galpin, *Syracuse University: The Pioneer Days* (Syracuse, 1952), Chap. 7. Harvard itself had in 1871 hired Charles Moore, a disciple of Ruskin, to teach drawing in the Lawrence Scientific School. Morison, *Three Centuries,* 130.

In the *history* of art, Harvard had already crept about as far as any institution by inducing Charles C. Perkins to give without salary University Lectures on Michelangelo and Raphael and on the history of engraving between 1871 and 1874. Corporation Records, 10 November 1873 and 25 May and 9 November 1874, HUA. Marshall College as early as 1850 required "Archaeology of Literature and Art," but this was pretty clearly ancillary to the study of Greek and Latin. Compare *Catalogue of Marshall College,* 1850–1851, 19, with 1851–1852, 17.

23. Lavin, *Eye of the Tiger,* 10–14; Wertenbaker, *Princeton,* 309. These courses were taught, respectively, by W. C. Prime, Allan Marquand, and Arthur Frothingham; in addition President James McCosh offered one on aesthetics.

24. Owing to the lack of respectable texts in English, Norton's courses imposed in the early years of his teaching the utopian requirement of "Ability to use a German text-book." In 1879 he arranged for a publisher to commission a translation by his student Joseph Thacher Clarke of Franz Reber's history of ancient art. This translation was soon adopted at Princeton and in all likelihood at other schools as well. *Harvard University Catalogue,* 1879–1880, 86; Contract Book 4: 9–12, and 5: 241–244; and Memorandum Book, 5: 70, Harper and Brothers Manuscript Collection, Butler Library, Columbia University; Lavin, *Eye of the Tiger,* 15, 29.

25. *Catalog of Carleton College for the Academic Year 1905–1906* (Northfield, Minn., 1906), 48–49; Craig Hugh Smyth and Peter M. Lukehart, eds., *The Early Years of Art History in the United States: Notes and Essays on Departments, Teaching, and Scholars* (Princeton, 1993), esp. 12–36, reproducing E. Baldwin Smith's 1912 survey of courses in art history in American colleges and universities.

26. For example, at Harvard in the 1840s students were assigned Arnold Heeren's *Ancient Greece* (translated from the German by Harvard's own recreant son George Bancroft and published in Boston by Charles C. Little and James Brown), along with Thomas Keightley's *History of Rome,* an old British standby (presumably in the edition printed by the Boston publishers Hilliard, Gray, and Co). For required texts, see *Catalogue of Harvard University,* 1844–1845 and 1845–1846.

27. Morison, *Three Centuries,* 264. "Seems" because one cannot be sure of Sparks's priority. College catalogs prior to 1838 sometimes mention history without specifying which history. Princeton, for example, required "history" of sophomores in 1830. *Catalogue of College of New Jersey,* 1830–1831, 10–11. Probably such requirements still envisaged students reciting from a manual of Greek or Roman history to their classics professor—a plausible inference because, in every pre-1850 catalog examined for this book where the subject is specified, it turns out to be ancient history; but silence is more common than clarification.

28. Caldwell, "Humanities at North Carolina," 16–17; Ruth Bordin, *Andrew Dickson White: Teacher of History,* Michigan Historical Collections, Bul-

letin No. 8 (Ann Arbor, 1958), 7–10; James Turner and Paul Bernard, "The Prussian Road to University? German Models and the University of Michigan, 1837–c.1895," *Rackham Reports,* 1988–1989, 13, 22.

29. *Catalogue of the College of New Jersey,* 1869–1870, 23–25, and 1870–1871, 26; Hugh Hawkins, *Pioneer: A History of the Johns Hopkins University, 1874–1889* (Ithaca, N.Y., 1960), 55–56; *Catalogue of Carleton College,* 1870–1871, 5 (faculty) and 12–13 (curriculum). Carleton had opened with only a preparatory department (not unusual) in 1868; 1870–1871 was its first year as a college. The Princeton courses were senior electives.

30. White in Rudolph, *Curriculum,* 125. On "utility" and "liberal culture" as competing paradigms for reforming higher education in the nineteenth-century United States, see Laurence R. Veysey, *The Emergence of the American University* (Chicago, 1965), Chaps. 2 and 4, and, for a somewhat different take on this conflict, see Turner and Bernard, "'German Model' and Graduate School," 71–72.

31. Andrew Dickson White's influential successor as professor of history at Michigan, Charles Kendall Adams (who taught perhaps the first American seminar in the subject), took the lead in organizing in 1881 a School of Political Science at the university, which included history. Turner and Bernard, "'German Model' and Graduate School," 81.

32. Trinity College divided instruction in the two subjects only in 1887. Chaffin, *Trinity College, 1839–1892,* 411.

33. Marsh was a student of Charles Eliot Norton and seems pretty faithfully to have echoed Norton's integrative approach to the teaching of art and literature against the background of intellectual, cultural, and social history. Graduating from Harvard College in 1883, he took over Norton's lecture course on ancient art during the latter's 1884–1885 sabbatical, then went to Kansas University as Professor of English and Belles-Lettres, 1886–1889. After studying in Europe on a Harvard fellowship in 1889–1891, he returned to Harvard as assistant professor of comparative literature. Though a popular teacher and promoted professor in 1898, he seems to have proved unsuccessful (or perhaps merely unfashionable) as a scholar and was unhappy enough at Harvard to resign from the university in 1899 to enter the cotton business, briefly in Texas, then as a broker in New York until his death in 1937. See Marsh's correspondence with Norton in NP; *Harvard University Quinquennial Catalog; Harvard Bulletin,* June 1, 1910; obituary in *New York Times,* September 17, 1937; material in biographical files, HUA; and Robert Morss Lovett, *All Our Years: The Autobiography of Robert Morss Lovett* (New York, 1948), 45, 47–48.

34. Earlier new curricula, such as the "scientific courses" that appeared after 1820, were erected as parallel programs to the "classical course"; they competed with it but did not threaten its integrity, such as that was. The real crumbling of the Greco-Latin-based curriculum itself began to become obvious with Eliot's inauguration at Harvard in 1869. Even marginal institutions had largely junked it by early in the new century, though for several years thereafter many colleges continued totemically to require a year or two of Greek or Latin for the B.A. degree. A revealing case is that of the Polytechnic College of the Methodist Epis-

copal Church, South, founded in Fort Worth in 1891. It began with a self-consciously traditional course, comprised completely of required studies and freighted with Greek and Latin (though already polluted with English literature); by 1905 the B.A. still required ancient languages, but students chose from many electives, including a wide selection of courses in history, sociology, economics, and psychology. Compare *Polytechnic College,* 1891–1892, 12–14, with *Polytechnic College,* 1904–1905, 11–20. Similarly, another small Texas school, Austin College, retained in 1878–1879 a fully required curriculum that, excepting the addition of history and English literature, closely resembled Princeton's in the 1830s. But by 1910 a B.A. degree required only two years of *either* Greek or Latin, and juniors and seniors chose courses from a varied menu of electives. Compare *Catalogue of Austin College,* 1878–1879, 9–11, with 1909–1910, 30–31.

35. Most colleges evolved without a clear rationale, gradually tacking new electives onto old required curricula, while simultaneously shifting old requirements into the elective column. This made for interesting flux even at the level of how curricula were presented in catalog tables. For a revealing cluster of cases, compare the catalogs of Princeton, Franklin and Marshall, and the University of North Carolina between 1870 and 1900 with those of Harvard (with its principled elective system) in the same period.

36. Charles Eliot Norton to C. W. Eliot, January 15, 1874 [copy], bMS Am 1826 [389], Houghton. Though addressed to Eliot, this letter seems to have been meant for the Harvard Corporation's eyes. Norton shared Eliot's enthusiasm for the elective system but, unlike his cousin, awaited the subsidence of educational flux and the emergence then of a cogent alternative to the old curriculum.

CHAPTER FIVE
THE BOON AND BANE OF SPECIALIZATION

1. *A Turning Point in Higher Education: The Inaugural Address of Charles William Eliot as President of Harvard College, October 19, 1869* (Cambridge, Mass., 1969), 21; Louise Stevenson, *Scholarly Means to Evangelical Means: The New Haven Scholars and the Transformation of Higher Learning in America, 1830–1890* (Baltimore, 1986); Stephen G. Alter, "William Dwight Whitney and the Science of Language," Ph.D. diss., University of Michigan, 1993. (Whitney himself was not an evangelical Christian.) It might be added that Ticknor's brother-in-law Andrews Norton began the first major American work of biblical criticism, his *Genuineness of the Gospels,* as a Harvard professor a few years earlier.

2. On conceptions of scholarship in Ticknor's milieu, see the early chapters of James Turner, *The Liberal Education of Charles Eliot Norton* (Baltimore, 1999); on Henry's conceptions of science, see Nathan Reingold, "Theorists and Ingenious Mechanics: Joseph Henry Defines Science," in Reingold, *Science American Style* (New Brunswick, N.J., 1991), 127–155, and Henry's own 1850 presidential address to the American Association for the Advancement of Science, first printed in *A Scientist in American Life: Essays and Lectures of Joseph Henry,* ed. Arthur P. Molella et al. (Washington, D.C., 1980), 35–50.

3. The most famous expression of this ideal was the "Yale Report" of 1828, commonly treated by historians as the work of Jeremiah Day but, as Caroline Winterer has pointed out, actually bearing the stronger mark of its coauthor, the classicist James L. Kingsley. Winterer, "Classics and Culture," 33–46.

4. Eliphalet Nott's "scientific course" at Union College in the 1820s and the founding of what became the Sheffield School at Yale twenty years later were perhaps the most widely noticed of many such efforts to develop degree programs that paid more attention to modern languages, history, natural science, and mathematics.

5. Winterer, "Classics and Culture," chapter 3; Turner and Bernard, "'German Model' and Graduate School," 73–77. Professional schools for law and medicine had existed in the United States since the late eighteenth century, with seminaries for training ministers making their appearance early in the nineteenth. These three areas—law, medicine, and theology—comprised three of the four traditional faculties of European universities. Some early proponents of graduate study in arts and sciences saw it as corresponding to the fourth traditional school, the faculty of philosophy. Probably Michigan's president Henry P. Tappan did; see his *A Discourse . . . on the Occasion of His Inauguration as Chancellor of the University of Michigan, December 21st, 1852* (Detroit, 1852). Others hoped to raise the undergraduate college to that dignity. Charles William Eliot certainly did. See *Turning Point,* 6–7.

6. See Robert A. McCaughey, *Josiah Quincy, 1772–1864: The Last Federalist* (Cambridge, Mass., 1974), 170–178; [Josiah Quincy], *Notice to Parents and Guardians in Relation to Elective System,* April 15, 1843, in Josiah Quincy Papers, HUA, and the printed Harvard College catalogs for 1843–1844 through 1846–1847.

7. Eliot, *Turning Point.* Quotations from pp. 1, 3, 9. Eliot assumed that, given the freedom to do so, students would concentrate on "the one subject which each may select as his principal occupation in life." This proved an astonishing overestimate of the maturity of the Harvard undergraduate of Eliot's day—astonishing because Eliot had spent four years as a Harvard undergraduate and then had taught the species as an assistant professor. Possibly only a Boston Unitarian could have indulged such optimism about the rationality and consistency of human nature.

8. On its origins see Amos Funkenstein, *Theology and the Scientific Imagination from the Middle Ages to the Seventeenth Century* (Princeton, 1986). This is not to deny that earlier thinkers believed knowledge to comprise a single whole, only to say that the intellectual presuppositions of the Aristotelian tradition and hence of Scholasticism were different and more qualified on this question. See Funkenstein, 6, 136, 142.

9. Douglas Sloan, *The Scottish Enlightenment and the American College Ideal* (New York, 1971); D. H. Meyer, *The Instructed Conscience: The Shaping of the American National Ethic* (Philadelphia, 1972); Daniel Walker Howe, *The Unitarian Conscience: Harvard Moral Philosophy, 1805–1861* (Cambridge, Mass., 1970); Mark A. Noll, *Princeton and the Republic, 1768–1822: The Search for a Christian Enlightenment in the Era of Samuel Stanhope Smith*

(Princeton, 1989); and a penetrating essay by Allen C. Guelzo in *Evangelicals and Science in Historical Perspective*, ed. David N. Livingstone, D. G. Hart, and Mark A. Noll (New York, 1999). In America the course was first fully developed at Princeton. Noll, *Princeton and the Republic*, 36–47.

10. G. Stanley Hall, *Life and Confessions of a Psychologist* (New York, 1923), 168.

11. Turner, *Norton*, passim, and more succinctly Turner, "Charles Eliot Norton," in *A Companion to American Thought*, ed. Richard Wightman Fox and James T. Kloppenberg (Oxford, 1995), 499–500; Stephen G. Alter, *Darwinism and the Linguistic Image: Language, Race, and Natural Theology in the Nineteenth Century* (Baltimore, 1999).

12. *Oxford English Dictionary*, s.v. *discipline*.

13. In the exceptional case, of course, a scholar could achieve competence in distinct disciplines by training in them. Child-Norton correspondence in NP; G[eorge]. L[yman]. Kittredge, "Francis James Child" [1898], in Child, ed., *The English and Scottish Popular Ballads*, 5 vols. (1882–1898; reprint, New York, 1956); Jo McMurtry, *English Language, English Literature: The Creation of an Academic Discipline* (Hamden, Conn., 1985). Technically, Child's Göttingen degree was an honorary one, but he had studied at the university a few years earlier, and the degree was awarded for scholarly achievement, so it was in a real sense "earned."

14. A suggestive isomorphism links disciplinary specialization with the late-twentieth-century idea that every social group's or community's knowledge is distinct from every other's and can be neither fully understood nor judged by outsiders. On the nineteenth-century retreat from the idea of a universal human nature, see Isaiah Berlin, "European Unity and Its Vicissitudes," in his *The Crooked Timber of Humanity* (New York, 1991), 175–179. Admittedly, not every academic study transformed itself into a proper discipline—classics is, so to say, the classical exception—while some made a pretty poor showing in their efforts; history's pretensions in this direction have always been embarrassingly feeble.

15. Horace Williams, Philosophy lectures (1898–1899, manuscript notes by F. W. Coker, Southern Historical Collection, Manuscripts Division, Wilson Library, University of North Carolina–Chapel Hill), September 23, 1898. (The Southern Historical Collection is hereafter cited as SHC.) This use of idealism was already authoritatively evident by 1871 in Noah Porter's *Elements of Intellectual Science*; see Herbert W. Schneider, *A History of American Philosophy* (New York, 1946), 444–445, and, for the phenomenon more generally, Part VII. Porter became president of Yale in the same year he published *Intellectual Science* and was, with McCosh of Princeton, the most prominent voice in the conservative wing of the university movement in the United States.

16. This affected the natural sciences and "hard" social sciences most powerfully but transformed academic knowledge generally. For an instance of the power of disciplinarity—even in methodologically less rigorous fields—see the symposium on Martin Jay's *Downcast Eyes: The Denigration of Vision in Twentieth-Century French Thought* (1993) in *Comparative Studies in Society*

*and History* 38 (1996): 370–394. Scholars from history, anthropology, art history, and sociology fumble over each other trying to get at the essence of Jay's book; if not otherwise informed, the naive reader would conclude that they were talking about entirely different books. Jay himself notes at the end (394) "the extent to which disciplinary prisms still refract the ways in which we read scholarship from other fields." This phenomenon seems "natural" to scholars now, but reading, say, the book reviews by established scholars from different fields in the *North American Review* in the 1860s shows how novel in fact it is.

17. Gilman quoted in Hawkins, *Pioneer,* 40 (after Hawkins has noted that Gilman "listed specialization first" in his hiring criteria); Charles W. Bain to Committee on Promotions, University of North Carolina, April 7, 1913, Charles W. Bain Papers, SHC; [University of Michigan] *University Record* 2 (1892): 79.

18. *Catalogue of North Texas Female College,* 1898–1899, 3; *Polytechnic College,* 1892–1893, 32.

19. William T. Harris, "The Use of Higher Education," *Educational Review* 16 (September 1898): 153–154, 161, quoted in John Higham, "The Matrix of Specialization," in *The Organization of Knowledge in Modern America, 1860–1920,* ed. Alexandra Oleson and John Voss (Baltimore, 1979), 6–7.

20. James McCosh, *The New Departure in College Education* (New York, 1885), quoted in Wertenbaker, *Princeton,* 306.

21. W. Bruce Leslie, *Gentlemen and Scholars: College and Community in the "Age of the University," 1865–1917* (University Park, Pa., 1992); Bliss Perry, *The Amateur Spirit* (1904), quoted in Graff and Warner, *Origins of Literary Studies,* 106. In 1904 Perry was editor of the *Atlantic Monthly,* but he had earlier studied philology in Germany and taught English at Williams and Princeton. In 1909 he returned to teaching, at Harvard.

22. J. David Hoeveler, Jr., *James McCosh and the Scottish Intellectual Tradition: From Glasgow to Princeton* (Princeton, 1981).

23. "General Introduction" to Adam Smith, *An Inquiry into the Nature and Causes of the Wealth of Nations,* ed. R. H. Campbell and A. S. Skinner, 2 vols., Glasgow Edition of the Works and Correspondence of Adam Smith (Oxford, 1976), 1: 4; Henry P. Tappan, *The University; Its Constitution: A Discourse Delivered June 22, 1858* (to the University of Michigan's Christian Library Association) (Ann Arbor, 1858), 17.

24. A. Hunter Dupree, *Asa Gray, 1810–1888* (Cambridge, Mass., 1959); Joseph Henry to Henry James, Sr., August 22, 1843, quoted in Paul Jerome Croce, *Eclipse of Certainty* (Vol. 1 of *Science and Religion in the Era of William James*; Chapel Hill, 1995), 64.

25. *Why* moral philosophy expired needs fuller explanation. Part of the reason must lie in the diminishing persuasiveness of the Scottish Common Sense realism that informed it (a development itself only partly understood). But this is hardly the whole story. There is no reason why philosophers could not have rebuilt a similar "integrating" course on, say, an idealist epistemological basis. More to the point, probably, are the reeling of natural theology from the aftershocks of Darwinism, which left no widely persuasive *system* for unifying

knowledge, and the growth in prestige of academic specialization, which sapped the widespread urge to do so.

26. Carl Diehl, *Americans and German Scholarship, 1770–1870* (New Haven, 1978); Turner, *Without God*, esp. Chap. 6 and Epilogue; Jon H. Roberts, *Darwinism and the Divine in America: Protestant Intellectuals and Organic Evolution, 1859–1900* (Madison, Wis., 1988); Croce, *Eclipse of Certainty*. It does not follow that agnostics were necessarily inclined to disciplinary specialization; Charles Norton was one.

27. Henry P. Tappan, *The University; Its Constitution: A Discourse Delivered June 22, 1858* (to the University of Michigan's Christian Library Association) (Ann Arbor, 1858), 17.

28. The generally Protestant character of almost all the leading universities in the latter half of the nineteenth century is abundantly clear in Marsden, *Soul of the American University*, Part II. If one were to survey all colleges and universities, Protestant and specifically evangelical hegemony would become overwhelming. State universities enjoyed perhaps even less leeway than a Princeton or Yale, since they answered to electorates deeply suspicious even of Catholics, much more of outright unbelievers.

29. A chair of "Biblical Instruction" was endowed at Princeton as early as 1866 and assigned to the president, though not until two years later does actual instruction appear in the catalog. (*Catalogue of the College of New Jersey, 1866–1867*, 4, and *1868–1869*, 26.) A tsunami of such courses began to surge in the 1880s. In 1888, for instance, Austin College in Texas decided to introduce a Bible course, later bragging that it "was one of the first in the West" to do so. (*Catalogue of Austin College, 1888–1889*, 12, and *1903–1904*, 11.) This claim was a Texan stretch: Carleton College, another western school, began requiring weekly "Bible-Study" seven years earlier, and by 1902 Carleton offered nine courses on the Bible (though by then students could, if assiduously single-minded in scheduling, elect out of Bible entirely). *Catalogue of Carleton College, 1881–1882*, 24, and *1902–1903*, 29–32, 34–35. Marsden, *Soul of the American University*, notes (p. 209) that Bible study courses became "a national trend during the 1890s" but (pp. 243–244) that this proved ambiguous for "Christianity in universities" since the Bible was frequently studied "scientifically" rather than as a source of religious truth.

There is an exception to the generalization about the novelty of distinct courses teaching Christianity in the later nineteenth century: a common, though not universal, antebellum course on "evidences of Christianity." This, however, was taught in the tradition of Paleyite natural theology and belonged to the moral-philosophical effort to unify all knowledge within a Christian framework, in contrast to the later courses that treated Christianity as, as it were, a distinct discipline. Colleges had earlier not neglected more specifically catechetical instruction but associated this with required Sunday religious services rather than with liberal arts classroom instruction. See, for example, *Annual Catalogue of Franklin and Marshall College and the Theological Seminary, Lancaster, Pa., 1879–1880* (Lancaster, 1880), 17.

30. Thomas Fitz-Hugh, *The Philosophy of the Humanities* (Chicago, 1897),

52. Now and then the rhetoric of specialization mixed incongruously with its antithesis; at Amherst the "laboratory method" was used "to get at the spirit of literature"! John F. Genung, "English at Amherst College," in Payne, ed., *English in American Universities,* 114.

CHAPTER SIX
TWO IDEALS OF KNOWLEDGE

1. Kimball, *Orators and Philosophers,* lucidly traces the competition between these two educational paradigms from antiquity to the North American present. His work contains much of direct relevance to the following paragraphs. But because the overriding concern in the book at hand is with the structure of academic knowledge (including research as well as instruction) rather than with pedagogy, the focus here falls on the different paradigms of *knowledge* that lay behind these programs of *education,* though admittedly any such distinction is artificial and cannot avoid much overlap.

2. The "Introduction" to Barbara J. Shapiro, *Probability and Certainty in Seventeenth-Century England: A Study of the Relationships between Natural Science, Religion, History, Law, and Literature* (Princeton, 1983), provides a helpful brief summary of these distinctions.

3. For something of the range of antique philology, see Georges Gusdorf, *Les origines de l'herméneutique* (Paris, 1988), Chap. 1; Robert Lamberton, *Homer the Theologian: Neoplatonist Allegorical Reading and the Growth of the Epic Tradition* (Berkeley and Los Angeles, 1986); Gian Biagio Conti, *Latin Literature: A History,* trans. Joseph B. Solodow, rev. Don Fowler and Glenn W. Most (Baltimore, 1994), 571–584.

4. *De ratione studii* (c. 1511), quoted in Kimball, *Orators and Philosophers,* xiv.

5. On this probabilistic revolution, see Shapiro, *Probability and Certainty;* Ian Hacking, *The Emergence of Probability: A Philosophical Study of Early Ideas about Probability, Induction and Statistical Inference* (Cambridge, 1975). The closest thing to a *locus classicus* is Locke's *Essay concerning Human Understanding.*

6. For instance, "comparative philology" and "linguistic science" sought general laws governing change in language, almost as if aping astronomy. In contrast, the methods of pre-Darwinian natural history resembled the work of classification and comparison typical of textual philologists far more closely than they did the law-seeking physical researches of Joseph Henry and Michael Faraday. Even the evolutionary schema of Darwin bore a similarity, exploited by Darwin and his disciples, to the historical "evolution" of textual variants as laid out in philology. Alter, *Darwinism and the Linguistic Image.*

7. The concept of scientific "law" itself underwent radical transformation, but this complication does not affect our concerns here.

8. Indeed, a sharpened perception of the cultural distinctness (as we would say) of the ancient world from the medieval was a precondition for the rebirth of philology in the Renaissance. *Culture* is used anachronistically here owing to the lack of any other brief term to signify the entire complex of beliefs, attitudes,

and practices that characterize a society, and to use the Victorian synonym *civilization* would mislead today's readers.

9. E. Harris Harbison, *The Christian Scholar in the Age of the Reformation* (New York, 1956), 92.

10. Dexter Lectures, Andrews Norton Papers, Houghton, especially Lectures 5 and 10; Andrews Norton, *Inaugural Discourse on the Extent and Relations of Theology* (1819), reprinted in Norton, *Tracts Concerning Christianity* (Cambridge, Mass., 1852), esp. 69–70. Most of this paragraph derives from James Turner, "Religion et langage dans l'Amerique du XIXème siècle: Le cas étrange de Andrews Norton," *Revue de l'histoire des religions* 210 (1993): 431–62.

11. Funkenstein, *Theology and the Scientific Imagination,* 11; Maurice Mandelbaum, "Historicism," *The Encyclopedia of Philosophy,* ed. Paul Edwards (New York, 1967) 4: 22 (Mandelbaum restating Ernst Troeltsch's definition). For a brief and helpful recent introduction to philological historicism (not his term) in the eighteenth and nineteenth centuries, see Paul Hamilton, *Historicism* (London, 1996), Chaps. 2–3. The classic work is Friedrich Meinecke, *Die Entstehung des Historismus,* 2 vols. (Munich and Berlin, 1936), English trans. J. E. Anderson (London, 1972).

12. *The New Life of Dante Alighieri* (Boston, 1867); *The Divine Comedy of Dante Alighieri,* 3 vols. (Boston, 1891–1892); "The Text of Donne's Poems," [Harvard] *Studies and Notes in Philology and Literature* 5 (1896): 1–19; *Historical Studies of Church-Building in the Middle Ages: Venice, Siena, Florence* (New York, 1880); "The Dimensions and Proportions of the Temple of Zeus at Olympia," *Proceedings of the American Academy of Arts and Sciences* 13 (1877): 145–70; "The Building of the Church of St.-Denis," *Harper's* 79 (1889): 766–776; "The Building of the Cathedral at Chartres," *Harper's* 79 (1889): 944–955.

13. See the student notes of Norton's courses, taken by several hands over some two decades, in Houghton and HUA. On Felton and the origins of "culture" as an educational program in the United States, see Winterer, "Classics and Culture," Chap. 3.

14. On the broader history of culture in this sense in the Anglo-American world, see Raymond Williams, *Culture and Society, 1780–1950* (New York, 1958), Part I. Despite its patent analogies to *culture* as Norton deployed the term, the German notion of *Bildung* seems to have had vanishingly little influence in the United States in the early years of the humanities. Norton's Boston Unitarian milieu had a closely analogous but indigenous tradition of self-cultivation, explicated in Turner, *Norton,* passim. By the turn of the twentieth century, however, recognizably Humboldtian language had begun to infiltrate; the eminent University of Michigan classicist Francis W. Kelsey, for example, speaks of "self-discovery, self-mastery, and self-direction" as goals of liberal education. Kelsey, "The Present Position of Latin and Greek," in Kelsey, ed., *Latin and Greek in American Education, with Symposia on the Value of Humanistic Studies* (New York, 1911), 17.

15. Norton's pencilled marginal notes on *Reports of the Joint Committee on the Organization of the University* (1907), HUG 1615.75, HUA; Norton, "The

Culture of the Imagination" (1899), t.s., Box 1, Miscellaneous Papers, NP; Norton, "Dante," in Charles Dudley Warner, ed., *Library of the World's Best Literature, Ancient and Modern* (New York, 1897), 4315; Norton, "History of Ancient Art" (1888–1889, manuscript notes by Harry Fletcher Brown, HUA), Vol. 1, Lecture 1. "The true conception of the Department of Fine Arts might be expressed," Norton argued to the Harvard Overseers, "by giving to it the name of the Department of Poetry,—using the word 'poetry' in its widest sense as including all works of the creative or poetic imagination." [Norton], *Report of the Committee on the Fine Arts,* bound in *Reports of Visiting Committees of the Board of Overseers of Harvard College, I to CIX,* HUA.

16. This presumably explains the family resemblance to Wilhelm von Humboldt's ideal of *Bildung. Bildung,* after all, emerged from a culture in which philology was the great model of erudition.

17. Notes by George McK. Bain of an unidentified course in Greek literature (manuscript notebook dated May 1881, Charles W. Bain Papers, SHC), 2; [William Cowper Prime and George B. McClellan], *Suggestions on the Establishment of a Department of Art Instruction in the College of New Jersey* (Trenton, N.J., 1882), 4–5, quoted in Lavin, *Eye of the Tiger,* 10; *Catalogue of the Pennsylvania State College, 1893–94* (State College, Pa., 1894), 19. The Virginia lecturer must have been Thomas Randolph Price, who was the professor of Greek there 1876–1882, for whom see Ward W. Briggs, Jr., ed., *The Letters of Basil Lanneau Gildersleeve* (Baltimore, 1987), 171, n. 4. (The Bain notebook may now be recatalogued, since as of June 1996 the notes were erroneously attributed to George Bain's younger brother Charles, who apparently used the remaining blank pages in 1886 for quite different notes.) And, yes, Prime's coauthor was the Civil War general.

18. Thomas G. Apple, "Philosophy of History" (n.d. [c. 1887], manuscript notes by C. Nevin Keller, Franklin and Marshall College Archives [hereafter cited as FMA]), 80–81; cf. John W. Nevin, "Lectures on Aesthetics" (1869, manuscript notes by Nevin M. Wanner, FMA), 119; *University of North Carolina Catalogue, 1893–1894,* 53; *The Pennsylvania State College Bulletin: General Catalogue, 1909–1910* (State College, Pa., 1910), 200; Joseph H. Dubbs, "Lectures on Ancient History" (1880, manuscript notes by unknown student, FMA), 1; Albert S. Cook, "The Province of English Philology," *PMLA* (1898), quoted in Graff and Warner, *Origins of Literary Studies,* 99. In the quotation from the Penn State catalog, "the sciences" is meant in the older sense of science as any body of organized knowledge.

19. *Catalogue of Carleton College, 1912–1913,* 50. "Textual philology" is specified because comparative or Indo-European philology retained an aura of "advanced" knowledge at the beginning of the twentieth century. Cf. John S. Stahr's comments on F. Max Müller and William D. Whitney in his "Lectures on Aesthetics" (c. 1910, manuscript notes by W. E. Weisgerber, FMA), 29—though citing Max Müller and Whitney also shows Stahr's distance from truly current scholarship.

20. On moral philosophy at Harvard in Norton's student days, see Howe, *Unitarian Conscience.* As a student Norton had also seen the early shadows,

though not grasped the implications, of the later collapse of integrated knowledge, during the brief experiment in broadening electives under President Josiah Quincy—an experiment squelched by Quincy's successor Edward Everett.

21. William Gardner Hale, *Aims and Methods in Classical Study* (Boston, 1887), 18; Norton to Leslie Stephen, December 20–23, 1897, Berg Collection, New York Public Library.

22. Hume, "Outlines of Lectures Delivered to the Post-Graduate Class in Literature [at Norfolk College]" (manuscript 1883–1884, Thomas Hume Papers, SHC), 6–13; "Notes on [Charles Eliot Norton's] Fine Arts 3: Compiled from Stenographic Reports by W. E. Weaver" (typescript 1898, Nor 5260.12F, Houghton), 2. Norfolk College was a finishing school for young ladies, and "Post-Graduate" should not be taken as meaning graduate education in the sense already current by 1883. Paul Hamilton Hayne was the threnodist of the Confederate South, study of his work being de rigueur on patriotic grounds.

23. Charles W. Shields, Lectures on the history of civilization and the philosophy of history (c. 1877–1878, manuscript notes by William R. Barricklo, Mudd), "Lecture I" and "Lecture II." The idea of a coherent European civilization is a product of the era of European expansion and imperialism in the obvious sense that one could conceive of "our" civilization only in contrast to others. At the same time, the idea of European civilization was not necessarily dismissive of others; Norton, for instance, held a low opinion of India's civilization but a high one of Japan's. Shields, rather confusingly, deployed alongside Guizot this newer concept of a specifically European civilization, whose superiority he took pains to stress.

24. Thomas Fitz-Hugh treated the relevant civilization specifically as Aryan in his *Philosophy of the Humanities,* 9. It is only fair to add, however, that the term *Aryan* had not taken on its Nazi connotations and could be used in a fairly neutral, descriptive way, which Fitz-Hugh did, though taking a Eurocentric attitude, if not implicitly assuming the superiority of Europe.

25. His actual phrase was "the sum of the acquisitions,—whatever they may be, moral, material—of a race at a given time." "Fine Arts 3: Compiled by Weaver," 12. The more neutral *people* is much closer to his meaning than either the late-twentieth-century meaning of *race* or the understanding by late-twentieth-century historians of the Victorian uses of *race.*

26. Norton explicitly distinguished "our civilization from the civilization of the Middle Ages." "Fine Arts 3: Compiled by Weaver," 12.

27. R. H. Dabney to Kemp P. Battle, August 23, 1891, in Battle Family Papers, SHC; "Fine Arts 3: Compiled by Weaver," 46–47; Norton, "The Work of the Archaeological Institute of America," *American Journal of Archaeology,* 2nd ser., 4 (January–March): 12.

28. Norton, "Dante. Lecture I" (typescript [1894?]), Box 13, Miscellaneous Papers, NP; Norton, "Fine Arts 3" (1892–1893, manuscript notes by George R. Noyes, HUA), Vol. 2, February 23, 1893; Norton, "Work of the Archaeological Institute," 15. Norton, for one, could specify improvements of the present over the past, chiefly material, and he did retain faith in a "very slow & irregular" rise "in the general morality of the race." Norton to Goldwin Smith, June 14,

1897, NP. But he was too chastened a moralist to voice any simple belief in progress.

The continuities between this project and twentieth-century courses in "Western civilization" would seem hardly to need mentioning; the actual term *Western civilization* was being used unselfconsciously by 1890. William M. Sloane, history lectures (c. 1890, unpaginated manuscript notes by W. S. Conant, Mudd), section on Crusades; Sloane said that the Crusades presaged "the unity of Western civilization." Yet Columbia's celebrated "Contemporary Civilization" course, in the wake of World War I, is commonly taken to be the first curricular appearance of "Western Civ." Peter Novick, *That Noble Dream: The "Objectivity Question" and the American Historical Profession* (Cambridge, 1988), 312, exemplifies the conventional view. If by "Western civilization course" is meant a course that explicitly uses the word *civilization* in its title and that runs from antiquity to the present, then the conventional view is right, though hardly to the point.

29. Norton, "Work of the Archaeological Institute," 8. Because of its purpose as a tool of culture, "civilization" required a list of "great books" for students to read. Victorian conventional wisdom already placed Homer, Dante, and Shakespeare above all others as repaying the student's attention. The canon as it descends to us, it scarcely needs saying, is not composed of some timeless crême de la crême, but of writers whose reputations happened to be at their highest in the later nineteenth century, when "liberal culture" was conceived. This truism should not be taken bizarrely to mean that canonical texts have no enduring qualities setting them apart, as if it were accident that the Victorians preferred Shakespeare to Tourneur or Dante to Cavalcanti.

30. Fitz-Hugh, *Philosophy of the Humanities,* 39–40: the student "will be present at the organization of society, and watch the growth of institutions. He will behold the birth of art and realize its function in culture. He will understand the beginnings of philosophy and see the separate sciences leap Minerva-like from its brow. He will incarnate the pure spirit of humanity in the highest sense of the '*Homo sum, humani nil a me alienum puto!*'" Fitz-Hugh was professor of Latin at the University of Texas. Curiously, Greece or Rome seemed to work especially well.

31. There is no systematic study; this comment is based on the catalogs read for this book.

32. Paul Shorey, "The Case for the Classics," in Kelsey, ed., *Latin and Greek in American Education,* 334n; Fitz-Hugh, *Philosophy of the Humanities,* 40. Again, we do not mean to suggest that the old idea of mental discipline as an end of college education disappeared; it was often cited as a subsidiary value of the humanities, especially language study.

33. Rev. James W. Strong, 1894, quoted in Leal A. Headley and Merrill E. Jarchow, *Carleton: The First Century* (Northfield, Minn., 1966), 9; *Polytechnic College,* 1898–1899, 21–22.

34. Gilman, *The Launching of a University* (1906), 239, quoted in Veysey, *Emergence of the University,* 181.

35. Harris, "Use of Higher Education," 153–154, 161.

CHAPTER SEVEN
FOR AND AGAINST SECULARIZATION

1. See additionally, for broader overview, Turner, *Without God,* Chaps. 2–3.

2. James B. Angell, "Lessons Suggested by Christ's Life to the Scholar," baccalaureate address, June 14, 1903, Angell Papers, Michigan Historical Collections, Bentley Library, University of Michigan. Cf. Marsden, *Soul of the American University,* esp. Chaps. 6, 10.

3. This paragraph and the next draw on James Turner, "Secularization and Sacralization: Some Speculations on the Origins of the Secular Humanities Curriculum, 1850–1900," in *The Secularization of the Academy,* ed. George M. Marsden and Bradley J. Longfield (New York, 1992), 81–82.

4. See the rather astonishing range of courses offered in 1886–1887 by Michigan's two philosophy professors, G. S. Morris and John Dewey: history of philosophy, logic, political philosophy, aesthetics, ethics, and metaphysics, as well as courses on individual philosophers from Plato to Herbert Spencer. *Calendar of the University of Michigan for 1886–87* (Ann Arbor, 1887), 51–52. ("Speculative philosophy" is assumed to be metaphysics.)

5. Veysey, *Emergence of the University,* 183, notes that "systematic idealism (which in educational terms allied itself to liberal culture) made major headway among American philosophers" in the 1880s. David Hollinger (personal communication [and cf. Schneider, *American Philosophy,* 444–445]) lists among college teachers of philosophy in this camp George T. Ladd of Yale, Charles E. Garman of Amherst, George H. Howison of Berkeley, Jacob G. Schurman and James E. Creighton of Cornell, George S. Morris and Robert M. Wenley of Michigan, and George H. Palmer and Josiah Royce of Harvard—to which group one should add Horace Williams of North Carolina.

6. On Garman, see Thomas Le Duc, *Piety and Intellect at Amherst College, 1865–1912* (New York, 1946), Chap. 8; George E. Peterson, *The New England College in the Age of the University* (Amherst, 1964), 134–136, 172–174; Cornelius Howard Patton and Walter Taylor Field, *Eight O'Clock Chapel: A Study of New England College Life in the Eighties* (Boston, 1927), 160–166. On Palmer, see Bruce Kuklick, *The Rise of American Philosophy: Cambridge, Massachusetts, 1860–1930* (New Haven, 1977), Chap. 12. On Williams, see Jane Ross Hammer, "Williams, Henry Horace," in *Dictionary of North Carolina Biography,* ed. William S. Powell (Chapel Hill, 1979–1996).

7. It is not positive that Williams intended to enter the ministry—no direct evidence of his early career plans seems to survive—but he did study principally theology at Yale (see his lecture notes from those years, in Henry Horace Williams Papers, SHC), and he took a B.D. there in 1888; his choices are otherwise puzzling. Unless otherwise noted, all biographical information about Williams is from Hammer, "Williams."

That quite a few American philosophers of this period were ministers or ministers manqué is important in understanding the link between philosophy and religious concerns. This claim rests on nothing more systematic than impressions from biographical accounts. But such a suspicion gains confidence from the closest thing to a prosopography: the collation by Bruce Kuklick of reasons given by Harvard Ph.D. candidates for undertaking graduate study in philosophy. In 1907–1911 almost two-thirds mentioned religious problems or doubts. The proportion was still over half in 1912–1916. Kuklick, *Rise of American Philosophy*, 464–465. There seems no reason why such concerns should have been less prominent in the late nineteenth century; if anything, the reverse. Allan Marquand, who became the first art historical scholar at Princeton, carried this career progression one step further: from ministerial studies, to a philosophy Ph.D. and teaching in the field, and *then* to art history. Lavin, *The Eye of the Tiger*, 8–10.

8. Although his Yale thesis (Williams Papers, Vol. 11) was on the Epistle to the Hebrews, Williams also produced at Yale a long "reproduction" of Hegel's philosophy of religion (Williams Papers, Vols. 9–10).

9. Williams's notes of Professor [Charles Carroll] Everett, "Theology," n.d., and Williams, Philosophy lectures (1898–1899, notes by Coker), September 14, 1898, Williams Papers. Another notebook from the years at Yale and Harvard (Williams Papers, Vol. 12) has detailed notes on Hindu religion. Strictly speaking, from 1890–1895 Williams held the old title of professor of mental and moral science, which in 1895 was modernized to professor of philosophy.

10. Williams, philosophy lectures, November 7, 1898, and February 20 and April 7, 1899.

11. Hammer, "Williams." Williams, philosophy lectures, April 17: "Christian dogmatism comes from Plato & Socrates, not from Christ. Dogmatism has no legitimate place in Christianity. Dogmatism is where you attempt to control my life by your theory."

12. Le Duc, *Piety and Intellect*, Chap. 8; letter from Garman to G. Stanley Hall, detailing the aims of his course, quoted in Patton and Field, *Eight O'Clock Chapel*, 162–163; words from memorial tablet to Garman in Amherst chapel, quoted in ibid., 166; George Herbert Palmer (another of the great idealist professors), quoted in Peterson, *New England College*, 173.

13. Fitz-Hugh, *Philosophy of the Humanities*, 55, 60–61; Edward C. Armstrong, "The Place of Modern Languages in American Education," in *The Languages in American Education: From the Proceedings of the Michigan Schoolmasters' Club and Classical Conference Held at Ann Arbor, Michigan, March 30, 1911*, Humanistic Papers, 2nd ser., No. 1, rep. from *School Review*, October–December 1911 (n.p., n.d.), 7.

14. *President's Report 1889–90*, Carleton College Archives.

15. Hiram Corson, *The Aims of Literary Study* (New York, 1901), 13.

16. Hiram Corson, "English at Cornell University," in Payne, ed, *English in American Universities*, 60–61; Fitz-Hugh, *Philosophy of the Humanities*, 22; "Fine Arts 3: Compiled by Weaver," 48.

17. Mark DeWolfe Howe and Charles Francis Adams, "Memoir of Charles Eliot Norton," *Proceedings of the Massachusetts Historical Society*, 3rd ser., 48 (1914): 66; Ellery Sedgwick, *The Happy Profession* (Boston, 1946), 71; William R. Thayer in Charles Downer Hazen, ed., *The Letters of William Roscoe Thayer* (Boston, 1926), 40; "Fine Arts 3: Compiled by Weaver," 1; Norton, "Work of

the Archaeological Institute," 8. Worry about materialism was not confined to North America. Iván Jaksic notes the insistent stress by the Uruguayan writer José Enrique Rodó in the almost cultishly influential *Ariel* (1900) on the need for (similarly vague) "spirituality," which Rodó set specifically against the technological materialism of modern democracy. Jaksic, "The Machine and the Spirit: Anti-Technological Humanism in Twentieth-Century Latin America," *Revista de Estudios Hispánicos* 30 (1996): 185–187. As Jaksic's work suggests, the international dimensions of this phenomenon merit serious investigation, and simply to categorize such impulses as "antimodern" is to (dis)miss their significance.

18. Lowell, "Address." Cf. his "Dante" and "Spenser," in *Literary Essays,* Riverside Edition of the Writings of James Russell Lowell, Vol. 4 (Boston, 1897). Some matter in the next few paragraphs is borrowed from Turner, "Secularization and Sacralization," 85.

19. Martin W. Sampson, "English at the University of Indiana," in Payne, ed., *English in American Universities,* 97–98; Arthur R. Marsh to Charles Eliot Norton, December 26, 1889, and November 27, 1888, NP; [Dwight C. Miner, ed.], *A History of Columbia College on Morningside* (New York, 1954), 25; Pierson, *Yale College,* 298. Woodberry was, like Marsh, Norton's student. For a typical "compendium," see James O. Murray, *Notes on English Literature: From Lectures Given by James O. Murray, D.D., Holmes Professor of English Literature in Princeton College* (Princeton; privately printed, 1882), copy in Mudd.

20. Quoted in Ian Ker, *John Henry Newman: A Biography* (Oxford, 1988), 574.

21. *Catalogue of Marshall College,* 1850–1851, 24.

22. Andrews Norton, 1823, quoted in Howe, *Unitarian Conscience,* 190; Lyman H. Atwater, moral philosophy lectures (1858, manuscript notes by George W. Ketcham, Mudd), 156; Kelsey, "Present Position of Latin and Greek," 37.

23. John W. Nevin, "Lectures on Aesthetics" (1869, manuscript notes by Joseph A. Reed, FMA), 58; T[homas]. G. Apple, "Lectures on Aesthetics" (c. 1880, manuscript notes by unknown hand, FMA), 1–2; John W. Nevin, "Lectures on Aesthetics" (1869, manuscript notes by Nevin M. Wanner, FMA), 121–123.

24. John Nevin, for example, derived a similar doctrine principally from German idealism.

25. Lyman H. Atwater, Metaphysics lectures (1875, manuscript notes by Charles R. Williams, Mudd). Cf. Atwater, Moral philosophy lectures (1858), 153–156.

26. Hiram Corson, *The University of the Future* (1875), 11, quoted in Veysey, *Emergence of the University,* 200; Thomas Hume, "Shakspeare as a Moral Teacher," *Journal of the Shakspeare Club of the University of North Carolina* (1886–1887), 12 (no volume number). Hume also warned that in *disordered* imagination conscience also finds "its deadliest enemy. There is danger in following it even through Shakspeare's magic realm."

27. Hume, "Lectures Delivered to the Post-Graduate Class," 73, 96.

28. Nevin, "Aesthetics" (notes by Reed), 74 (a Raphael Madonna being the case at hand); Kelsey, "Present Position of Latin and Greek," 36–38 (internal quotation from the geologist Archibald Geikie). It hardly needs saying that "the best which has been thought and said in the world" comes from the Preface to Matthew Arnold's *Culture and Anarchy* (1869) (p. 6 in the 1932 Cambridge University Press reprint).

29. *Catalogue of Pennsylvania State College,* 1893–1894, 19; Vernon L. Parrington, letter to the Regents of the University of Oklahoma [1908], quoted in John L. Thomas, review of H. Lark Hall, *V. L. Parrington: Through the Avenue of Art,* in *William and Mary Quarterly,* 3rd ser., 53 (1996): 424; James W. Strong, 1894, quoted in Headley and Jarchow, *Carleton,* p. 9.

30. Overseers' Records, April 14, April 28, and May 5, 1875, HUA; C. W. Eliot to Norton, May 5, 1875, in Box 16, Miscellaneous Papers, NP; Norton to John Simon, May 15, 1875, NP; *The Christian,* November 1908 (clipping in NP, Box 6).

31. Patton and Field, *Eight O'Clock Chapel,* 227.

32. Patton and Field, *Eight O'Clock Chapel,* 20. The quoted words are actually President Eliot's, as given by Patton and Field.

33. See, for example, Stahr, "Lectures on Aesthetics," 7, where the Incarnation becomes "the pivot on which all history turns"—an utterly orthodox Augustinian position (in this case given a Hegelian gloss) utterly at odds with the historicism that Stahr was trying to assimilate.

34. One observes an analogous tendency among Catholic college leaders in the early twentieth century to regard their own curricula, centered on classical language (the first, humanistic level of the Jesuit *Ratio Studiorum* apparently being the ideal type), as somehow achieving "an almost perfect synthesis of religious and educational values," when in fact the basic course of studies was just as compatible with a pagan world (whence it ultimately originated) as with Catholicism. Philip Gleason, *Contending with Modernity: Catholic Higher Education in the Twentieth Century* (New York, 1995), 35.

35. William Gardner Hale, "The Practical Value of Humanistic Studies," in *Languages in American Education,* 51.

36. This particular formulation is from Erik Cohen, "Radical Secularization and the Destructuration of the Universe of Knowledge in Late Modernity," *Knowledge and Society: Studies in the Sociology of Culture Past and Present* 7 [1988]: 213.

37. [Andrews Norton], "Character of Rev. Joseph Stevens Buckminster," *General Repository and Review* 1 (1812): 307–308.

38. And at least in principle for its mother, Judaism, and younger sister, Islam, though these do not concern us here.

39. See Turner, *Without God,* Chaps. 2–3, 5.

40. Technically Parker, arriving at Harvard Divinity School after Norton had resigned, was not Norton's student, but he drew on Norton's expertise and personal library and was schooled in the tradition that Norton had established. The quoted words are from the title of Parker's famous or notorious "A Discourse

of the Transient and Permanent in Christianity" (1841), though in 1841 Parker had not yet discarded every Christian particularity.

41. W. L. Garrison, Jr., to Norton, December 30, 1895, NP; Norton to Paul Elmer More, April 25, 1898, Paul Elmer More Papers, Princeton University Library. Veysey, *Emergence of the University,* 204, believes that in "the larger universities, most of the advocates of culture" still accepted "some form of Christianity" but "had divorced themselves from the piety of an earlier day." As agnostics he cites only Norton, George Woodberry, and Irving Babbitt—possibly unaware that the last two were students of the first.

42. William Gardner Hale, *Aims and Methods in Classical Study* (Boston, 1887), 16; *Catalogue of Austin College,* 1903–1904, 31–32; student notes by S. G. Morley on Professor George Foot Moore's History of Religions, 1906, HUC 8906.338.56, HUA; Norton to Goldwin Smith, June 14, 1897, NP. At Austin College as early as 1891 the Bible was deemed to deserve a place in the curriculum on the strikingly modern grounds that "the history and customs of the Jews deserve their full place in secular education, and the understanding of the principles of Christianity which enter so fully into our civilization is so highly important that no education is complete and practical that omits this study." *Catalogue of Austin College,* 1891–1892, 31.

43. *Catalogue of Austin College,* 1891–1892, 30–31; *Catalogue of Austin College,* 1899–1900, 23–24.

44. The quoted phrase is from *Catalogue of Austin College,* 1903–1904, 11. For a typical statement of "Christian Culture," see *Annual Register of Franklin and Marshall College and the Theological Seminary, Lancaster, Pa., 1891–92* (Lancaster, 1892), 20–21; compare this with the notably different concerns expressed in the paragraph on the college's Reformed affiliation in *Catalogue of Franklin and Marshall College,* 1879–1880, 17.

# INDEX